D1256337

Crisis Counseling, Intervention, and Prevention in the Schools

SCHOOL PSYCHOLOGY

A series of volumes edited by
Thomas R. Kratochwill and James E. Ysseldyke

Crisis Counseling, Intervention, and Prevention in the Schools

edited by

Jonathan Sandoval
University of California, Davis

LEA LAWRENCE ERLBAUM ASSOCIATES, PUBLISHERS
1988   Hillsdale, New Jersey   Hove and London

LB
1027.55
.C74
1988

Fairleigh Dickinson University Library

TEANECK, NEW JERSEY

Copyright © 1988 by Lawrence Erlbaum Associates, Inc.
All rights reserved. No part of this book may be reproduced in
any form, by photostat, microform, retrieval system, or any other
means, without the prior written permission of the publisher.

Lawrence Erlbaum Associates, Inc., Publishers
365 Broadway
Hillsdale, New Jersey   07642

Library of Congress Cataloging-in-Publications Data

Crisis counseling, intervention, and prevention in the
  schools.

  (School psychology)
  "Half of the chapters in the book are revisions and
expansions of articles that were published in the fall
1985 issue of School psychology review"—P.
  Includes bibliographies and index.
  1. School psychology—United States. 2. Crisis
intervention (Psychiatry)—United States. 3. Mental
health counseling—United States. I. Series.
LB1027.55.C74 1988   370.15   87-17341
ISBN 0-89859-823-0

Printed in the United States of America
10 9 8 7 6 5 4 3

Contents

Contributors

John M. Davis, Department of Education, University of California, Davis, Davis, CA 95616

Marvin J. Fine, Department of Educational Psychology and Research, University of Kansas, Lawrence, KS 66044

Robert B. Germain, Worthington Public Schools, Worthington, OH 43085

Ruth K. Goldman, Department of Psychology, San Francisco State University, San Francisco, CA 94132 and Center for the Family in Transition, Corte Madera, CA 94925

Barbara Hardy, St. John Parish, Reserve, LA 70084

Colette L. Ingraham, Department of Counselor Education, College of Education, San Diego State University, San Diego, CA 92182

Mari Griffiths Irvin, Department of Educational and Counseling Psychology, School of Education, University of the Pacific, Stockton, CA 95211

Mariam J. King, Private Practice, Berkeley, CA and Center for the Family in Transition, Corte Madera, CA 94925

Gary Ross-Reynolds, Department of Psychology and Counselor Education, Nicholls State University, Thibodaux, LA 70310

Linda D. Roberts, Department of Educational Psychology and Research, University of Kansas, Lawrence, KS 66044

Jonathan Sandoval, Department of Education, University of California, Davis, Davis, CA 95616

Barbara Sommer, Department of Psychology, University of California, Davis, Davis, CA 95616

Margaret S. Steward, Department of Psychiatry, School of Medicine, University of California, Davis, Davis, CA 95616

Pamela G.H. Wilson, Private Practice, San Rafael and School Psychologist, Reed School District, Tiburon, CA 94920

Preface

This book had its origins in my experiences as a young school psychologist in trying to reconcile the needs of students I served with my professional skills and orientation. It was clear that I did have a direct service role to pupils as well as an indirect service role centering around consultation. Exactly what direct services I was to deliver, other than assessment, was never explicit. Much of what I did was vaguely labeled as *counseling*. When I examined the needs of the students and responded with the counseling I had been trained to do, I found myself encountering children's issues and conflicts that were very much reality based and urgent. My nondirective tools did not fit either the children's problems or their developmental status. As I encountered students who were being abused, who were suicidal, who had strong conflicts in adolescence with their parents, and who were in other kinds of crises, I evolved ways of adapting my counseling technique to their level of cognitive, social, and emotional development.

Although successful to a degree, at the time I was unsure that I was "counseling." The crisis cases were the ones I most often dealt with, not the archtypical "client." There was simply no time for me to take those referrals from teachers who believed a child needed "some sort of counseling to help him adjust."

Beyond the time problem, the model of services delivery I was following was predicated on finding ways to prevent problems from occurring and facilitating the development of children and schools. My belief was that the school psychologist is a part of the regular education component of the school as well as the special education program. I struggled successfully to find time to visit all of the school's classrooms, sought to consult with teachers about difficulties they were having, and collaborated with teachers and administrators to establish policies and procedures that would contribute to student development. These activities, it seemed to me, were more worthy of my efforts than one-to-one counseling.

It is only in retrospect and as an educator of school psychologists that I have come to understand how involved school psychologists and other school personnel are in crisis counseling, intervention, and prevention. Much of what we do is to support other professionals in the schools as they interact with children in crisis. For our role of consultant, we need to know as much as possible about the psychology of the crisis events we commonly encounter. In addition, we need to think developmentally about children, not assuming that preschoolers will react to a given crisis the same as sixth graders, and we need to be able to distinguish usual reactions from pathological ones. The more we know about the psychology of crisis, the better able we will be to plan programs to prevent them from occurring or to facilitate their swift resolution.

We also need to learn and think about the counseling interventions we may deliver directly to a child in crisis. Crisis counseling has a sufficient history at this point that some general principles may be put forward. These overarch, to some extent, the particular kind of hazardous event effecting the student. As a result, the first section of the book is devoted to general principles and conceptions of crisis counseling. Particular attention has been given to self-theory in helping school psychologists and other school personnel be prepared for children's needs in time of crisis. Although we have written this book with the school psychologist in mind, all of the authors intend that other mental health professionals working in schools as well as teacher and principals find this information useful.

The second and third sections of the book have been devoted to discussions of particular hazardous events that may result in crises for school children. Insofar as possible each author has discussed the prevalence of the crisis, the psychological dynamics of the event and reactions to it, individual and group work with children, as well as secondary and primary prevention activities. Topics range from relatively common events such as geographical moves, the death of a loved one, or divorce, through relatively rare crises such as adolescent suicide and pregnancy. Taken together, however, at least one of the hazardous situations described in this book will occur for most of the children in a given school. Many children experience several. There is much for school guidance personnel to do. The authors and I hope this volume will be of help.

ACKNOWLEDGMENTS

In conclusion, I wish to thank a number of people who have contributed to the genesis of this book. Half of the chapters in the book are revisions and expansions of articles that were published in the fall 1985 issue of *School Psychology Review*. I would like to thank

SPR editor Steve Elliott for his support. A number of Davis students, now school psychologists, have made important contributions to my thinking. I thank Gay Bourgignon, Liz Boyer, Valjean Bryant, Susan Craig, Cathi Cristo, Lisa French, Rob Martinez, Connie Muschetti, Cindy Orrett, Karen Russell, Doris Takayama, and Lynn Trittipo.

I especially wish to thank Mary Cambell, another Davis school psychology alumnus who has acted as an editorial assistant.

Jonathan Sandoval

I

THEORY

Crisis counseling differs from other forms of counseling on a number of dimensions. First, the primary goal of crisis counseling is to restore the client to equilibrium. As a result, it is more limited in its scope and briefer in its duration than traditional nondirective counseling. Encounters ranging from one meeting to eight sessions are common. A second goal is that of taking action rather than listening and allowing the client gradually to take responsibility for his or her own decision making and understanding. Accordingly, crisis counseling is far more directive than usual. A principal goal in traditional counseling is to avoid dependency on the counselor. In crisis counseling there may be times when temporary dependency is to be encouraged when it is necessary to help a person survive extreme disequilibrium. Another feature that is different is the amount of talk by the counselor. In typical counseling the counselor listens, reflects, and summarizes, whereas in crisis counseling the counselor takes a much more active role in giving information and offering strategies to the client as well as giving advice and suggestions. Of course the crisis counselor does use active listening techniques, too.

Other techniques having to do with the confrontation of a client and the use of self-disclosure and modeling probably have very little place in crisis counseling. These techniques are probably more relevant to personality change and thus are not as applicable, because the emphasis in crisis counseling is to restore equilibrium and to free the individual from troubling symptomatic behavior.

Naturally, many similarities exist between crisis and traditional counseling. Certainly the active listening skills that characterize normal counseling are important to use in crisis counseling. It is very important to establish empathy and trust in the client, and the counselor has no better tools than reflecting feelings, restating the client's ideas, and summarizing. Carl Rogers' basic ideas of empathetic understanding, genuineness, and warmth all have their place in crisis counseling as well as traditional forms of counseling.

The two chapters in this section explore the basic ideas underlying crisis counseling and intervention. Sandoval (chapter 1) explores the history of crisis counseling, and makes some important conceptual distinctions. In addition, he outlines a taxonomy of crisis and some general approaches to helping children in crisis. The framework for crisis counseling and intervention described in this chapter has applicability for each of the varieties of crises described in the other two sections of the book.

Perhaps the most important body of research and theory bearing on the individual in crisis is that related to attitudes about self. In the second chapter, Ingraham explores this literature and applies it to the individual in crisis, particularly those crises related to school learning. Central to all crisis counseling, however, is exploration, preservation or alteration of the child's sense of self. Self-esteem must be maintained and protected at all times.

Other notions and theoretical approaches are explored in the chapters in the second and third sections, in the context of particular crises. Both general skills and specific information about the particular crisis are necessary to be effective with clients.

Conceptualizations and General Principles of Crisis Counseling, Intervention, and Prevention

Jonathan Sandoval
University of California, Davis

Perhaps the feature of a crisis that is most dramatic to witness is the effect on individuals. Children in crisis suddenly function with greatly diminished capacity in meeting everyday demands. Students whom others have seen only behaving competently and efficiently suddenly become disorganized, depressed, hyperactive, confused, or hysterical. Customary problem-solving activities and resources seem to evaporate. Individuals who are in what Caplan (1964) terms a state of *psychological disequilibrium* often behave irrationally and withdrawn from normal contacts. They cannot be helped using usual counseling or teaching techniques. Nevertheless, children in crisis are usually also in school. School psychologists and other guidance personnel must be able to support teachers, parents, and the children themselves during periods of crisis for children. In addition, school personnel must be forward thinking and anticipate that crises will occur in children's lives. They must be prepared to act and find ways to help children master the challenges of crises when they occur.

A History of Crisis Intervention Theory

The earliest work on crisis intervention is usually attributed to Erich Lindemann (1944) and his studies of the aftermath of Coconut Grove nightclub fire. This disaster, which occurred in Boston in the late 1930s took a large toll of human life. For the first time, a social scientist conducted systematic observations of the reactions of victims and their families to a natural disaster. This study, plus Lindemann's efforts in opening a mental health agency in Wellesley, Massachusetts, formed the basis of his ideas about crisis and crisis intervention.

In Wellesley he was able to study such problems as children's entry into kindergarten and the process by which individuals become prepared to assume the position of nurse. From this work, he was able to link notions of crises of transition with ideas about helping people cope with crises springing from traumatic events.

Erik Erikson (1962) contributed the next major milestone in crisis intervention theory with the 1950 publication of *Childhood and Society*. Erikson's theory revolves around the notion of specific crises characterizing each developmental stage of an individual's life. His contribution was the notion of crisis as a normal developmental phenomenon and that intervention which leads to a balanced resolution at the time of a crisis would prevent later problems in emotional development and maturation.

The third early pioneer was Gerald Caplan whose formulations about the primary prevention of emotional disorders and mental health consultation led to the notion of an entirely new field of preventative psychiatry (Caplan, 1961, 1964). Caplan's data came from early work with Peace Corps volunteers, with parents reacting to premature birth, and with families coping with the affliction of tuberculosis. His (and others' associated with the Harvard School of Public Health) adoption of ideas from public health and the application of them to mental health settings had an enormous influence that led to the blossoming of crisis intervention centers throughout the country.

Caplan's work came at a time when there was a great push on the part of the federal government for community mental health agencies and at a time of great social unrest in our country. The 1960s brought unprecedented illegal use of psychoactive drugs on the part of adolescents and young adults. These forces, particularly drug abuse, led to the creation in the community and on college campuses of crisis counseling agencies, often nontraditional in nature, which could deal with the problems of alienated youth, especially drug overdose (Beers & Foreman, 1976). During this time, the use of telephone crisis lines also came into widespread use, spurred on by a growing interest in suicide prevention services (Golan, 1978).

The late 1970s and early 1980s saw the burgeoning of a great deal of interest in brief psychotherapy (e.g., Bellak & Small, 1978; Davanloo, 1978). This trend emerged as a result of cuts in mental health funding and of new techniques and procedures for dealing rapidly with mental health problems. Mental health workers began to appreciate that as much could be accomplished in six to eight sessions as had earlier taken years.

Another recent trend has been an interest in stress and its impact on physical and mental health. Theorists such as Hans Selye (1974) and Adolph Meyer (cited in Moos & Schaefer, 1986) have noted how a variety of environmental events may have broader effects than previously believed. Physical events may have emotional sequelae and vice versa. Normal life events such as graduation from school, birth of a child, marriage, not to mention unpleasant events such as job failure, a death in the family, or divorce may foreshadow the development of symptoms and disease. Moreover, stressful events are additive or perhaps multiplicative in their action, in that the more events with which the individual must cope, the more likely an illness response will develop (Moos & Schaefer, 1986).

Although crisis theory has had a relatively brief history, sufficient research findings and clinical observations exist for school psychologists and other school mental health workers to begin to apply the ideas and techniques to the school setting.

Definitions and Distinctions

Donald C. Klein and Erich Lindemann (1961) offered the following definition:

> An *emotionally hazardous situation* (or emotional hazard) refers to any sudden alteration in the field of social forces within which the individual exists, such that the individual's expectations of himself and his relationships with others undergo change. Major categories of hazards include: (1) a loss or threatened loss of significant relationship; (2) the introduction of one or more new individuals into social orbit; (3) transitions in social status and role relationships as a consequence of such factors as (a) maturation, (e.g., entry into adolescence), (b) achievement of a new social role (e.g., marriage), or (c) horizontal or vertical social mobility (e.g., job promotion). (p 284)

Klein and Lindemann use the term *hazard* to capture the notion that many individuals are able to pass through such alterations with little difficulty or with a minimum amount of stress. Others, however, find themselves immobilized or damaged by the hazard.

Klein and Lindemann (1961) reserve the term *crisis* "for the acute and often prolonged disturbance that may occur in an individual or social orbit as a result of an emotional hazard" (p. 284). Emotional hazards faced by school children include losses in significant relationships associated with the death of a parent; parental divorce and remarriage; death of a sibling or the loss of a parent to illness; maturational challenges such as the beginning of puberty; and transitions such as those accompanying movement into new schools, or new educational programs. Nonpromotion is a hazard, but so is promotion to a new grade with its separation from a known, possibly favored teacher and the adjustment to change and an unknown, new teacher. Some children will navigate these hazards with little or no ill effect. Others will develop crisis reactions and come to the attention of school psychologists and other school personnel.

Caplan (1964) offers a general view of an emotional crisis as a "psychological disequilibrium in a person who confronts a hazardous circumstance that for him constitutes an important problem which he can, for the time being, neither escape nor solve with his customary problem solving resources" (p. 53). Caplan views a crisis as being a period when the individual is temporarily out of balance. This state of of disequilibrium provides an opportunity for psychological growth as well as a danger of psychological deterioration. Although there are great risks that may occur to the future mental well-being of an individual who passes through a crisis, there is also an opportunity for an individual to change. It is an old but traditional cliché to point out that the Chinese character for crisis includes ideographs related to the concept of danger as well as the concept of opportunity. The primary goal in helping an individual who is undergoing a crisis is to intervene in such a way as to use the situation to enhance personal growth, or at least to restore the individual to a previous level of functioning. The goal is not to reorganize completely the individual's major dimensions of personality, but to restore the individual to creative problem solving. Of course by successfully resolving a crisis an individual will most likely acquire new coping skills that will lead to improved functioning in new situations, but that is only a desired, possible outcome, not the sole objective of the process.

Because failure to cope is at the heart of a crisis, and the promotion of coping is an overall objective of crisis intervention, it is useful to consider what normal coping entails. Moos and Billings (1984) have identified a taxonomy of coping skills organized into three domains, each with three skills. The first is *appraisal-focused coping*. The three skills in this domain enable the individual to find mean-ing and to understand the crisis, that is, to apprehend it in a productive manner. They are (a) logical analysis and mental preparation, (b) cognitive redefinition, and (c) cognitive avoidance or denial. Thus, in first becoming aware of a hazardous event, a child may think it through rationally, step by step, and prepare for what will probably happen next, may re-frame the hazard in a variety of ways, or may keep all or part of it at a distance, mentally, until he or she is ready to deal with it.

The second domain is *problem-focused coping*. The three skills in this domain enable the individual to confront the reality brought about by the crisis. These are (a) seeking information and support, (b) taking problem-solving action, and (c) identifying alternative rewards. This last skill involves changing activities and relationships so there may be substitutions for the sources of satisfaction lost by the hazardous event.

The third domain is *emotion-focused coping*. Here, the three skills enable the child to manage the feelings generated by the crisis and to maintain affective equilibrium. The three skills are (a) affective regulation, (b) emotional discharge, and (c) resigned acceptance. These skills allow one to maintain control of emotions, or to vent them in a way that brings relief. Many situations cannot be controlled, however, and resigned acceptance may lead to avoidance and withdrawal as a way to protect the self. As we see later in the chapter, and in this book, much of crisis intervention is directed at stimulating one or more of these coping skills, or even teaching them depending on the individual and the type of hazard he or she is attempting to negotiate.

TYPES OF CRISES

Although there are a number of ways that the crises may be defined and outlined, perhaps the most comprehensive taxonomy has been developed by Baldwin (1978). Baldwin noted six major types of emotional crises drawing on his work in a mental health clinic at the student health service at the University of North Carolina.

Dispositional Crises

Baldwin (1978) calls his first class of crises *dispositional crises*. These crises are "distress resulting from a problematic situation in which the therapist responds to the client in ways peripheral to a therapeutic role; the intervention is not primarily directed at the emotional level" (p. 540). In a dispositional crisis an individual typically lacks both information and the encouragement to go about solving a problem in an unusual way. The school psychologist who helps a pupil learn about a local program for overweight teenagers might be dealing with such a crisis.

In general, the major counseling strategy with these pupils is to provide information, particularly information that would be difficult for the child or adolescent to obtain on his or her own. If the client is capable of doing most of the "research," the counselor merely points the way. The act of obtaining the information on one's own builds self-confidence and increases the chance of the information being believed.

Another specific strategy is to rule out possible hidden, serious emotional implications of the seemingly innocent request for information. The counselor must be sure the current problem is not an offshoot of another, more serious situation.

The school psychologist should also consider referring the client on. Another expert may provide either information that is more comprehensive or more authoritative than is available at the school. If the real reason for the request is to discuss a more serious problem outside of the scope of solution in the school, a referral for long-term therapeutic intervention may be required.

Anticipated Life Transitions

Baldwin's (1978) second category subsumes crises of *anticipated life transitions*. These are crises "that reflect anticipated but usually normative, life transitions over which the client may or may not have substantial control" (p. 542). Common transitions for children are entering school, moving from grade to grade, moving to another school, or moving from a self-contained special education classroom to a mainstreamed one. The birth of a sibling or pregnancy in a teenager also fit this category in as much as they are transitions from one status (only child or adolescent) to another (sibling or mother).

One approach to dealing with crises related to life transitions is to provide information about what is about to occur in the person's life. As a preventative technique, I discuss anticipatory guidance in another major section, but a child in the middle of a transition also needs to know what is likely to occur next and what the normal experiences and emotions are for those going through such a transition. This kind of normative information can be provided by school personnel.

An alternative is to let peers supply the information. Another strategy is to establish support groups consisting of a number of children facing the same transition. If the group functions well, it may facilitate the expression of feeling and the acquisition of productive coping mechanisms as members share experiences and join in mutual problem solving. Even young children can do productive group problem solving through devices such as a Magic Circle, or other structured approaches to classroom discussions of children's self-identified conflicts and problems (Jones, 1968).

Traumatic Stress

A third class of crises result from *traumatic events*. These are "emotional crises precipitated by externally-imposed stressors or situations that are unexpected and uncontrolled, and that are emotionally overwhelming" (Baldwin, 1978, p. 543). Traumatic events for children in school include the sudden death of a family member, catastrophic illness, hospitalization, parental disablement, parental divorce, physical abuse, pregnancy, sexual assault, and academic failure. Often, the pupil facing one or more of these events is emotionally overwhelmed and unable to bring into play previously learned coping strategies.

The counselor's first goal is to help the child understand the impact of what has occurred. Because of the suddenness of occurrence, the counselee probably has not had time to think through all of the impacts of what has happened. Exploration of the event and the attendant feelings will get the child to gain needed perspective and overcome defensive reactions. Traditional nondirective helping interviews (Benjamin, 1981) can accomplish this task and can stimulate appraisal-focused coping (Moos & Billings, 1984).

Another goal for helping in this kind of crisis is to mobilize any existing coping mechanisms the child may have. If the individual has characteristic ways of dealing with stress in other situations, the counselor can remind the child of these, be they appraisal-, problem-, or emotion-focused, and facilitate the transfer of the old skills to the new crisis (Brenner, 1984).

If the counselee is not coping at all, it may be possible to provide the pupil with new coping mechanisms. Brenner (1984) refers to the process as teaching new coping strategies, and believes the new technique will be more easily learned if it is close to the child's initial reaction.

For example, Joshua's teacher helped him substitute sublimation for impulsive acting out as a coping technique after his mother deserted him. Josh's first impulse was to express his anger by running around the classroom, pushing furniture and people out of his way. His teacher helped him to think of several vigorous physical activities which would not be destructive but which would still serve to release his pent-up emotions. (p. 173)

Another way of helping victims of traumatic crisis is to relieve them of other, unrelated stressors (Brenner, 1984). A child whose parents are divorcing may be relieved of certain expectations at school if those expectations are adding to the child's sense of being overwhelmed. If, however, the child is using school work in a sublimation strategy, it might be wiser to search for other potential stress sources that need to be eliminated.

Maturational/Developmental Crises

Crises in this fourth category result "from attempts to deal with an interpersonal situation reflecting a struggle with a deeper (but usually circumscribed) issue that has not been resolved adaptively in the past and that represents an attempt to gain emotional maturity" (Baldwin, 1978, p. 544). Focal issues for this class of crises include dependency, value conflicts, sexual identity, capacity for emotional intimacy, responses to authority, and attaining reasonable self-discipline. All of these issues may erupt in school children but are more visible during adolescence. These crises are different from others in that they usually occur as another episode in a pattern of relationship problems that have similar dynamics. In secondary schools, the attainment of sexual maturity by young people precipitates a number of these crises, as does adolescence in general. Struggles with parents and teachers often develop to the point of crisis in this class. A special case of such a crisis is the discovery in adolescence of a homosexual orientation (Ross-Reynolds & Hardy, 1985; chapter 13, this volume).

Once again, the counselor can be of help with clients in this kind of crisis by facilitating the exploration of thoughts and feelings. In this instance, however, the hope is to identify issues underlying the crisis. This strategy will be particularly attractive to dynamically oriented counselors. What thoughts and feelings does the client have about significant others and the self? What value conflicts are being experienced and what are their origins? What themes and conflicts appear to be unresolved? Are these issues related to trust, acceptance and control of aggression, attitudes toward learning, separation, accepting limits from others, and so on?

Next, the counselor works to support the individual in crisis to redefine relationships and develop adaptive interpersonal skills. Because most of these crises involve creating new ways of acting with other people in the student's social environment, helping them learn new prosocial strategies is effective. Strategies for making friends may be taught directly (Stocking, Arezzo, & Leavitt, 1980) but providing models to observe (or even read about, e.g., Fassler, 1978) is also beneficial.

Crises Reflecting Psychopathology

Baldwin (1978) describes the fifth category: "These are emotional crises in which a preexisting psychopathology has been instrumental in precipitating the crisis or in which psychopathology significantly impairs or complicates adaptive resolution" (p. 546). The problems of a child hallucinating in school or a severely depressed adolescent might well achieve crisis proportions. These kinds of crises, although present in the school, are rarely the kind that special services practitioners are trained for and thus usually result in a referral to outside community resources. School personnel do have a role in preventing a worsening of the child's adjustment by keeping him or her functioning academically as well as possible. In addition, the special services personnel may assist teachers and administrators to appreciate that the child has problems that cannot be resolved in school yet can be managed in a reasonable way in the classroom.

Generally, with children experiencing this kind of crisis, it is wise not to respond to the underlying problem. This in-depth treatment is a task for professionals.

What can be done is to support the child's attempts to respond to the stressful situation as adaptively as possible. Whatever the child is doing in school that is appropriate and productive can be acknowledged and encouraged. At the same time, the counselor can search for ways to reduce stress, especially by eliminating any stressors that may be pushing the child beyond his or her capacity to cope.

In addition, the counselor must look for ways to support other school staff and even parents who will also undergo trauma in dealing with a psychopathological child. Consultation skills and techniques are particularly valuable in this respect.

Psychiatric Emergencies

This sixth class consists of "crisis situations in which general functioning has been severely impaired and the individual rendered incompetent or unable to assume personal responsibility" (Baldwin, 1978, p. 547). Examples include acutely suicidal children, alcohol intoxification, drug overdoses, reactions to hallucinogenic drugs, acute psychoses, and uncontrollable anger. These are all "classic" crises of the type where the individual is often dangerous to him or herself or others.

The counselor's efforts in this type of crisis are directed at assessing the danger by attempting to learn the physical or psychiatric condition of the pupil. Facts must be gathered to clarify the situation so that action may be taken quickly and appropriately. Much of this information may need to be determined from persons other than the child.

The first principle in psychiatric crises is to intervene quickly so as to reduce danger. The school professional must be willing to mobilize all medical or psychiatric resources necessary and thus must be familiar with state law and local community agencies. Prior to the need for such information, school practitioners should familiarize themselves with community resources. Not only must they know about existing agencies, they must learn the detail of what services are offered and they must know the key personnel to contact (Sandoval, 1985a).

Learning which pupils to refer to outside experts takes a novice a long time because of the need to follow up on referral cases, and the difficulty in evaluating one's own competence. School practitioners must routinely review their cases with supervisors and peers. In the review, not only does counselor knowledge and skill need to be examined but so, too, does counselor objectivity.

CRISIS COUNSELING AND INTERVENTION

Crisis Counseling Goals

One approach to considering the goals for work with children in crisis is to consider tasks the children must accomplish if they are to manage the crisis situation successfully and emerge intact. Moos and Schaefer (1986) identify five major adaptive tasks as follows.

1. *Establish the meaning and understand the personal significance of the situation.* The child must come to view the event personally. He or she must realize all of the short- and long-term ramifications of what has occurred and to assign it a meaning. This meaning will undoubtedly be limited by the child's cognitive and emotional development.

2. *Confront reality and respond to the requirements of the external situation.* The child must marshal resources in able to continue or in the conventional social roles remaining. The victim still must go to school, play in the neighborhood, and be part of a family in spite of the crisis.

3. *Sustain relationships with family members and friends as well as with other individuals who may be helpful in resolving the crisis and its aftermath.* The child, particularly, must depend on others for assistance in dealing with the crisis situation. The child must keep lines of communication open to parents and friends and look to them for support. Where adult authorities are involved, such as other school personnel, or medical or social agency helpers, the child must be able to cooperate and use the assistance rendered.

4. *Preserve a reasonable emotional balance by managing upsetting feelings aroused by the situation.* The powerful emotions stemming from a crisis must be mastered. Through a combination of appropriate expression and the use of strategies to manage or block the full impact of the event, children can achieve a sense of hope that will enable them to continue functioning.

5. *Preserve a satisfactory self-image and master a sense of competence and mastery.* The child must search for new roles in which to be competent or to return to old arenas where he or she has been successful in the past in order to

achieve a sense of competence. Because many crises threaten a sense of self, the individual must work particularly hard to find compensating ways to feel good about the self.

Generic Counseling Principles

Given that crisis counseling is different from usual school counseling and has the aforementioned goals, it is useful to indicate a general strategy for helping people in a crisis situation. What follows will be a generic model taken from the work of Lindemann (1944), Caplan (1964), and Rusk (1971) and others (see Golan, 1978; or Slaikeu, 1984 for an exhaustive model). An individual counselor will change and adapt these techniques depending on the type of crisis, the age of student, and the specifics of the type of crisis. Although I have outlined the principles in the general order that they are applied in a crisis, they are not necessarily sequential in practice.

In working with a pupil in crisis:

1. *Begin counseling immediately.* By definition, a *crisis* is a time when a child is in danger of becoming extremely impaired emotionally. The longer the pupil remains in a hazardous situation and is unable to take action, the more difficult it will be to facilitate coping and a return to equilibrium. When a person remains in a state of confusion without any kind of human support, anxiety and pain are sure to result.

2. *Be concerned and competent.* The pupil will need a certain amount of reassurance during a crisis situation. The more the counselor can present him or herself as a model of competent problem solving and demonstrate the process of taking in information, choosing between alternatives, and taking action, the more the child will be able to begin to function appropriately. This higher functioning will come about both from a sense of safety and security and from observing a clear model. The counselor does not call attention to his or her competence but keeps it in the background as the counseling goes on.

3. *Listen to the facts of the situation.* Before proceeding, the counselor must carefully gather information about the events leading up to the crisis, eliciting as many details as possible. Not only will solutions come from these facts, but concrete knowledge of the situation will also put into perspective the pupil's behavior—Is this child behaving rationally or irrationally? Such a determination allows the counselor to judge the severity of the crisis and to proceeding accordingly.

4. *Reflect the individual's feelings.* The counselor should explicitly focus the discussion on the pupil's affective experience and encourage its appropriate expression. The objective here is not only to create empathetic understanding, but also to legitimize affect. The child must learn that feelings can be discussed and are an important part of problem solving. By reflecting feelings the counselor

also "primes the pump" in that it gives the counselee a way to begin and continue exploration of what occurred.

5. *Help the child realize that the crisis event has occurred.* Do not accept the child's defensiveness or let the mechanisms of denial or other defensives operate and prolong the crisis situation unnecessarily. Some denial may actually be coping, in that it gives the child a chance to be desensitized to what has occurred. Prolonged or complete denial may not lead to coping. Encourage the pupil to explore the crisis events without becoming overwhelmed. By asking appropriate well-timed questions, the counselor can control the pace of exploration.

6. *Do not encourage or support blaming.* This strategy also is a way of avoiding the pupil's defensiveness and of encouraging coping. If one can put blame aside, and focus on what has occurred, the child may more quickly move on. Dwelling on being a victim leaves one in a passive position rather than moving on to an active role. The focus should be shifted to self-esteem issues and internal strengths rather than remaining oriented toward external causation and guilt.

7. *Do not give false reassurance.* The counselor should always remain truthful and realistic, even though it is tempting to offer unrealistic comfort. The individual in crisis will always suffer anxiety, depression, or tension, and the counselor must acknowledge that the discomfort will probably continue for some time. At the same time, it is possible to provide some sense of hope and expectation that the person will ultimately overcome the crisis. The counselor should be clear that there will always be scars and tenderness resulting from a crisis. Nevertheless, the child or adolescent will be able to get on with his or her life eventually, and may even develop new strengths.

8. *Recognize the primacy of taking action.* The individual will need real assistance in accomplishing everyday tasks during the time of crisis. Every crisis counseling interview should have as an ultimate outcome some action that the client is able to take. Restoring the client to the position of actor rather than victim is critical to success, because taking effective action helps to restore a sense of self.

Generic Crisis Intervention Principles

In addition to interviewing the child, the counselor also must take action, with or without the participation of the person in crisis. These interventions may be within or outside of the counseling setting. With younger children, particularly, it will be expeditious to make changes in the environment, in the classroom, or at home to reduce stress.

1. *Facilitate the re-establishment of a social support network.* If possible, get the child to accept some help from others. It is usually possible to find either a group of peers or family members who can provide emotional support and temporary physical assistance during the crisis. In this way the pupil's energies may

be devoted to coping with the crisis. If family is not available, there are often community resources available and the counselor should be knowledgeable about them (Sandoval, 1985a).

2. *Engage in focused problem solving.* Once the counselor has been able to formulate an accurate, comprehensive statement about the counselee's perception of the situation, identifying all of the sources of concern, it will be possible to begin the process of exploring potential strategies to improve or resolve the emotionally hazardous situation. Jointly, the counselor and pupil review the strategies explored and select one for trial. This is much like the problem solving that occurs in other kinds of counseling but must be preceded by the steps previously mentioned. Moving too quickly to problem solving is a common mistake of novices (Egan, 1986). However effective the problem solution is, the very process of turning attention to the future, away from the past, is beneficial in and of itself. Some solutions may involve actions by others such as teachers or school administrators. To the extent necessary, the counselor may act as an intermediary communicating with authorities on the child's behalf.

3. *Focus on self-concept.* Any action strategies must be implemented in the context of what the client thinks it is possible for him or her to accomplish. The crisis situation often leads to a dimunition in self-esteem and the acceptance of blame for the crisis. With an emphasis on how the person did cope well given the situation so far and how the person has arrived at a strategy for moving forward, there can be a restoration of the damaged view of the self. Counselors can emphasize what positive there is in the situation, even if it seems relatively minor. However, even the victim of a sexual assault can be congratulated for at least surviving physically. The next chapter is devoted to ways to assist in the development of healthy self-concepts.

4. *Encourage self-reliance.* During the process of crisis counseling, the counselee will have temporarily become dependent on the counselor for direct advice, for stimulating action, and for supplying hope. This is a temporary situation and before the crisis intervention interviews are over, the counselor must spend some time planning ways to restore the individual to self-reliance and self-confidence. Typically in counseling this is done by the counselor consciously moving into a position of equal with the counselee, sharing the responsibility and authority. Although earlier the counselor has taken charge, eventually he or she must return to a more democratic stance. Techniques such as onedownsmanship, where the counselor acknowledges the pupil's contribution to problem solving while minimizing the counselor's own contribution (Caplan, 1970), permit the counselee to leave the crisis intervention with a sense of accomplishment. Helping individuals to find alternative rewards and sources of satisfaction (i.e., using problem-focused coping, is most helpful).

Although these principles may generally apply to all crisis counseling and intervention, it is important to realize that there are specific techniques that are

TABLE 1.1
General Principles:
Counseling Goal Interventions Particularly Relevant to
Baldwin's Six Classes of Emotional Crisis

Crisis Type	Goals	General Intervention
1. Dispositional crises	Confront reality	• Provide information—educate • Rule out hidden, serious emotional implications • Refer to expert
2. Anticipated life transitions	Confront reality	• Anticipatory guidance • Provide support groups
3. Traumatic stress	Establish meaning Preserve emotional balance Preserve self-image	• Help client understand the impact of what has occurred • Mobilize existing coping mechanisms • Provide new coping mechanisms
4. Maturational/ developmental crises	Sustain relationships	• Identify issues underlying • Support client in redefining relationships and developing adaptive interpersonal responses
5. Crisis reflecting psychopathology	Preserve self-image Confront reality	• Support attempts to respond to stressful situation as adaptively as possible • Find ways to reduce stress • Refer to experts • Do not respond to underlying problems
6. Psychiatric emergencies	Preserve self-image Establish meaning	• Intervene quickly to reduce danger • Assess medical or psychiatric condition • Clarify situation • Mobilize all medical or psychiatric resources necessary

appropriate to a given kind of crisis. Table 1.1 lists goals and general intervention techniques that seem most appropriate for each of Baldwin's crisis types. Other chapters in this volume contain a number of specific ideas for particular crises.

The Counselor in Crisis

Not much has been written about the counselor's feelings and adaptive behavior at a time of crisis. In a sense, a crisis in a child is also a time of crisis for the counselor. Because the event may have come up suddenly and unexpectedly and because the child's problem may be quite serious, the counselor is likely to experience heightened anxiety and momentary disorganization. A number of principles for the counselor's behavior may also be identified.

1. *Remove distractors and other stressors acting on you.* Set aside your other duties and roles. Order your priorities and realize your limit. Give as much time as you can to the crisis and put off what is not urgent.

2. *Avoid impulsive action.* You must act quickly but you should also take time to plan in a time of crisis. Gather your thoughts and think through the possibilities prior to seeing the affective parties in a crisis situation.

3. *Delegate authority.* The medical response to a crisis is the triage process. Not only are the most important risks to the patient assessed and identified but also roles are assigned to various medical personnel. In the schools there is the ideal of the multidisciplinary team, and with effort it can be a reality. In times of crisis, by delegating authority among school psychologists, counselors, social workers, school nurses, administrators, and teachers, there will be a minimum of duplication of effort and a greater likelihood that professionals will be tackling those tasks they can do best.

4. *Model calmness in a way consonant with your personality.* Although Carl Rogers (1957), for example, argues that the counselor should always be genuine and honest with the client, there are times when such openness may not be in the best interest of the client. If the counselor is overly upset and angry about the child's predicament and acts it out in front of the client, it may have the effect of getting in the way of emotion-focused coping.

5. *Be prepared.* The Scout motto is still valuable. The more one is informed about the particular crisis the child is experiencing, the easier will be the process of working with him or her. One aim of this book is to provide school psychologists and other school personnel with the knowledge base to begin to work with the common crises they will encounter. Be prepared has another meaning, however, and that is to anticipate that various crises will occur and to expend some energy into planning and executing prevention programs that will keep hazardous situations from developing into crises for large numbers of children.

PREVENTION PROGRAMS

Many of the early pioneers in crisis intervention (e.g., Caplan, 1961; Klein & Lindemann, 1961) came from a background in public health and stressed the prevention of crises. At least five general strategies have been used in the schools to prevent various kinds of crises from occurring. They are educational workshops, anticipatory guidance, screening, consultation, and research (Sandoval, 1985b).

Educational Workshop

An educational workshop is a short intensive course of study on a topic that generates feelings and emotions. As a result, workshops emphasize student participation and discussion. It is preventive to the extent that the topic of the workshop is intended to forestall future mental health problems. A number of programs exist for children under the general heading of psychological education. Programs such as classroom meetings, Magic Circle, and others (Miller, 1976) help children express their feelings about what is occurring in the social environment of the classroom, and attempts to free them from the anxiety that may occur from crises that may develop in the classroom. Others have pointed out the value of a psychologist's role in all curriculum designs (e.g., Jones, 1968), because so many school subjects can bring up unpleasant emotions. Specific curriculum materials have been developed on topics such as death, dying, suicide, and illness as is pointed out in later chapters in this book.

Anticipatory Guidance

The second technique, anticipatory guidance, also has a variant called *emotional innoculation*. Offering anticipatory guidance consists of orienting a student intellectually to events that are likely to occur in the future and helping him or her prepare effective coping strategies. Emotional innoculation puts the emphasis on future feelings rather than on the cognitive. Events in question are ones that experience has shown are difficult for individuals to cope with and may influence educational performance. Examples of anticipatory guidance are programs that are designed to help children adjust to new institutional settings, or programs that inform students as to what can be expected, both intellectually and emotionally, when a new sibling is born.

Screening Programs

A third preventive technique involves setting up procedures to identify children who are vulnerable to particular hazardous situations so that they might receive special assistance at the appropriate time. Screening programs consist of designing means (usually questionnaires, rating scales, or group tests) to determine who is at a high risk of not coping. The followup intervention might be anticipatory guidance, a workshop, a special remediation program, or preventive counseling. Screening has been particularly effective in identifying children who are at risk of educational failure but it is conceivable that screening could be designed to identify children who are also at risk for other kinds of crises. An example would be an effort to learn which families, in the near future, plan to enlarge their numbers so that children might be identified for workshops designed to facilitate the adjustment to a new sibling.

Consultation

Serving as a consultant is another important way that school psychologists and other special services personnel can act preventively in crises. *Consultation* is defined as one professional helping a second professional be more effective in his or her job (Caplan, 1970). In this context, a consultant is defined as a special services worker collaborating with teachers, administrators, or parents to help them deal more effectively with the child or teacher in crisis. By working with teachers, and possibly with parents, a mental health professional can help these key adults support children when they become involved in a crisis situation and be sensitive to the various emotional needs a child may have during times of crisis.

Research

Doing research is not usually conceived of as a preventive activity. Nevertheless, the more that is known about a phenomenon through research, the better able we are to predict and control that phenomenon. The more we understand about crises, the more effective we will be in creating workshops, educational curriculum, anticipatory guidance programs, screening programs, and consultation interventions. Evaluative and case study research on crises and crises intervention programs are within the capability of the school psychologist and should be thought of as important preventive activities.

DEVELOPMENTAL ISSUES IN CRISIS COUNSELING

A number of texts on counseling, even texts focusing solely on counseling children, ignore an important point. A child of 5 and an adolescent of 16 have radically different faculties for dealing with information and reacting to events. Differences in cognitive, social, and emotional development mean that they will respond differently to hazards and will need to be counseled differently should they develop a crisis reaction. The same event, the death of a parent, for example, may be a crisis for a preschooler as well as a high school senior, but each will react and cope with the event differently. Counseling with younger children often involves the use of nonverbal materials, many more directive leads in order to elicit and reflect feelings, and a focus on concrete concerns as well as fantasy.

Traditional talk therapists such as nondirective counseling capitalize on a client's capacity for rational thought and high level of moral development and are more likely to be effective with adolescents. With adolescents, the school psychologist can also acknowledge and use the age-appropriate crisis of establishing an identity.

In reviewing the generic crisis counseling principles just outlined, it seems reasonable to expect that younger children would have a greater difficulty acknowledging a crisis, and would be more prone to use immature defenses such as denial and projection to avoid coping with a crisis. In contrast, an adolescent might use more advanced defenses such as rationalization and intellectualization. In counseling children, more time might be spent on exploring reactions and feelings to the crisis situation and establishing support systems that engage in lengthy problem solving. With older adolescents, then, it may be possible to focus much more on establishing reasonable expectations and avoiding false reassurance, as well as spending more time on focused problem-solving activities.

CONCLUSION

School psychologists have a powerful role to play in helping children cope with and regain equilibrium after a crisis response to a hazardous situation. Adding together exemplars of Baldwin's six classes of crisis yields a large number of events that occur in the school-age population and that undoubtedly interfere with the effective learning of children in schools. The techniques and theories of crisis counseling have a relatively short history of being applied and evaluated. Much of what is done with a child in crisis depends on what kind of crisis it is, the age of the child, the time available to the counselor, and the counselor's skills. To be efficient, group interventions that are preventative in nature may be necessary to cope with the strong need for crisis counseling in the schools. The next two sections of this book deal with crisis counseling and intervention in particular kinds of situations. School psychologists and others in the schools can have an enormous impact on the mental health of children if they are aware of and act immediately in helping students develop positive coping responses in times of crisis.

Children may regain equilibrium, not lose precious time away from learning to emotional disorganization, and possibly even develop successful new coping strategies as a result of successfully passing through a crisis. They will be able to face emotional hazards throughout their lifetimes with a greater degree of confidence and success. If we are successful in developing our crisis counseling and intervention skills, and in implementing prevention, programs, future children surely must benefit.

REFERENCES

Baldwin, B. A. (1978). A paradigm for the classification of emotional crises: Implications for crisis intervention. *American Journal of Orthopsychiatry, 48,* 538–551.

Beers, T. M. Jr., & Foreman, M. E. (1976). Intervention patterns in crisis intervention. *Journal of Counseling Psychology, 23,* 87–91.

Bellak, L., & Small, L. (1978). *Emergency psychotherapy and brief psychotherapy* (2nd ed.). New York: Grune & Stratton.

Benjamin, A. (1981). *The helping interview* (3rd ed.). Boston: Houghton Mifflin.

Brenner, A. (1984). *Helping children cope with stress.* Lexington, MA: D. C. Heath.

Caplan, G. (1961). *An approach to community mental health.* New York: Grune & Stratton.

Caplan, G. (1964). *Principles of preventative psychiatry.* New York: Basic Books.

Caplan, G. (1970). *Theory and practice of mental health consultation.* New York: Basic Books.

Davanloo, H. (1978). *Basic principles and techniques in short-term dynamic psychotherapy.* New York: Spectrum.

Egan, G. (1986). *The skilled helper* (3rd ed.). Monterey, CA: Brooks/Cole.

Erikson, E. (1962). *Childhood and society* (2nd ed.). New York: W. W. Norton.

Fassler, J. (1978). *Helping children cope.* New York: The Free Press.

Golan, N. (1978). *Treatment in crisis situations.* New York: The Free Press.

Jones, R. M. (1968). *Fantasy and feeling in education.* New York: New York University Press.

Klein, D. C., & Lindemann, E. (1961). Preventive intervention in individual and family crisis situations. In G. Caplan (Ed.), *Prevention of mental disorders in children* (pp. 283-306). New York: Basic Books.

Lindemann, E. (1944). Symptomatology and management of acute grief. *American Journal of Psychiatry, 101,* 141-148.

Miller, J. P. (1976). *Humanizing the classroom.* New York: Praeger.

Moos, R., & Billings, A. (1984). Conceptualizing and measuring coping resources and processes. In L. Goldberger & S. Breznitz (Eds.), *Handbook of stress: Theoretical and clinical aspects* (pp. 109-145). New York: Macmillan.

Moos, R.H., & Schaefer, J. A. (1986). Life transitions and crises. A conceptual overview. In R. H. Moos & J. A. Schaefer (Eds.), *Coping with life crises. An integrated approach* (pp. 3-28). New York: Plenum.

Rogers, C. R. (1957). The necessary and sufficient conditions of therapeutic personality change. *Journal of Consulting Psychology, 21,* 95-103.

Ross-Reynolds, G., & Hardy, B. S. (1985). Crisis counseling for disparate adolescent sexual dilemmas: Pregnancy and homosexuality. *School Psychology Review, 14,* 300-312.

Rusk, T. N. (1971). Opportunity and technique in crisis psychiatry. *Comprehensive Psychiatry, 12,* 249-263.

Sandoval, J. (1985a). Notes on teaching school psychologists about community resources and agencies. *Trainers' Forum, 5*(2), 1-4.

Sandoval, J. (Ed.). (1985b) Mini-series on crisis counseling in the schools. *School Psychology Review, 14,* 255-324.

Selye, H. (1974). *Stress without distress.* New York: The New American Library.

Slaikeu, K. A. (1984). *Crisis intervention. A handbook for practice and research.* Boston: Allyn & Bacon.

Stocking, S. H., Arezzo, D., & Leavitt, S. (1980). *Helping kids make friends.* Niles, IL: Argus Communications.

Self-Esteem, Crisis, and School Performance

Colette L. Ingraham
San Diego State University

The experience of crisis is in the eye of the beholder. Crisis is idiosyncratically defined by each person and under differing circumstances, even by the same individual. What may be a crisis this month may not be experienced by the person as a crisis next month. A crisis may be characterized as anything that is contrary to expectation or that is not anticipated *both* cognitively and emotionally. For example, even though a teenager knows that a parent has a terminal disease and will probably die within a year, the emotional reaction to the death may still be experienced as a crisis. Perhaps the most debilitating types of crises are those that threaten self-esteem.

The purpose of this chapter is to develop a conceptual framework for understanding the cognitive–affective processes associated with mastery of challenges confronting children, with special attention to the impact of crisis on self-esteem and school learning. The chapter begins with a discussion of self-concept development with special reference to school learning, followed by an examination of normal and dysfunctional processing. Attention is then directed to the cognitive–affective dynamics of a crisis reaction, the impact of crisis on development, and suggestions for the role of the crisis counselor.

THE DEVELOPMENT OF COGNITIVE–AFFECTIVE PROCESSES

The child's self-concept, self-esteem, and patterns of processing information are important contributors to the cognitive–affective dynamics associated with school functioning. An understanding of the development and functioning of self-concept and its relationship with information processing is particularly important for planning successful interventions with children in crisis.

Self-Concept Development and School Learning

Self-concept is generally defined as a multifaceted construct that is organized into categories of beliefs one maintains about self. *Self-concept* consists of the cognitive dimensions of self-perception, whereas *self-esteem* is composed of affective dimensions associated with global feelings of self-worth. There are several components of self-concept, each of which relates to different aspects of the person, depending on the maturity and interests of the individual. For example, the self-concept of a junior high student might contain separate categories for self-concept in the areas of social (peer and adult relations), physical (appearance and ability), academic (math, English, social studies, science, etc.) and emotional self-concept. Within each of these self-concept areas, the student groups information about self obtained from interactions with significant others and the environment. For example, within academic self-concept, the student maintains self-perceptions associated with each of the main subject areas. The same student might have a postitive self-concept of math, a negative self-concept of English, and an average self-concept of science ability. Several successes in English classes might raise the self-concept of English ability without necessarily changing self-concept of math or science. In other words, self-concept can change over a period of time, depending on the experiences of the individual.

The accuracy and completeness of self-concept are thought to increase with age. Although the young child may have a simplistic impression of "I am good at math," the more mature child is better able to specify various strengths and weaknesses and might say "I am good at two-place addition and subtraction, but I have trouble borrowing." Self-concept accuracy and specificity are important for healthy functioning in school. A student who has an accurate self-concept is able to take appropriate risks, to identify areas of needed assistance, to make realistic predictions about the chances of success or failure, and to utilize problem-solving strategies to resolve difficulties. Simply stated, the more information one has about one's skills, the better one can assess a task and successfully apply one's abilities.

One of the key features in the development of an accurate self-concept is the ability to attribute correctly the causes of success and failure. When failure occurs, the student who can analyze the situation and determine the reason for failure is in a good position to handle the situation in a more successful way next time. For example, when Bill gets a failing score on the spelling test and wants to do better on the next test, he can try to assess the situation to find the causes for his failure. Did he study? Did he feel rested on the day of the test? Was he paying attention as the teacher read the spelling words? Through logical information processing, he is able to find the reasons for his failure and to modify his self-concept of spelling ability. Now his self-concept might contain the statement "I can be a good speller if I pay attention to the teacher when she is reading the words." If Bill's attribution for the spelling test failure is accurate, he now knows the conditions for future success.

Cognitive–Affective Dynamics of School Learning

The development of an accurate self-concept is enhanced through the use of logical information processing and correct attributions for success and failure. As the student evaluates the reasons for successes and failures, he or she accumulates more information about (a) one's own strengths and weaknesses, and (b) how to manage one's skills in a variety of experiences to increase chances for success (Covington, 1984; Harari & Covington, 1981). Successes generally lead to pride and satisfaction, especially when one is able to attribute the success to internal sources of ability and effort. These positive feelings increase one's self-confidence and one's willingness to try new tasks and situations. In other words, success breeds motivation to try other tasks. Failure may lead to initial feelings of self-doubt or disappointment. The student with self-confidence and positive self-concept may overcome these initial reactions and begin searching for the reasons for the present failure. This student knows that by finding the reasons for failure this time, modifications in behavior are possible so that the next attempt may be successful. A healthy recovery from failure often includes the "I'll try" attitude, combined with information about how to try differently next time. The student can then take this information and incorporate it into the self-concept so that the self-concept becomes more accurate and complete.

Another aspect of cognitive–affective dynamics of school learning involves the ability to balance emotional and thinking processes. A certain amount of excitement and motivation is helpful for sustaining attention. Teachers are well aware of the benefits of creating a mental set for an activity to increase motivation. When the teacher says, "Now this will really help you on the test" most students will pay closer attention to the subsequent discussion. On the other hand, too much anticipation may interfere with attention. The child who has test anxiety may become so worried about the upcoming test when the teacher mentions it, that the student is unable to concentrate on the explanation given by the teacher. Successful learning requires the student to selectively attend to certain emotions and ignore "off-task" feelings. Anticipation, excitement, and arousal need to be within a constructive range for each student, or achievement may suffer. Also, the student needs to be able to focus attention on the task at hand and not be distracted by off-task thoughts. Thinking about what snack to have after school may cause the student to miss the teacher's directions for an assignment. Similarly, the student who empathizes with the feelings of the character in the story may begin to recall personal experiences. The memory of the student's own emotions and experiences may interfere with concentration needed to complete the reading task.

The Perceptual Filter: Protector and Distorter

Human beings seem to have a perceptual filter that serves to protect feelings of self-worth and self-esteem. We have a natural tendency to want to think positively about ourselves, and we may become defensive when there is a hint that we are not worthwhile. When someone makes an accusation, for example that we are inconsiderate, we might react with "I am not" followed by an explanation or reframing of the situation.

Within attributional research, *attributional egotism* is a term used to describe the tendency to believe positive things about ourselves and to disregard or explain away negative things (Snyder, Stephan, & Rosenfield, 1978). Specifically, attributional egotism is the tendency to accept responsibility for positive outcomes and to externalize responsibility for negative outcomes. When a student does poorly on a term paper, placing the blame for the low grade on an unjust teacher, "the luck of the draw," or other external causes, the student is denying responsibility for the outcome. The same student who gets an "A" on a term paper and attributes the success to his or her own superior ability or extra effort in preparing the paper is accepting responsibility for the success. A person who makes internal attributions for success and external attributions for failure is demonstrating attributional egotism.

The consequence of attributional egotism is that attributions of low ability are deflected at the expense of self-concept accuracy. By attributing the causes of failure to external sources, the student is able to maintain the belief that "I'm OK. It was just that the teacher was overly strict." The problem is that the student is not making use of the performance feedback to make modifications in the preparation of term papers, hence the same poor performance may be repeated. The student may continue to believe that she or he can write fine term papers and thus perpetuate an inaccurate self-concept. Although the student has a positive self-concept of writing ability, this self-concept does not match the school performance, and no changes are made to bring the student's self-concept into closer congruence with the situation. The more the student uses egotistical attributions, the further self-perception is from classroom experience. The protection of feelings of self-esteem, in this situation, creates distortion of self-perception. Information is not accurately processed and assimilated into the developing self-concept. Instead, feelings of self-esteem may be protected, but the student does not learn from the experience. Future achievement in writing term papers is in jeopardy.

Clearly, healthy functioning involves accurately attributing the causes of successes and failures. A good understanding of the reasons for success and failure enables one to know what to do to ensure future successes. Knowing what one did to contribute to the success allows the person to feel pride and self-efficacy. Similary, knowing what one did to contribute to failure gives one clues for self-improvement. A healthy self-perception allows one to attribute accurately the causes of both success and failure, without severely threatening one's feelings of self-worth. "Yes, I made a mistake. Now that I know why I did poorly, I can do it differently next time. I'm still a good person" would be a healthy response to a failure.

Dysfunctional Patterns of Information Processing

Students who typically respond to failure in an adaptive way may react differently during times of crisis. Students who are experiencing crisis may interpret achievement feedback in ways similar to students with dysfunctional patterns of information processing. There are several dysfunctional patterns of attribution and information processing that adversely affect school performance.

Some students distort performance feedback to protect their feelings of self-worth and self-esteem, or they may stop trying as a way to avoid failure (Covington, 1984; Covington & Beery, 1976; Covington, Spratt, & Omelich, 1980). An example of this dysfunctional pattern is seen in the case of Clarisa. She wants to believe that she is academically capable. She is afraid that if she tries hard in school and fails, it would show that she is not bright, so she prefers to avoid trying. She tells her teacher that she did not do the assignment because "it was boring," or because "I already know how to do it, so why do I have to do it over and over." Clarisa is really not trying as a way to avoid the possibility of negative performance feedback about her academic abilities.

Other students develop symptoms of learned helplessness. They stop trying because they have lost hope that their efforts can produce success (Andrews & Debus, 1978; Diener & Dweck, 1980; Dweck, 1975; Dweck, Goetz, & Strauss, 1980; Weisz, 1979). Kevin demonstrated this type of pattern. In the second grade, he tried repeatedly to do well in reading. He paid attention, he practiced making the sounds for the letters in reading group, and he stayed in at recess to finish his work. Even with all his efforts, Kevin still did poorly in reading. By about January, he became so frustrated that he stopped trying to read. He felt that he was doomed to be a poor reader, despite anything he tried to do to improve. He lost hope that he could do anything to improve his reading ability, so he stopped trying.

A third dysfunctional pattern occurs in students with low self-esteem who take responsibility for failure, but not success—just the opposite pattern from attributional egotism. For these students, negative self-perception is supported because when failure occurs, they attribute it internally to low ability. If they do succeed at a task, they externalize responsibility, believing that they were "just lucky" or "the teacher was just in a good mood." In this way, they perpetuate the belief that they have low ability and will never succeed because of their own effort or skill. For these students, low self-esteem is maintained by distorted information processing.

WHEN CRISIS THREATENS SELF-ESTEEM

Any crisis can affect school learning, especially if it threatens self-esteem. When self-esteem is threatened, the student may be less willing to take risks, to initiate, to take a stand, or to do anything that might further jeopardize feelings of self-worth and self-esteem. The reduction in feelings of self-confidence, emotional strength, and ability to cope with events limits the emotional energy available to take on new challenges or to attempt academic tasks.

A person experiencing a crisis may show marked emotionality and greatly reduced cognitive functioning in the areas of memory, concentration, articulation of thoughts, organization and planning ability, and other areas important for school learning. The ability to ignore distracting emotions or thoughts and the ability to focus attention on learning tasks may be greatly reduced. Behavior, social interaction, play, creative thinking, and fine motor abilities such as writing may also be seriously affected by a crisis reaction. Logical information processing is probably not in operation, and the normal perceptual filter that serves to protect self-esteem may be altered in one of two ways.

One reaction to crisis is for defense mechanisms to *overcompensate* for the threat to self-esteem and become so rigid that the student does not take in any information suggesting personal responsibility or involvement with the failure. "I'm good at writing. I got a 'D' because the teacher was having a bad day," might be expressed by an overly defensive student in the face of school failure. Research that explains the difference between coping processes and defenses that prevent adaptive conflict resolution is found in the areas of ego psychology (Block & Block, 1980; Haan, 1969, 1977; Lazarus, 1970; White, 1974) and attribution research (Covington, 1981; Snyder, Stephan, & Rosenfield, 1978; Weiner, 1979).

An alternative reaction to crisis is when a flood of negative feedback enters one's awareness and causes instant pervasive loss of self-esteem, self-worth, self-efficacy, and hope. Students in crisis may feel like there is no point in expending effort because success is out of their reach. Children who had a positive, healthy self-perception before the crisis may now respond much like the unmotivated, paralyzed, "learned helplessness" children who have experienced repeated failures. One devastating experience can produce behaviors and feelings similar to those of chronic failers (Jonas & Hayes, 1984; Maddux & Rogers, 1982; Orbach & Hadas, 1982).

Effects of Crisis Reaction on Student Development

There are several ways in which a crisis may affect student development. The impact of a crisis on information processing and self-concept development can be tremendous. A student in crisis may be unable to focus attention on the important pieces of information for solving problems, learning, and relating with others.

A child in crisis may have difficulties on the playground and in peer interactions, due to an inability to follow the conversation, feelings of insecurity or emotionality, and lack of self-confidence. Acting-out or withdrawn behaviors may increase during times of crisis, increasing the student's feelings of isolation, and loss of self-efficacy. Friends may not understand the sudden unpredictability of behavioral changes of the child in crisis. The same behaviors and difficulties with logical information processing can affect classroom performance. Inability to concentrate, restlessness, or lethargy may increase during times of crisis.

Patterns of behavior may develop out of the child's reaction to a crisis. For example, children of divorce may not talk about the family or may pretend that both parents live at home because they do not want others to know about the divorce. Similarly, a child who is experiencing a crisis over a reading disability may attempt to cover up the perceived weakness in reading and find ways to avoid reading aloud. Keeping "the problem" a secret is one way a child might try to protect an outer image of "being OK" while internally feeling lacking or unworthy in some way. On the other hand, students who are so engrossed in their own crisis that they talk about it endlessly may lose friends and begin to feel like no one understands or cares about them. In this case, the expression of internal feelings and thoughts may contribute to the loss of a support network of friends.

Whatever way the child reacts behaviorally, the internal loss of self-confidence and self-esteem that so often accompany crisis can significantly affect the child's personal development. The impact of many of the emotions experienced during crisis—perceived loss of control, inability to cope and master, insecurity and reluctance to take risks, lowered self-esteem—can affect student development in a variety of ways.

Experiences That Can Threaten Self-Esteem

The types of experiences that threaten self-esteem are thought to be associated with developmental and individual differences (Ingraham, 1983, 1985/1986). The areas of life most important to one person may not be very significant for another. For example, a student who wants to become a scientist may go into a crisis reaction upon receipt of a "C" grade on a science project, whereas another student may be quite content with an average grade in science. In other words, failure in an area of life that is very important to the individual (called *high valuation*) may threaten self-esteem much more than a failure in an area in which the person places little importance (called *low valuation*; Ingraham, 1980, 1983, 1985/1986). Following this reasoning, a person is most susceptible to threat of self-esteem in areas that have high valuation. Failure in an area of high valuation presents a potential for a crisis reaction.

Other potential threats to self-esteem are situations that involve a great deal of uncertainty. New situations, new tasks, or environments with which we are unfamiliar can threaten self-confidence because the rules and expectations for the new experience are unknown. Certainly, some persons are more vulnerable than others. Nevertheless, for many people, trying a new game, joining a new group, starting a new schedule, or moving to a new environment can make them uncomfortable and uncertain. A person with an unstable self-concept of ability may feel very threatened when he or she is called to demonstrate his or her skills with a new textbook, a new reading group, or a new teacher. The student who lacks confidence may ask "Can I do it? What if I don't succeed? What will the new teacher think if I forget the answer?"

The Role of the Crisis Counselor

Knowledge of the cognitive–affective dynamics associated with crisis is useful in planning effective interventions for students experiencing a crisis. Of course, specific intervention plans will depend on the developmental level of the student and the unique features of each case, however, some general principles are involved. A main goal of crisis intervention is to help the student regain perspective and cope with the crisis, thereby preventing further deterioration of self-esteem, self-efficacy, or other qualities central to school functioning. At the time of the crisis, the counselor can help restore adaptive functioning by using two levels of intervention directed at self-esteem dynamics (Ingraham, 1985).

In the first level of intervention, the counselor listens for the student's perspectives about the causes of the crisis and any coping strategies the student has considered. The main function of the crisis intervention at this level is to reduce the student's anxiety, feelings of isolation, and confusion—without challenging the student's attributions or otherwise adding to the threat to self-esteem. This is a critical step in establishing rapport, as in other types of counseling, and in gathering information about how the student thinks and feels.

Diagnostic assessment of key cognitive–affective dynamics is the second level of crisis intervention. The crisis counselor gathers information about the student's patterns of processing information, general level of self-esteem, areas of self-perceived strengths and weaknesses related to the self-concept, and any coping resources available to the student. Through counseling and informal assessment techniques, useful information about the child's functioning is collected in the following areas:

1. attributional patterns (along dimensions of perceived controllability and stability);
2. level of self-esteem (generally high, medium, or low, both before the crisis and presently);
3. self-concept in several dimensions (achievement, social, physical, etc.)
4. level of defensiveness in processing success and failure feedback (i.e., does the student make internal or external attributions for each type of achievement situation);

5. typical patterns of coping and resources available under the current crisis situation; and
6. the chronic versus acute nature of the current crisis.

An assessment of these areas will help the crisis counselor know if this is a normally confident student who has fallen into a sudden state of crisis, or if the student has chronically dysfunctional patterns of processing information. Similarly, a student with a vast array of coping resources may regain access to them through intervention, whereas a student without many coping skills will need to learn adaptive strategies.

Through the counselor's assessment of the student's functioning in all of these areas, it is possible to collect a great reservoir of diagnostic information that is useful for planning the appropriate intervention. For example, Sue has a high self-concept of math ability, and Mark has a low self-concept of math ability. Both Sue and Mark are changing schools soon, and they are both very nervous about the move because they will lose contact with their friends. If the receiving teacher gets both students involved in math assignments right away, Sue may come out of her crisis and regain her confidence due to her high math self-concept. She will probably succeed in the math task. In contrast, starting with math might increase Mark's feelings of crisis because math is an area of low self-concept for him. A more useful intervention for Mark might involve a non-academic task with a partner to help him establish peer relations. The more information the crisis counselor has about self-concept and coping, the better the chances for planning a successful intervention.

REFERENCES

Andrews, G. R., & Debus, R. L. (1978). Persistence and the causal perception of failure: Modifying cognitive attributions. *Journal of Educational Psychology, 70,* 154–166.

Block, J. C., & Block, J. (1980). The role of ego-control and ego-resiliency in the organization of behavior. In W. A. Collins (Ed.), *Development of cognitions, affect, and social relations: The Minnesota Symposia on Child Psychology* (Vol. 13, pp. 39–101). Hillsdale, NJ: Lawrence Erlbaum Associates.

Covington, M. V. (1981, June). Motivated cognitions: On why children are studying less and smoking more. *Proceedings of the Institute on Learning and Motivation in the Classroom.* Ann Arbor: University of Michigan.

Covington, M. V. (1984). The motive for self-worth. In R. Ames & C. Ames (Eds.), *Research on motivation in education* (Vol. 1, pp. 77–113). New York: Academic Press.

Covington, M. V., & Berry, R. G. (1976). *Self-worth and school learning.* San Francisco: Holt, Rinehart & Winston.

Covington, M. V., Spratt, M. F., & Omelich, C. L. (1980). Is effort enough or does diligence count too? *Journal of Educational Psychology, 72,* 717–729.

Diener, C. I., & Dweck, C. S. (1980). An analysis of learned helplessness: II. The processing of success. *Journal of Personality and Social Psychology, 39,* 940–952.

Dweck, C. S. (1975). The role of expectations and attributions in the alleviation of learned helplessness. *Journal of Personality and Social Psychology, 31,* 674–685.

Dweck, S., Goetz, T. E., & Strauss, N. L. (1980). Sex differences in learned helplessness. IV. An experimental and naturalistic study of failure generalization and its mediators. *Journal of Personality and Social Psychology, 38*, 441–452.

Haan, N. (1969). A tripartite model of ego functioning values and clinical research applications. *The Journal of Nervous and Mental Disease, 148*, 14–30.

Haan, N. (1977). *Coping and defending processes of self-environment organizations.* San Francisco: Academic Press.

Harari, O., & Covington, M. V. (1981). Reactions to achievement behavior from a teacher and student perspective: A developmental analysis. *American Educational Research Journal, 18*, 15–28.

Ingraham, C. L. (1980). *Self-concept: A critical analysis of the construct and a refinement of the theory.* Unpublished manuscript, University of California, Berkeley.

Ingraham, C. L. (1983, April). *Valuation and school success: A cross-sectional study of student values, self-esteem and self-concept dimensions.* Paper presented at the Annual Convention of the Western Psychological Association, San Francisco.

Ingraham, C. L. (1985). Cognitive-affective dynamics of crisis intervention for school entry, school transition and school failure. *School Psychology Review, 14*, 266–279.

Ingraham, C. L. (1986). Dimensions of self-concept and valuation and their relationship with self-esteem, effort and grades: A cross-sectional analysis. (Doctoral dissertation, Unversity of California, Berkeley, 1985). *Dissertation Abstracts International, 47*, 837A.

Jonas, E. D., Jr., & Hayes, L. G. (1984, April). *The effects of exit-exam failure on students' self-concept.* Paper presented at the Annual Meeting of the American Educational Research Association, New Orleans.

Lazarus, R. S. (1970). Cognitive and personality factors underlying threat and coping. In S. Levine & N. A. Scotch (Eds.), *Social stress* (pp. 143–164). Chicago: Aldine.

Maddux, J. E., & Rogers, R. W. (1982, March). *Prediction motivation and self-efficacy: Toward a general expectancy-value model of attitude change.* Paper presented at the Annual Meeting of the Southeastern Psychological Association, New Orleans.

Orbach, I., & Hadas, Z. (1982). The elimination of learned helplessness deficits as a function of induced self-esteem. *Journal of Research in Personality, 16*, 511–523.

Snyder, M. L., Stephan, W. G., & Rosenfield, D. (1978). Attributional egotism. In J. H. Harvey, W. Ickes, & R. F. Kidd (Eds.), *New directions in attribution research* (Vol. 2, pp. 91–117). Hillsdale, NJ: Lawrence Erlbaum Associates.

Weiner, B. (1979). A theory of motivation for some classroom experience. *Journal of Educational Psychology, 71*, 3–25.

Weisz, J. R. (1979). Perceived control and learned helplessness among mentally retarded and nonretarded children: A developmental analysis. *Developmental Psychology, 15*, 311–319.

White, R. W. (1974). Strategies of adaptation: An attempt at systematic description. In G. V. Coelho, D. A. Hamburg, & J. E. Adams (Eds.), *Coping and adaptation* (pp. 47–68). New York: Basic Books.

II

CRISES THROUGHOUT CHILDHOOD AND ADOLESCENCE

This section consists of chapters devoted to hazardous events that can occur at any age. Each of the authors has devoted space to the crisis-relevant differences in cognitive, social, and emotional development that the school psychologist or guidance worker will encounter in working with children from preschool through high school. Even at a given age or grade level, children will differ in their developmental level and will differ across domains of development (i.e., a child's social developmental level may be different from his or her cognitive, emotional, or physical developmental level). An underlying assumption of this book is that effective counseling, intervention, or prevention must be directed at the child's appropriate developmental status.

The events described in many of the following chapters are hazardous to parents as well as to childern. Divorce, maltreatment, handicap, death, and moving are all events that are likely to leave the parent, as well as the child, in a state of crisis. Although it may be out of the school's sphere of influence to offer help directly to parents, the school should be prepared with outside referral sources should the parents request help. In addition, school personnel should realize that because parents may well be in crisis at the same time as their children, they are thus unavailable to provide them with needed emotional support. The burden falls even more on the schools for regularizing and improving the environment for the child. It is important to realize, however, that in intervening with children in crisis we are assuming roles that in the past have been the roles of others. We must be sensitive that other support systems such as church, extended family, and neighborhood may still exist and we must not preempt natural prerogatives. Nevertheless, increasingly these alternative resources are not available for children.

In this section, Ingraham (chapter 3) writes on school-related crises. These are school entry, changes in educational placement, academic failure, and difficulties springing from a learning handicap. In her discussion of these difficulties, she stresses the need to rebuild carefully the student's sense of self-efficacy and mastery.

King and Goldman (chapter 4) focus their chapter on assisting children of divorce and remarriage. A special feature of their chapter is an extensive discussion of group work with children in the schools centering on the common experience of divorce. Their model serves a prototype for programs that have helped or could be designed to help children in other crises such as death of significant other or maltreatment.

Chapter 5 by Germain is an overview of intervention with children who have been maltreated. This topic has received a great deal of attention as of late, and Germain has summarized a great deal of recent thought and research. It is an excellent starting point for more study on this heartbreaking topic.

Irvin (chapter 6) has written about children with handicapped parents. Parents who are injured, contract a physical or mentally debilitating disease, or who become addicted to alcohol or drugs are often not able to provide the basic conditions necessary for children to thrive. Irvin stresses the need to be sensitive to the existence of such children and to actively identify them so that appropriate school accommodations can be made.

Increasingly, chronically ill children are finding their way into the classroom, as medical technology and societal attitudes toward them improves. Illness is not only a crisis of children, but, as recent cases related to AIDS in school children have shown, may also be a crises all for school personnel and classmates. Steward (chapter 7) reviews notions from behavioral medicine and developmental models of children's understandings of illness in an effort to facilitate the formation crisis interventions for ill children. In this and the following chapter the movement from understandings of children's conceptualizations at different ages to crisis counseling is most clear.

In chapter 8, Wilson reviews the literature of helping children cope with the death of significant people in their lives. In addition to children's conceptions of death, she describes the process of grieving and grief reactions. She suggests that crisis counseling is directed at facilitating the bereavement process. School prevention efforts may consist of special curricula or in increased willingness to discuss death in conventional academic subjects.

Moving is a hazard that may occur by itself on in connection with another hazardous event such as death or divorce. Sandoval (chapter 9) discusses variables that may be related to a move becoming a crisis for a child and emphasizes programatic ways to prevent the event from becoming harmful.

All of these crises may produce a great deal of anxiety in all concerned, including school personnel. It does no good to ignore anxiety and the most adaptive way to respond to it is to move forward systematically and to gain as much detailed knowledge as possible to reduce the unknown or uncertainty.

School-Related Crises

Colette L. Ingraham
San Diego State University

There are many crises that affect the lives of children. Almost all affect the school learning and performance of children in some way. Some crises are directly related to what happens in school. This chapter identifies four common school-related crises and describes students who are at risk of each crisis. The first section discusses who is at risk of crises associated with school entry, transition, perceived academic failure, and learning handicaps. The second section describes several strategies for intervention and prevention of crises in school learning.

WHO IS AT RISK

Four types of crises that impact student learning are the sources of numerous referrals to school professionals. The competent professional who understands the dynamics associated with each type of crisis is better able to provide rapid, effective intervention.

School Entry

Entry to school involves a wide range of new experiences for any child. The adjustment from home to school includes learning a whole set of new skills, rules, expectancies, and so on. Classroom rules may differ from the rules of the home, and the methods and consistency with which rules are enforced may also be different. Social interaction takes place with new adults, peers, and perhaps new languages and cultures, and with a much larger number of same-aged persons than previously experienced. There are expectations for learning concepts, fine motor movements, sharing, demonstration of knowledge, and so on that may represent new patterns of behavior. In fact, everything about school may be new and unfamiliar.

Most children are able to make all of the adjustments needed to adapt to entrance to school. But for some, school entry becomes a crisis sometimes called *school refusal* or *school phobia*. Gordon and Young (1976) define *school phobia* as "a partial or total inability to attend school" (p. 783). Unlike the truant, the authors explain, the school phobic child stays at home with the parents and is absent for consecutive days or weeks at a time.

The incidence of school phobia is relatively low, ranging from 3 to 17 cases per thousand school-age children per year (Gordon & Young, 1976). Johnson (1979) cites several studies in which school phobics account for less than 8% of the cases seen in psychiatric clinics. Referrals for school phobia are most common around the age of 11, but they are also frequent for ages 5–6 and 7–8 (Johnson, 1979).

The etiology of school phobia continues to generate controversy (Atkinson, Quarrington, & Cyr, 1985; Gordon & Young, 1976; Johnson, 1979), although most theorists tend to agree that school phobia or school refusal are more accurately described as a manifestation of separation anxiety from the mother than as a fear of school. Some authors describe the school phobic child as having an over-inflated feeling of importance in the family (Leventhal & Sills, 1964) and preferring the security of home to the ambiguities and newness of the school environment. Other writers identify a classification scheme for school refusal to characterize the various types of etiologies and descriptions of school refusal (Atkinson, Quarrington, & Cyr, 1985). This scheme suggests a complex phenomenon and considers several variables: extensiveness of disturbance, mode and age of onset, fear sources, and gender.

In other words, the school phobic child may evidence symptoms of idiosyncratic defense mechanisms that attempt to protect an inaccurate self-concept. The self-concept is threatened by the realities, competition, and uncertainty of the school environment. Staying home with a supportive parent protects the child's feeling of self-worth and self-efficacy by limiting the incoming information about the child's abilities and comparison with other children that is typical at school.

Gordon and Young (1976) and Johnson (1979) both review numerous intervention studies that report varying degrees of success in treating the school phobic child. Brief intervention approaches such as behavior modification, systematic desensitization, and similar techniques appear to be successful for treating school phobic children and providing rapid reentry into school. The need for long-term psychotherapy is still being debated in the literature.

Once the child is attending school regularly, the crisis counselor can work with the teacher and parent to improve gradually the accuracy of the child's self-perception and to increase feelings of belongingness with the class. Interventions may include group participation; responsibilities such as monitor, partner, or tutor; and by pairing the student with peers for achievement tasks. The goals of follow-up interventions are to increase the child's sense of self-efficacy in the school environment and to maintain feelings of self-worth, while modifying the accuracy of the child's self-image so that it more appropriately matches the real world. This type of follow-up is designed to promote continued positive mental health and information processing once the behavioral symptoms of school attendance have been addressed.

School Transition

School transition refers to changes from one educational placement to another. These changes can include changes from one school, building, or classroom to another. Students whose families move from one location to another, a similar type of school transition, are discussed in chapter 9.

The prevalence of crisis associated with school transition is great. The numbers of children who change grades, schools, or educational placement each year vary considerably from district to district. Factors such as military or mobile populations, redistricting, bussing, and program stability all contribute to the number of school transitions children make. There are many predictable school transitions that may lead to crisis for vulnerable children. Any change in school, class, playground, grouping, educational program, or teacher can be problematic. When multiple changes are made simultaneously, the potential for crisis increases. For example, a special education student who is being transferred from a special day class in a special school into a regular school with a Resource program is changing schools, teachers, programs, time mainstreamed, peer groupings, and possibly curriculum.

Although some children greet these transitions as challenges and welcomed rites of passage, others experience feelings of anxiety, confusion, insecurity, anger, and/or fear that can precipitate psychological crisis. The student knows the old familiar classroom, rules, peers, social norms, and so on, must be given up, yet the future is a mystery. The unknown and new reference group, environment, rules, and patterns of behavior can all generate great anxiety and a loss of coping strategies. The student may fearfully wonder: Will the new kids accept me? What if I get lost? What if I do something stupid?

School professionals can take an active role in seeking appropriate placements for students in transition and at risk of crisis or school failure. McFadden (1978) demonstrated that even as early as first grade, the instructional strategies of a teacher and school climate can alter student achievement motivation. Matching the student's needs for structure, reward system, ability grouping, peer compatibility, and teacher characteristics can greatly reduce the chances that the student will experience severe crisis during the transition.

Other studies highlight social comparison with peers as an important factor to consider in the adjustment of students to new educational environments. The student's relative standing with the academic performance of classmates significantly impacts the student's feelings (McLoughlin, 1983; Schwarzer & Schwarzer, 1982; Zarb, 1984). The student may have higher feelings of self-worth and self-efficacy and show greater task persistence when placed with students of similar or lower ability than when placed with high-achieving students in an environment that does not match his or her attributional and motivational patterns.

Crisis related to school transition can be minimized through anticipatory guidance activities that help reduce anxiety and fear of the unknown by providing information and concrete expectancies. As anxiety is reduced, strategies to build social supports such as a buddy system or a tour of the new setting are useful. Teachers who receive new students can assign a partner to show the new student around at recess and introduce him or her to other children. Teachers can foster the building of peer relationships by assigning group projects where students have to work on a task together, thereby providing some initial structure to their interactions.

Perceived Academic Failure

It is relatively easy to point to environmental changes such as school entry and school transition as contributors to the onset of a crisis. In contrast to crises with school entry and school transition, which occur at relatively predictable times and are readily defined by the change in environment, crises associated with academic failure are more difficult to define and to predict. Perceptions of academic failure vary from person to person and can occur at any point during one's schooling. Additionally, the antecedents and consequences of perceived failure for any individual vary greatly. When viewed from the cognitive–affective processing framework discussed in chapter 2, however, the dynamics of perceived academic failure are much clearer.

A crisis associated with a perceived academic failure may be any event that the individual interprets as a failure in school and that is connected with the individual's feelings of self-esteem. The number of students who experience some form of perceived academic failure each day is great. Every day some students experience their first low grade on an assignment, some are placed in the slowest reading group, some are sent home with notes of reprimand, and some must miss recess for misconduct or unfinished work. Depending on the student's perception, any of these experiences could be interpreted as an academic failure. The same "B+" grade on a spelling test may be cause for celebration for the average student and cause for perceived failure for the student accustomed to grades of "A+." The impact of any of these experiences on the student's feelings of self-esteem, self-worth, and coping and defending strategies determines the extent to which the experience may result in a crisis situation for the student.

There are many populations that are at risk of academic failure. In the past 10 years, several theories have emerged that help identify groups of students that are susceptible to academic failure. Theories of self-efficacy (Bandura, 1977), self-worth (Covington & Beery, 1976), and school-related attribution (Weiner, 1979) all suggest that students who do not feel a sense of personal control and responsibility for achievement are at risk of both negative self-perception and school failure. Snyder, Stephan, and Rosenfield (1978) posit that self-esteem may be threatened by a failure experience if the reason for failure is attributed to the person (internal causality), and if the task is relevant to the person's self-esteem. Similarly, valuation theory (Ingraham, 1980, 1985/1986) hypothesizes that self-esteem is most threatened when the person receives negative feedback about self in an area of self-concept that is highly valued by the individual. Students who base their self-worth on their success in the classroom are more likely to experience crisis related to perceived academic failure, compared with students who do not care much about school performance because their social life (or other area of interest) is the basis for their self-worth.

Among students who base at least some of their self-esteem on their success in school, school failure may be particularly distressing when the failure is attributed to stable internal causes such as low ability (Covington, 1984; Covington & Omelich, 1981; Covington, Spratt, & Omelich, 1980). Students with a history of academic failure are likely to have lower self-concept of ability, lower expectancies for future success, fewer problem-solving strategies (Johnson, 1981; Stipek & Hoffman, 1980; Wiegers & Frieze, 1977) and feelings of helplessness (Diener & Dweck, 1980). Some studies show that girls attribute failure to internal causes such as low ability more often than boys (Dweck, Goetz, & Strauss, 1980; Stipek & Hoffman, 1980; Wiegers & Frieze, 1977), suggesting that girls may be more susceptible to feelings of school failure and lowered expectancies for school success despite their levels of actual achievement. In one study, girls in Grades 4–6 attributed failure more often to low ability at the beginning of the school year when there were minimal performance cues, but as the year progressed, the girls developed more accurate and hopeful expectancies and attributions; boys, on the other hand, seem to be more prone to overdefensiveness and overestimation of their chances for success (Dweck, Goetz, & Strauss, 1980).

Students with ineffective coping strategies may also be candidates for crisis in the face of school failure. Covington (1980), Ingraham (1985a), and Licht (1983), among others, have highlighted the importance of knowing the right problem-solving strategy for the problem at hand. Students who continue to use ineffective strategies increase feelings of frustration and may eventually reduce school effort. Learning-disabled students (Cullen & Boersma, 1982; Licht, 1983), retarded students (Weisz, 1979), and culturally disadvantaged students (McLoughlin, 1983; Raviv, Bar-Tal, Raviv, & Bar-Tal, 1980) may not have effective problem-solving strategies in their repertoire of coping resources for school tasks. Similarly, students with a history of school failure who have not received special assistance are more at risk of debilitating cognitive–affective dynamics than students who have received remedial help at the high school level (Zarb,

1984). Finally, students who experience test anxiety are at risk of crises related to school failure. The prevalence of test anxiety is estimated to be approximately 30% of school-age children (Johnson, 1981; Stevens, 1980).

In addition to certain types of students who are at risk of school failure, as previously described, there are also indentifiable developmental transitions that are predictive of populations at risk of school failure. The concurrence of cognitive, social, and emotional developmental transitions, coupled with environmental changes at school, creates times of developmental crisis (Ingraham, 1985b). For example, students in Grades 3 and 4 are typically expected to concentrate longer, remember more, and demonstrate more academic skills than students in earlier grades. These increased performance expectations occur at the same time that students are cognitively more aware of how they compare with peers, and, with the emergence of cognitive decentration, they may be more aware of how others perceive their abilities. Poor achievement, coupled with the alarm of parents, teachers, or even chiding peers, can lead to crisis at this age due to the clear feedback that the student is not performing well. The student who is not doing well in school may begin forming cognitive–affective patterns that are not conducive to healthy information processing or a negative self-evaluation that may lead to feelings of helplessness and decreased motivation to try.

Given the potential for self-doubt in the classroom, the simultaneous change from the primary playground to the upper grade playground at recess may further contribute to the child's insecurity. Now the fourth grader may be playing with older students, sometimes with new games and social rules for conduct, thus increasing the unfamiliarity and potential threat to self-esteem. It is no surprise that students are often referred for difficulties with academics, self-esteem, peer relations, frequent absences, and so forth around this age. The frequency of referrals for school refusal is also not surprising, given the cognitive–affective dynamics taking place. Whenever the student is in transition from one developmental phase to another, especially when developmental transitions are accompanied by changes in the school environment, expectations, and social groupings, self-esteem may be more vulnerable to threat due to perceived academic failure (Ingraham, 1985b).

Learning-Handicapped Students and School Crises

Students with learning handicaps represent a special population that is at risk of school failure and potential school-related crises. There are several ways in which learning-handicapped students are particularly vulnerable to crises in school.

According to present classifications, learning-handicapped students are typically learning disabled or mildly mentally retarded. Mildly mentally retarded students are at risk of failure at school both socially and academically because they may not be as intellectually agile as their peers, both on the playground and in class. Academically, the student may have difficulty learning at the same rate as agemates, and unless special instruction or curriculum is provided, the student may be subject to academic frustration and/or failure.

Learning-disabled students, by definition, have difficulty in one of the basic psychological processes, frequently in the area of auditory and/or visual information processing. The learning-disabled student may experience difficulty following directions, comprehending information, remembering, or articulating thoughts. Many of these areas of difficulty are exactly the types of skills needed to succeed in the typical educational program. These are also the same skills that are needed to use logical information-processing and problem-solving strategies in solving non-academic, personal problems. Consequently, the learning-disabled student also may be handicapped in the use of strategies to cope with crisis. Difficulty with making a plan, sustaining concentration, and ignoring distractions, are common in many learning-disabled students. The ability to contain emotional frustration over a failure, to put a failure into proper perspective, and to continue experimenting with alternate strategies may be very difficult for the handicapped student.

The self-esteem and self-confidence of learning-disabled students may be threatened by feelings of being different from peers and by difficulties with social interaction. Learning-handicapped students often have difficulty in social judgment, in understanding cause–effect relationships, and/or in articulating their thoughts to others. Problems in anticipating events and in self-expression can interfere with satisfying peer relations and social behaviors.

When a student is initially diagnosed as having a specific learning disability or evidence of mild mental retardation, for some people, there is relief in the discovery of some "reason" for the frustrations and difficulties in school. For others, however, the initial diagnosis may be perceived as a crisis. Sometimes the parent or student expresses feelings of denial, guilt, or depression at the time of diagnosis. For some, placement into a special education program may be perceived as a failure or crisis, whereas for others, it may be a welcomed opportunity for assistance. The individualized educational program (IEP) team can provide useful assistance as the diagnostic information is shared with parent and student, helping to support both during this critical time. Careful monitoring of the student's attitudes and behavior, once placed in special education, is also important in order to provide early intervention when needed, before the student experiences a crisis.

Interventions that involve both cognitive and affective approaches are especially important for the learning-handicapped student. Licht (1983) describes effective interventions that teach learner strategies and effort attributions to learning-disabled students. Waters (1983) reports that peer interactions, with supportive counseling groups, helped improve the grades and attitudes of failure-prone students. Robinson (1986) offers excellent suggestions for teaching learning-disabled teenagers to focus attention on the learning process and to reinforce their own learning. Robinson's intervention combined consultation with teachers and cognitive training for students into a successful confluent education model that involved both cognitive and affective aspects of learning.

Adjusting to transitions, new environments, new teachers or routine, and new social groupings may be especially problematic for learning-handicapped students. Unless they have good coping strategies, positive self-esteem, and high self-confidence, learning-handicapped students may be vulnerable to self-esteem threats associated with uncertain or unfamiliar educational experiences. Learning-handicapped students may benefit from extra support during times of change and transition in order to prevent experiences of crisis. Because these students are commonly identified for special education services, it is relatively easy to anticipate and plan ways to ease the transitions for learning-handicapped students.

INTERVENTION FOR SCHOOL-RELATED CRISES

Effective intervention for students experiencing a crisis involves attention to the cognitive–affective processes described in chapter 2. Attention to self-concept, self-esteem, and patterns of processing information is especially important.

School professionals who are knowledgeable about the cognitive–affective processes associated with a crisis reaction are able to provide intervention services that go beyond the traditional crisis intervention strategies of calming affect and restoring stability in functioning. A variety of approaches may be used to actually teach students effective coping strategies, thereby assisting their successful recovery from the immediate crisis and developing skills for mastery over potential crises in the future.

First- and Second-Level Crisis Intervention

During the initial steps in crisis intervention, the crisis counselor provides emotional support and structuring (Sandoval, 1985) and uses the diagnostic techniques outlined in the previous chapter. This information is useful in planning the appropriate second-level intervention. Some students will be ready to begin problem solving shortly after crisis counseling begins, whereas other students may have experienced devastation that leads to immobilization and pervasive feelings of self-doubt and helplessness. The types of goals appropriate for second-level intervention will depend on the nature of the crisis, the developmental level of the student, and the crisis counselor's assessment of the student's cognitive–affective processing.

For students who are experiencing a debilitating reaction to a school-related crisis, the early goals of the intervention involve carefully rebuilding the student's sense of self-efficacy and mastery. The first tasks should involve small goals with reasonable opportunities for success, outcomes that are clearly attributable to the student's own efforts, and a noncompetitive setting (Ingraham, 1985a). Depending on the intensity of the perceived crisis, early tasks could include simple accomplishments such as organizing a physical education equipment box, cleaning out a desk, or watering the plants. With these initial tasks, the goal is to take some action that breaks the anxiety/depression/immobilization cycle while producing some visible form of accomplishment. Simple, tangible accomplishments offer concrete proof of one's efforts and symbolize mastery and order over one's environment. If the student is ready for tasks in the academic realm, intervention might include planning a schedule to complete the night's homework assignment, or dividing the book report assignment into manageable pieces and deciding what to do first. The level of complexity of the task and the amount of independent effort involved will depend on two factors: (a) the crisis counselor's assessment of the amount of coping resources available in the student's repertoire at the time of the crisis, and (b) the perceived magnitude of the failure that resulted in the crisis.

Once the student overcomes the initial emotional reaction to the crisis, other strategies can be used to redirect the cognitive–affective processing into constructive patterns. For example, attribution retraining is useful for students who show dysfunctional information-processing characteristics such as learned helplessness. The goal of the training is to reinforce students for attributing the causes to internal attributions such as effort. When the student fails, the student is encouraged to think that it was due to insufficient effort rather than inability or external causes. Attribution retraining is effective with learned-helplessness children (Dweck, 1975) and in increasing task persistence in regular education elementary (Andrews & Debus, 1978) and junior high students (Reiher & Dembo, 1984).

Research on attribution retraining also highlights the types of reinforcements that are most effective for students with different attributional patterns. Children who tend to attribute failure to internal causes such as low ability—the most common attributional pattern for children who have a history of failure—benefit from programs that use social reinforcement or tutoring (Bugental, Whalen, & Henker, 1977; Cullen & Boersma, 1982; Johnson, 1981; Licht, 1983) as opposed to programs that rely on self-instruction. Children in regular or special education who attribute achievement internally and who have high levels of perceived control, on the other hand, achieve better with reward systems and classroom structures that are noncontrolling (Harpin & Sandler, 1979) and use self-talk or self-controlling motivational approaches (Bugental, Whalen, & Henker, 1977).Once again, the crisis counselor's assessment of the attributional patterns of the student are key to selecting the most effective type of reinforcement during recovery from the crisis.

Another intervention strategy that is effective after the student has emotionally recovered from the immediate crisis is instruction in problem-solving strategies. Effective instruction in problem solving teaches students how to try, so that their increased efforts are directed in ways that can lead to success. Linking task strategies with achievement beliefs of self-efficacy (Schunk & Gunn, 1984) and establishing rewards that are contingent on performance (Schunk, 1983) are two recommended approaches. These strategies teach students to identify which strategies are working and to take credit for their successes, thereby building self-concept of ability and feelings of mastery. The modification of self-concept and self-confidence requires meaningful reinforcement and repeated experience, especially in the initial phases of overcoming a crisis.

Attribution retraining and problem solving are only two recommended approaches for intervention with children who have experienced failure in school. More information about these and other approaches is available in Henker, Whalen, and Hinshaw (1980) and Licht (1983). Additionally, special issues of the *School Psychology Review* are devoted to research on cognitive–behavioral interventions (Hynd, 1982) and social competence and social skill development (Carroll & Elliott, 1984).

Whatever approach the crisis counselor uses in the second level of intervention, the underlying counseling goals are similar. The student is encouraged to modify self-concept to match reality, to gain broader perspective on the situation, and to plan steps to cope with the previous crisis. As the student regains access to coping strategies (and possibly learns new ways to handle situations), the counselor helps articulate what the coping strategies are and how the student is developing mastery over his or her feelings, thoughts, and behaviors. This process helps the student conceptualize the coping strategies that were useful and develops internal attributions for their successful use. Finally, the counselor helps the student transfer effective coping strategies from other areas of life to the problematic situation.

Steve's case is an example of a frequent type of school crisis. His IEP team is moving him from a special day class to a regular fifth grade class and a Resource Specialist Program. He is afraid of the change because he has grown accustomed to the special class, and he feels unsure of how he will survive most of the day with 30 other students in his new class. He remembers, with terror, his experiences in school before his placement into a special class in the second grade. During the second level of intervention, the counselor helps Steve focus on the coping skills he already has, helping him realize how to apply these to the fearful transition. The counselor might ask questions such as:

> How did you learn the rules of your special class? What are the rules in your class? What happens when you do something right? How did you learn what the teacher expects of you? What do you do if you need help?

The counselor directs Steve's attention to his knowledge of rules, expectations, and his clues for learning these. Then the counselor helps Steve anticipate what to expect in the new class and how to use his coping strategies to adjust more smoothly. Finally, it is important for Steve to have a very concrete awareness of the resources and strategies to assist him in the new class if he needs help or feels panic. Rehearsing strategies for getting help, regaining his composure, and using tools such as lists or written reminders will assist him during the transition period.

Early Intervention and Prevention of School Crises

Many types of school-related crises can be reduced through anticipatory guidance and well-timed intervention. The following three guidelines are central to planning effective prevention and early intervention services for children at risk of crises associated with school.

1. *Intervene early in the child's development.* There appears to be a critical age in the child's development when lasting attitudes and patterns of processing information are formed. Comparison of developmental theories (Ingraham, 1978, 1985b) and numerous developmental studies (Harari & Covington, 1981; Nicholls, 1975, 1979; Weiner, Kun, & Weiner, 1980) suggest that around the age of 10, children are susceptible to some of the dysfunctional self-perception and attribution patterns that perpetuate school failure. Once patterns of low self-esteem, lack of internal success attributions, or overly defensive protection of self-esteem set in, they are very difficult to modify. Prevention activities in the second and third grade might teach students coping skills and productive information-processing patterns, prior to the critical cognitive–affective transition that takes place around age 10 (Ingraham, 1985b).

2. *Develop a school-wide prevention program.* The major emphasis of a program designed to prevent school crises is one that supports the development of self-esteem and coping skills. An effective prevention program has several components. First, the philosophy and actions of the school staff and community communicate the worth of each student, regardless of their level of achievement. Students need an opportunity to develop their self-concept in a variety of areas— academic, social, physical, and other domains. Specific performance feedback about what parts are done well, what needs improvement, and suggestions for how to improve helps students to develop an accurate self-concept and to identify strategies for improvement. Academic material at the appropriate level for each student is important for success to be within reach, thereby reducing feelings of frustration, avoidance, and failure.

Students need to develop and practice coping strategies. The school curriculum can offer students instruction and practice in analyzing, searching for causes of events, determining all the steps involved in a task, and making use of problem-solving strategies and a variety of thinking skills. This includes practice in planning and carrying out multi-step solutions. An important component in a school-wide prevention program is specific instruction and practice in seeking support when needed. The first step is to teach students how to know when they need help. Then students need to know how to seek help when there is a need so students do not feel isolated and without support when they get stuck.

Several resources may be useful in the planning of a school-wide program to prevent school crises. Schilling (1986) offers excellent suggestions and resource lists for building positive self-esteem in the classroom. *Communicating to Make*

Friends (Fox, 1980) is a wonderful book full of resources and classroom activities that are well-suited for elementary and middle grades. The *Productive Thinking Program* (Covington, Crutchfield, Davies, & Olton, 1974) is useful for developing the cognitive strategies needed in problem solving at the preadolescent and adolescent levels. *The Human Development Program* (Bessell, 1972) has many uses for developing self-awareness, communication, and social skills for Grades K-12. An examination of many of the recent media and curriculum catalogues reveals a wide variety of books, films, software programs and materials, that can be used for a school-wide prevention program.

    3. *Plan early intervention for at-risk populations.* Anticipatory guidance prior to major transitions, developmental crises, and other predictable times of difficulty is a cost-effective and logical intervention strategy. Groups of students who are identified as at-risk of school crises, such as students changing schools, students failing classes, or students showing early signs of dysfunctional cognitive-affective processing are obvious targets for early intervention. Students who make statements such as "I can never do anything right," "Why should I even try—I won't get it anyway," "I have to get a 'B' or I might as well have failed" could be identified for early intervention programs. Statements like these show perceptions of low self-efficacy, low self-concept of ability, or unrealistic expectations for performance.

    There is some evidence to suggest that interventions for at-risk populations are more effective when they address both informational and social needs. Junior high students who participated in weekly Peer Intervention Network groups demonstrated improved grades and interpersonal skills (Kehayan, 1983). Alienated high school students benefited attitudinally and behaviorally from a psychology course and cross-age tutoring at the elementary school (Zeeman, 1982). Additional research suggests that training in problem-solving and coping skills is more effective than group counseling alone (Stevens & Pihl, 1982). Other programs have included intervention for teachers as part of the program. For example, Ryals (1975) reported the success of Achievement Motivation Training for teachers in improving math and science achievement of junior and senior high school students. Robinson (1986) provided direct instruction and group counseling for high school students, combined with regular training for their teachers. She reported gains academically and socially for learning-disabled students in the project. The general conclusion of many of these studies is that intervention for at-risk populations is most effective when students are taught strategies to solve problems and are given the emotional supports to sustain motivation and develop coping strategies.

    In general, prevention of school-related crises is enhanced by programs that foster accurate, well-articulated, and diversified self-concept development. Logical processing of performance feedback allows the student to assess the causes of school success and failure and to modify strategies based on achievement feedback. Students who know how to seek out performance information are better prepared to solve problems and reduce anxiety associated with the unknown, new situations, and changes in routine. Students who have an array of personal resources and coping strategies at hand are more resilient. Students who know when they need help and how to seek assistance have an invaluable strategy to prevent crises.

Finally, when the school professionals are knowledgeable about the dynamics of healthy and dysfunctional cognitive-affective processes, they are better equipped to intervene. School-related crises are often integrally associated with perceived threats to self-esteem and self-worth. The crisis counselor who understands the relationship of crisis with self-esteem and information processing is prepared to carefully assess the dynamics of the crisis and plan effective interventions. The prevalence of crises with school learning can be greatly reduced with prevention and early intervention.

REFERENCES

Andrews, G. R., & Debus, R. L. (1978). Persistence and the causal perception of failure: Modifying cognitive attributions. *Journal of Educational Psychology, 70,* 154–166.

Atkinson, L., Quarrington, B., & Cyr, J. (1985). School refusal: The heterogeneity of a concept. *American Journal of Orthopsychiatry, 55,* 83–101.

Bandura, A. (1977). Self-efficacy: Toward a unifying theory of behavioral change. *Psychological Review, 84,* 191–215.

Bessell, H. (1972). *Methods in human development: Theory manual.* San Diego, CA: Human Development Training Institute.

Bugental, D. B., Whalen, C. K., & Henker, B. (1977). Causal attributions of hyperactive children and motivational assumptions of the two behavior-change approaches: Evidence for an interactionist position. *Child Development, 48,* 874–884.

Carroll, J. L., & Elliott, S. N. (Eds.). (1984). Social competence/skills [Special issue]. *School Psychology Review, 13*(3).

Covington, M. V. (1980, October). *Strategic thinking and the fear of failure.* Invited address presented at the National Conference on Thinking and Learning Skills, University of Pittsburg.

Covington, M. V. (1984). The motive for self-worth. In R. Ames & C. Ames (Eds.), *Research on motivation in education* (Vol. 1, pp. 77–113). New York: Academic Press.

Covington, M. V., & Beery, R. G. (1976). *Self-worth and school learning.* San Francisco: Holt, Rinehart & Winston.

Covington, M. V., Crutchfield, R. S., Davies, L. B., & Olton, R. M. (1974). *The productive thinking program: A course in learning to think.* Columbus, OH: Merrill.

Covington, M. V., & Omelich, C. L. (1981). As failures mount: Affective and cognitive consequences of ability demotion in the classroom. *Journal of Educational Psychology, 73,* 796–808.

Covington, M. V., Spratt, M. F., & Omelich, C. L. (1980). Is effort enough or does diligence count too? *Journal of Educational Psychology, 72,* 717–729.

Cullen, J. L., & Boersma, F. (1982). The influence of coping strategies on the manifestation of learned helplessness. *Contemporary Educational Psychology, 7,* 346–356.

Diener, C. I., & Dweck, C. S. (1980). An analysis of learned helplessness: II. The processing of success. *Journal of Personality and Social Psychology, 39,* 940–952.

Dweck, C. S. (1975). The role of expectations and attributions in the alleviation of learned helplessness. *Journal of Personality and Social Psychology, 31,* 674–685.

Dweck, S., Goetz, T. E., & Strauss, N. L. (1980). Sex differences in learned helplessness. IV. An experimental and naturalistic study of failure generalization and its mediators. *Journal of Personality and Social Psychology, 38*, 441–452.

Fox, C. L. (1980). *Communicating to make friends.* Rolling Hills Estates, CA: Winch.

Gordon, D. A., & Young, R. D. (1976). School phobia: A discussion of etiology, treatment, and evaluation. *Psychological Reports, 39*, 783–804.

Harari, O., & Covington, M. V. (1981). Reactions to achievement behavior from a teacher and student perspective: A developmental analysis. *American Educational Research Journal, 18*, 15–28.

Harpin, P. M., & Sandler, I. N. (1979) The interaction of sex, locus of control, and teacher control: Toward a student-classroom match. *American Journal of Community Psychology, 7*, 621–632.

Henker, B., Whalen, C. K., & Hinshaw, S. P. (1980). The attributional contexts of cognitive strategies. *Exceptional Education Quarterly, 1*(2), 17–30.

Hynd, G. W. (Ed.). (1982). Cognitive-behavioral interventions for classroom and academic behaviors [Special issue]. *School Psychology Review, 11*(1).

Ingraham, C. L. (1978). *Self-concept development and psychosocial, cognitive, and moral theories of development.* Unpublished manuscript, University of California, Berkeley.

Ingraham, C. L. (1980). *Self-concept: A critical analysis of the construct and a refinement of the theory.* Unpublished manuscript, University of California, Berkeley.

Ingraham, C. L. (1985a). Cognitive-affective dynamics of crisis intervention for school entry, school transition and school failure. *School Psychology Review, 14*, 266–279.

Ingraham, C. L. (1985b, March). *Reducing developmental crises: Preventing school failure and building student self-esteem.* Paper presented at the Annual Meeting of the California Association of School Psychologists, Los Angeles.

Ingraham, C. L. (1986) Dimensions of self-concept and valuation and their relationship with self-esteem, effort and grades: A cross-sectional analysis. (Doctoral dissertation, University of California, Berkeley, 1985). *Dissertation Abstracts International, 47*, 837A.

Johnson, D. S. (1981). Naturally acquired learned helplessness: The relationship of school failure to achievement behavior, attribution, and self-concept. *Journal of Educational Psychology, 73*(2), 174–180.

Johnson, S. B. (1979). Children's fears in the classroom. *School Psychology Digest, 8*(4), 382–396.

Kehayan, A. V. (1983, March). *Peer intervention network: A program for underachievers.* Paper presented at the Annual Convention of the American Personnel and Guidance Association, Washington, DC.

Leventhal, T., & Sills, M. (1964). Self-image in school phobia. *American Journal of Orthopsychiatry, 34*, 685–695.

Licht, B. G. (1983). Cognitive-motivational factors that contribute to the achievement of learning-disabled children. *Journal of Learning Disabilities, 16*, 483–490.

McFadden, C. L. (1978). Academic achievement motivation as a function of classroom responsiveness. *Journal of Experimental Education, 46*(4), 41–44.

McLoughlin, W. (1983). Understanding how schools fail children. *International Review of Education, 29*, 59–72.

Nicholls, J. G. (1975). Causal attributions and other achievement-related cognitions: Effects of task outcome, attainment value, and sex. *Journal of Personality and Social Psychology, 31*, 379–389.

Nicholls, J. G. (1979). Development of perception of own attainment and causal attributions for success and failure in reading. *Journal of Educational Psychology, 71*, 94–99.

Raviv, D., Bar-Tal, A., Raviv, A., & Bar-Tal, Y. (1980). Causal perceptions of success and failure by advantaged, integrated and disadvantaged pupils. *British Journal of Educational Psychology, 580*, 137–146.

Reiher, R. H., & Dembo, M. H. (1984). Changing academic task persistence through a self-instructional attribution training program. *Contemporary Eductional Psychology, 9*(1), 84–94.

Robinson, C. A. (1986). The case for confluence and LD teens. *Academic Therapy, 21*, 323–329.

Ryals, K. (1975). Achievement motivation training for low-achieving eighth and tenth grade boys. *Journal of Experimental Education, 44*(2), 47–51.

Sandoval, J. (1985). Crisis counseling: Conceptualizations and general principles. *School Psychology Review, 14*, 257–265.

Schilling, D. E. (1986). Self-esteem: Concerns, strategies, resources. *Academic Therapy, 21*, 301–307.

Schunk, D. H. (1983). Reward contingencies and the development of children's skills and self-efficacy. *Journal of Educational Psychology, 75*, 511–518.

Schunk, D. H., & Gunn, T. P. (1984, April). *Modeled importance of learning strategies and children's achievement behaviors.* Paper presented at the Annual Meeting of the American Educational Research Association, New Orleans.

Schwarzer, R., & Schwarzer, C. (1982). Achievement anxiety with respect to reference groups in school. *Journal of Educational Research, 75*, 305–308.

Snyder, M. L., Stephan, W. G., & Rosenfield, D. (1978). Attributional egotism. In J. H. Harvey, W. Ickes, & R. F. Kidd (Eds.), *New directions in attribution research* (Vol. 2, pp. 91–117). Hillsdale, NJ: Lawrence Erlbaum Associates.

Stevens, R. (1980, September). *At-risk for school failure: A comparison for competence and performance of under stress at-risk and normal seventh graders.* Paper presented at the Annual Convention of the American Psychological Association, Montreal.

Stevens, R., & Pihl, R. O. (1982). The remediation of the student at-risk for failure. *Journal of Clinical Psychology, 38*, 298–301.

Stipek, D. J., & Hoffman, J. M. (1980). Children's achievement related expectancies as a function of academic performance histories and sex. *Journal of Educational Psychology, 72*, 861–865.

Waters, M. K. (1983). "I've been tested, rejected and neglected." *Academic Therapy, 18*, 547–554.

Weiner, B. (1979). A theory of motivation for some classroom experience. *Journal of Educational Psychology, 71*, 3–25.

Weiner, B., Kun, A., & Weiner, M. B. (1980). The development of mastery, emotions, and morality from one attributional perspective. In W. A. Collins (Ed.), *Development of cognitions, affect, and social relations, The Minnesota Symposia on Child Psychology* (Vol. 13, pp. 103–129). Hillsdale, NJ: Lawrence Erlbaum Associates.

Weisz, J. R. (1979). Perceived control and learned helplessness among mentally retarded and nonretarded children: A developmental analysis. *Developmental Psychology, 15*, 311–319.

Wiegers, R. M., & Frieze, I. H. (1977). Gender, female traditionality, achievement level, and cognitions of success and failure. *Psychology of Women Quarterly, 2*, 125–137.

Zarb, J. M. (1984). A comparison of remedial, failure, and successful secondary school students across self-perception and past and present school performance variables. *Adolescence, 19*, 335–348.

Zeeman, R. D. (1982). Creating change in academic self-concept and school behavior in alienated secondary students. *School Psychology Review, 11*, 459–461.

4

Crisis Intervention and Prevention with Children of Divorce and Remarriage

Mariam J. King
Center for the Family in Transition

Ruth K. Goldman
San Francisco State University

INTRODUCTION

Divorce and marital separation are second only to the death of a parent as stressful events for youngsters (Coddington, 1972). The distinctive nature of these marital crises has led researchers to investigate how crisis intervention techniques can best be adapted to ameliorate the negative, long-term effects of familial disruption on youngsters (Goldman & King, 1985; Kalter, Pickar, & Lesowitz, 1984; Pedro-Carroll & Cowen, 1985; Stolberg & Cullen, 1983; Wallerstein & Kelly, 1980).

In this chapter, we describe our efforts at adapting a spectrum of preventive mental health techniques, including those of crisis intervention, to fit the unique aspects of marital crises as they affect children and school systems. The program described here attempts to treat children with families at different stages of resolution to the marital crisis—the newly separated or divorced family, the remarried family, and the chronically embattled divorced family.

Divorce, separation, and remarriage are processes that introduce rapid, multiple structural changes and require adaptation of all family members. Anxiety experienced at this time increases a child's need for a stable "holding environment" (Winnicott, 1971), while the nature of these familial changes temporarily undermines the capacity to parent (Wallerstein & Kelly, 1980), leaving the child vulnerable to even greater anxiety and depression. Because the changes required are of such great magnitude, it is likely that the family system will have difficulty in providing nurturance, sustaining intimacy, and containing anxiety. For some families, this failure is transitory, with the family structure restabilizing 2 to 3

51

years postseparation. For others, there is a permanent familial disequilibrium, resulting in what Hunter and Schuman (1980) have described as the "chronically reconstituting family."

Unlike other stressful events, such as a death in the family, the announcement of a divorce does not rally the support of the community. In fact, the members of the divorcing family may find themselves excluded from the social/familial network that provides support in other crisis situations. Bain (1978) hypothesizes that the capacity of a family to cope with a transition is proportional to the ability of formal social organizations at the boundary of the transition to deal with the transition as a psychosocial event. Important formal organizations in an individual's life often deny the pain experienced by the individual in an effort to protect staff against the experience of anxiety associated with the individual's pain. As a result "it becomes *that* individual or *that* family which is not able to cope, rather than an experience which includes the institution and where possible difficulty in coping is commonly confronted" (p. 677).

At times of familial disruption, school can offer children a source of nurturance and continuity as well as a place where age-appropriate developmental tasks can be pursued while family life is in disequilibrium.

> One 7-year-old whose parents had recently divorced was having nightmares. In his dollhouse play he showed a little boy awake at night while everyone else slept. The boy runs around the house from room to room. "I dream that the house is falling apart, but sometimes I have good dreams. I dream that I'm in school and I'm making things."

For this child, the school environment was a supportive one in which he could move ahead with his life less hindered by the preoccupations that plagued him at home.

Our interest in working in the schools is rooted in the belief that an individual's capacity to cope with familial change and the resulting stress is partially dependent on the quality of support and guidance available from extra-familial organizations in which that person functions (Peterson, Leigh, & Day, 1984; Stolberg & Cullen, 1983). The single most important formal institution providing such support outside the home is the school (Drake, 1981; Kelly & Wallerstein, 1979).

Because the school as a system is confronted with large numbers of families attempting to cope with the transitions brought about by divorce, strategies for intervention must be designed to address the needs not only of the individual student so affected, but also those of the classroom teacher and the school as a whole. In this chapter, we describe programmatic efforts designed to accommodate the organizational structure of the school to the structure of the postdivorce family.

WHO ARE THE CHILDREN OF DIVORCE?

Recent statistics from the Bureau of the Census estimate that of the children born in 1983, 45% will experience the divorce of their parents and 35% will experience the remarriage of their parents, while 20% will experience the redivorce of the remarried family before the age of 18. In the United States, two-thirds of the women who divorce are under 30, and most children are under age 7 at the time of their parents' divorce or separation (Beal, 1980). These dramatic figures indicate the changing nature of the familial configuration in the school-age population.

The schools, however, are faced with problems in being able to offer support to students from these families. In addition to dealing with anxiety and depression in the students (which commonly induce strong countertransference reactions in teachers and administrators, some of whom are also coping with marital changes of their own), many of these youngsters develop learning and behavioral problems secondary to the stress of the familial disruption. Numerous writers have described the behavioral changes and disruption in the children's ability to learn associated with the stress of parental separation and divorce (Gardner, 1976; Guidubaldi, 1984; Hetherington, 1979; Wallerstein & Kelly, 1980). Teachers report an increase in restlessness, aggression toward peers, tendency to daydream, and inability to concentrate. For adolescents, a marked increase in absenteeism and tardiness is often present (Goldman, 1981). In longitudinal research on 131 children from divorcing families (Kelly & Wallerstein, 1977), close to half were reported to experience school-related difficulties in the postdivorce period. These were youngsters with no prior history of emotional difficulties or learning problems

Opinion has been divided as to whether it is appropriate for schools to intervene in family-related crises (Drake, 1981; Goldman, 1981). This has clearly been reflected in the dearth of training programs, teacher consultation, and on-site direct services offered to youngsters. However, both parental and professional attitudes appear to be changing with regard to the need for offering an array of school-based services to students from divorced families (Clay, 1981; Elam & Gough, 1980; Gallup, 1980).

YOUNGSTERS AT RISK

This section draws heavily upon findings reported in four major studies. The pioneering and most comprehensive of the studies conducted over 10 years by Wallerstein and Kelly, while limited in some design respects (60 families with 131 children from Northern California), continues to yield the richest source of clinical and conceptual material (Wallerstein, 1983, 1984; Wallerstein & Kelly, 1980). Five years postdivorce, they noted that approximately one third of the children in their study were faring well and considered themselves happy. Approximately one third were doing reasonably well and were able to pursue academic goals, but the remainder were depressed.

Hetherington, Cox, and Cox (1978) conducted a more limited 2-year study of 48 preschool children and their families. Although this design included a control group matched for age, sex, birth order, and numerous parent variables, it, too, lacks social class and geographic representativeness. According to them, within 2 years of divorce the majority of debilitating factors that encumber children have subsided and equilibrium is in the process of being restored.

More recently, Kurdek and Berg (1983) and Kurdek, Blisk, and Siesky (1981) have been following 74 families from an Ohio chapter of Parents without Partners in an attempt to assess and contrast children's and parents' postdivorce adjustment. As in the previously cited studies, sample selection and restriction and a variety of methodological problems continue to be present.

Guidubaldi, Perry, Cleminshaw, and McLoughlin (1983) and Guidubaldi (1984) have attempted to resolve a number of the design limitations of past studies through employing a randomly selected national sample of elementary school youngsters, controlled for age, sex, race, IQ, family income, and geographic location. Currently, the authors have 2- and 3-year follow-ups of two subsamples for the original group of 699 first, third, and fifth graders.

Risk Factors Linked to Sex

Of special concern are the consistent findings that divorced-family boys, "in comparison with both girls from divorced homes and boys from intact homes, have a behavioral profile indicating high frequencies of negative acting out including aggression, opposition, and impulsivity" (Guidubaldi et al., 1983, p. 32). In their 2-year follow-up with a cohort of the original sample, girls clearly improved on social–emotional and academic criteria while boys deteriorated (Guidubaldi, 1984). Others report similar findings for boys (Hess & Camara, 1979; Hetherington et al., 1978). In a survey of approximately 400 teachers, Goldman (1981) noted that fighting with peers was one of the most frequently cited divorce-related behaviors.

Kelly and Wallerstein (1977) describe the extent to which the school functioned as a primary source of gratification for students who had been doing well in school prior to the familial disruption. These students used the school as a sanctuary and, in particular, turned to teachers who provided sympathy and attention. Their teachers were frequently the only stable and continuing force in an environment filled with uncertainty. Kelly and Wallerstein (1979) concluded that girls, rather than boys, were able to utilize teachers in these ways.

Risk Factors Linked to Age

Research findings regarding the risk factors correlated with the child's age at the time of divorce and the length of time spent in the divorced household are contradictory. The work of Hetherington et al. (1978) suggests that more detrimental effects are associated with children of younger ages, a finding supported by Kurdek and Berg (1983), who report that older children have fewer adjustment problems. The Guidubaldi study (Guidubaldi et al., 1983) indicates that older girls adjust better to divorce than younger girls do, with the reverse being true for boys. This finding is further supported by a 2-year follow-up in which fifth grade girls from divorced families were most indistinguishable from those in intact homes, whereas fifth grade boys show an increase in problems over those presented in first grade (Guidubaldi, 1984). Kalter and Rembar (1981), however, conclude that there is no relationship between degree of adjustment and age of the child. Current preliminary findings by Wallerstein (1984) in her 10-year follow-up show that "children who are very young at the marital breakup are considerably less burdened in the years to come than those who were older at the time of the divorce" (p. 457), and that "by virtue of their own immaturity at the time and the repressive processes at work, [they] have emerged less consciously troubled than their older siblings" (p. 468).

Risk Factors Linked to Parental Adjustment and Environment

Closure or resolution of the divorce happens at both the level of the family as a whole and at the individual level. Wallerstein (1983) has conceptualized the child's resolution of the divorce as a series of developmental tasks. She believes that this follows a particular time sequence beginning with the critical events of the parental separation and culminating in young adulthood. Although resolution of the divorce at the level of the individual child is influenced by the resolution of the disruption at the family systems level, she notes "there is no necessary *determining* relationship between the resolution and adjustments achieved by either of the adults . . . and the outcome for any particular child . . . it is the child who must carry the burden of mastery and resolution on the way to a successfully achieved adulthood" (p. 231).

   Wallerstein and Kelly (1980) conclude that a positive relationship with the father appeared to be more critical for boys than girls. Other investigators have reported that both positive relations between the parents and availability of the noncustodial parent contributed to the good adjustment of the child following the stressor of divorce (Hess & Camara, 1979; Jacobson, 1978a, 1978b, 1978c).

   More recently, Kurdek and Berg (1983) have identified parent-related factors that influence positive adjustment following marital breakup. They found that "children's divorce adjustment is significantly related to their mothers' use of social support systems, to their mothers' own divorce adjustment, to low maternal stress levels, and to low interpersonal conflict" (p. 58). The quality of the interaction with the noncustodial parent figured significantly, whereas the frequency and regularity of the visits were not significantly related to good adjustment.

   Controls for socioeconomic status (SES) have been inadequate in past studies making it difficult to discern whether negative effects following divorce were primarily attributable to decreased family income (Brown, 1980). In Kurdek and Berg's (1983) continuing study parents' social status did not emerge as a significant predictor of postdivorce adjustment. However, they recognize that their middle-class sample may not have had to endure great financial distress thereby limiting the extent to which generalizations could be made from their study. In the work of Guidubaldi et al. (1983) and that of Guidubaldi, Cleminshaw, and Perry (in press), the authors clearly distinguish socioeconomic factors that separately and interactively with other postdivorce variables negatively effect boys. Of the different SES measures, reduced family income had the most adverse effect (primarily on boys) and particularly in areas of academic achievement.

Other studies have consistently reported the interruption in or reduced ability to function well academically, with no clear time limit on the extent of the effect (Goldman, 1981; Guidubaldi, Perry, & Cleminshaw, 1983; Kelly & Wallerstein, 1979). Factors such as orderly and predictable school environment, traditional classroom structure, and general school attitudes, which stress student achievement, were all related to more successful school adjustment in latency-aged children (Guidubaldi, Perry, Cleminshaw, & McLoughlin, 1983).

COMMON AGE-SPECIFIC REACTIONS TO DIVORCE

Preschoolers

In Wallerstein and Kelly's (1980) initial study, which focused on postseparation reactions, they noted that 2½- and 3½-year-olds regressed in their behaviors. These toddlers, struggling with issues of mastery, often lost recently acquired toilet-training skills and showed signs of separation anxiety, such as clinging behavior, or the converse of reaching out too quickly to strangers. Children between 3¾ and 4¾ years frequently displayed bewilderment, irritability, aggressive behavior, and self-blame (Gardner, 1976; Hetherington, 1979).

Although Wallerstein and Kelly have addressed themselves primarily to the affective component in divorce-related responses, Neal (1983) has extended their work into the cognitive domain. He found that the youngest group (3- to 6-year-olds) understands parental divorce entirely from an egocentric perspective. They link feelings of attachment to physical closeness, and therefore when one parent moves away from the child, the syllogistic assumption is that the child did something wrong to cause this physical distance.

Latency-Age Children

Wallerstein and Kelly (1980) reported that early elementary school-aged children (ages 7 to 8) appeared sad, were observed to be deeply grieving, and were torn with feelings of split loyalty, fantasies of responsibility and reconciliation. Despite their greater understanding of the divorce, they seemed unable to lessen their suffering. By contrast, older latency-aged children (9 to 10 years), while experiencing feelings of loneliness, shame, intense anger, rejection, and helplessness, along with continued loyalty conflicts, appeared more able to utilize adult interventions. According to Neal (1983), children between the ages of 5 and 8, although continuing to construe the marital disruption egocentrically, could additionally understand that conflicts existed between their parents that did not involve them.

Young Adolescents

Neal (1983) found that young adolescents saw the divorce in terms of parents' bad intentions and/or irreconcilable differences or personality problems. They could not make sense of good intentions that did not lead to the stability of the parental relationship. They believed that the parents were responsible for unanticipated negative effects on others. This age group has the advantage of being able to distance themselves from the home conflict through varying techniques: pseudo-maturity, social activities, or turning to friends.

Kurdek and Berg (1983) report that 9- to 12-year-olds could adjust to the divorce better if they experienced an internal locus of control and if they had good interpersonal understanding. Favorable adjustment was positively related to children's perceptions that factors were under their control and that they understood issues in terms of psychological feelings and relationships rather than along concrete dimensions.

Springer and Wallerstein (1983) examined the responses to divorce of a non-clinical population of young adolescents, ages 12–14. They described five hallmarks of these young peoples' reactions to the marital rupture: (a) keen ability to attend to parental relationships and burgeoning ability to judge each parent and his or her behavior as individual; (b) a deep sense of loss of the intact family and loss of hope for what that family might have been; (c) profound concern that overt parental conflicts will become public, leading the adolescent to experience shame and embarrassment; (d) increased rivalry with siblings accompanied by an increased dependency on the intact sibling subsystem; and (e) an ability to maintain distance from the parental discord by sporting a ''cool'' stance, use of sarcasm and humor, and use of extra-familial sources of interest and support. In those cases where the adolescent was not able to maintain distance, there was a strong alliance or identification with one parent. These young people became drawn into loyalty conflicts and experienced a sense of excitement in their involvement in the parental discord. Their continued normal development was considered to be very much at risk.

CONCEPTUALIZING A COMPREHENSIVE MODEL OF PREVENTION

Earlier crisis intervention studies have helped us to better understand emotional responses to loss (Caplan, 1981). Lindemann's (1944) pioneering work was aimed at reducing the traumatic effects of catastrophic loss when individuals were the victims of natural disasters. Bowlby (1980, 1982); Ainsworth (1969); and Mahler, Pine, and Bergman (1975) studied the impact of attachment, separation, and loss on the child. Special attention was given to the young child's attempt to master the temporary or permanent loss of the primary caretaking figure at particular developmental phases.

Children experiencing the crisis of divorce frequently have to deal with ongoing or repeated experiences of loss coupled with feelings of rejection. In many cases, the decision to divorce is preceded by one or more parental separations involving the departure of one parent from the existing family (Bloom, Asher, & White, 1978). The child faces the additional complexity of knowing that the parental decision to separate and divorce was made by choice, which at some level is experienced by the youngster as a rejection. Typically, the youngster is called upon to master relationships with subsequent parent substitutes and newly acquired siblings, all of whom are struggling to obtain sufficient and/or equal affection from one another.

Although many writers have described efforts at treating children of divorce in groups, little has been written that conceptualizes the activity group as part of an overall preventive approach to children as members of schools and communities (Drake, 1981).

As the realization becomes clearer that the "typical" American family is no longer the "norm," the need for organizational changes to accommodate the multiplicity of actual family structures also becomes clearer. Although a direct counseling service with students represents one way of helping them cope with stress, a broader preventive perspective is necessary.

Through the School Services Program of the Center for the Family in Transition, a school-based intervention incorporating activity groups for children of divorced families along with ongoing teacher training and consultation plus parent involvement has been designed. Through collaboration with administrators and faculty, the group interventions become an avenue for helping to create system changes for families in transition at both the school and family level.

Effective Administrative Changes

At the administrative level we have attempted to help educators look critically at their policies toward nonresidential parents. We have addressed such issues as the re-design of registration forms to include both parents and the establishment of uniform policies encouraging issuance of duplicate report cards, school calendars, and so forth.

Administrators need to develop guidelines for faculty members faced with the complexities of conducting parent–teacher conferences with parents who do not reside together. School events should be planned taking into account the growing number of students with stepparents and stepbrothers and stepsisters so as not to leave students in a position in which they feel forced to choose between inviting one household or another to school-related events.

As Ricci (1979) points out, children continue to need both parents. The refusal of social institutions such as the schools to open up avenues that encourage responsible relationships on the part of both parents with their children only serves to weaken family ties in the postdivorce family.

It is through administrative consultation aimed at effecting such changes that school psychologists and counselors can best apply a model of primary prevention in their schools.

Working with Teachers

In a preventive intervention, it is clear that one cannot work effectively within a system by offering service to one segment without understanding the nature of the impact on the related segments and without developing plans to address the impact. It is only by helping teachers acquire greater understanding of a child's classroom behavior as a response to this disruption and by developing more effective strategies for aiding a student's learning, despite the disruption, that one is able to support individual or group work with the child.

The following serves as an illustration of how our collaborative efforts with teachers led to a better understanding of a child's school performance, increased empathy for the youngster, and enhanced the possibility of reaching the student educationally through the use of alternative strategies.

A frustrated teacher complained of the immature quality of one girl's illustration for an essay, using it as an example of the generally poor quality of the student's work. The clinician was able to reframe the "immaturity" in this particular illustration of a house and a bunny rabbit in a sunny field by talking about this 12-year-old's desperate need for mothering and comfort which were triggered by the assigned topic, "Those were the Good Ol' Days." When seen in light of a longing for the predivorce family, this child's "immature" work was less frustrating to this teacher.

In-service training for teachers has been used to educate them about children's reactions to marital crisis. We have found that Wallerstein's (1983) conceptualization of the child's resolution of the divorce as a *series of developmental tasks* is a useful concept to teach. Elucidating common age-specific postdivorce behaviors and how these might be seen in the classroom is equally important.

Vignettes and case presentations are used as a way of helping groups of teachers think about how they cope with troublesome classroom behavior and how they deal with nonresidential parents. For example, one often-voiced complaint on the part of teachers is the difficulty in handling the anger of the latency-age boy that often surfaces as "acting up" in class and refusing to do school work. In several cases where these youngsters' nonresidential fathers were invited by the teacher to discuss the problem and become an active part of the teacher–parent team, the children's troublesome behavior lessened.

COUNSELING INTERVENTIONS

General Considerations

References are drawn primarily from the seminal work of Wallerstein and Kelly, which remains the richest source of clinical data regarding age-specific risk and postdivorce interventions. In their article on brief interventions (1977), Wallerstein and Kelly described the divorce-specific assessment (particularly useful to school psychologists). They evaluated the following factors: (a) each child's overall developmental achievements; (b) each child's unique responses to and experiences with the divorce; and (c) the support systems available to each child. In particular, they were concerned with how the child understood the meaning of the divorce. Drake (1981) has encouraged utilization of this divorce-specific assessment in intervention strategies with students in schools.

In formulating school-based interventions for children with familial disruptions, the following must be considered: (a) a youngster may be experiencing a chronic and highly stressful series of events lasting in some cases for the entirety of the youngster's school years; (b) a youngster may be experiencing a set of indirectly related transitions such as loss of home, change in neighborhood or school, and so on, increasing the stress of the actual familial disruption; (c) a youngster may simultaneously lose the support of extra-familial figures and be particularly needy of nurturance from empathic adults with whom he or she spends time; and (d) a youngster's capacity to cope with stress is dependent on his or her sex, age, developmental temperament, and problem-solving skills.

Interventions with Preschoolers.   Wallerstein and Kelly (1980) suggest that interventions with preschoolers, who do not have a history of emotional difficulties, should focus primarily on the parents. The central intent should be to help parents communicate more effectively with their preschooler and understand better the causes of the child's distress. Frequently, preventive interventions involve stabilizing aspects of both the caretaking situation and visits with the noncustodial parent.

Interventions with Young Elementary School Children.   Interventions for this age group need to take cognizance of the child's realistic understanding of the basis for the divorce. Just as children of this age generally have difficulty in talking about issues involving strong feelings, they have considerable trouble in talking about their parents' divorce. Wallerstein and Kelly (1980) found it necessary to develop an indirect technique for discussing the multiple and complex feelings that arose from the marital disruption. For example, the therapist would recount what such an experience was like for other youngsters of the same age, while specifically utilizing familial information unique to this child's situation in order to help the child express the painful feelings. Thus, the "divorce monologue" was born. Similar storytelling approaches utilizing fantasy, displacement, and projection are described by Kalter, Pickar, and Lesowitz (1984) and by Gardner (1976).

Interventions with the Older Elementary School Children and Adolescents. These youngsters frequently turn to counselors for their support and assistance because they often are able to understand their own conflicts and discuss them (Wallerstein & Kelly, 1980; Goldman, King, & Lamden, 1983). Counselors often are perceived as empathic advocates who could help make sense of many issues in which split loyalty offered no opportunity for discussion with either parent. Brief interventions proved helpful with them when the problems were primarily divorce-related and concerned a variety of more external or environmental considerations. For example, frequently a child's concern over a parent's welfare could be first addressed with a counselor and then taken up with the parent.

GROUP INTERVENTIONS

Research in crisis theory and its application has shown that individuals who receive cognitive guidance and emotional support for coping with a stressful situation have a reduced risk for developing mental and physical illnesses. The use of group techniques in meeting the needs of individuals in stressful situations has proven successful.

Beginning with the work of Cantor (1977, 1979), time-limited counseling groups have been used to help students whose parents recently were separated or divorced and who showed signs of behavioral disruptions. Typically, these groups are offered to older elementary school students of both sexes. Content centers on a child's confusion concerning the reasons for the divorce, loyalty conflicts, visitation issues, problems with stepparents and siblings, and so on. Children report that sharing reactions to typical divorce-related issues offers them support and comfort. When postgroup interviews are held, group members uniformly indicate that the groups were of help to them. (The reader may refer to Drake & Shellenberger, 1981, for a more extensive review of early efforts at using group models with children of divorce.) Recent reports of successful school-based group intervention programs are those described by Kalter, Pickar, and Lesowitz (1984), Stolberg and Cullen (1983), Stolberg and Garrison (in press), and Pedro-Carroll (1985).

Kalter and his associates have developed an 8-week group for older school-aged students. Operating as outside consultants within four public school districts, they characterize their groups as using a "displacement format" to help youngsters deal with anxieties and cognitive confusions in the postdivorce family.

These investigators advocate using a male and female co-leader in order to give youngsters same-sex role models and report having two adults present as advantageous for group management. In their groups, which are highly structured, the adult leaders often take on roles of "Mom" and "Dad," acting out prewritten dialogues characterizing typical situations in the pre- and postdivorce family. Using the adults as the primary actors and allowing the children to comment and elaborate on the scenes enacted serves to engage children in lively discussions without raising their anxiety levels so high that the group becomes hard to manage.

Themes that are used as focal points for each week's 50-minute meeting are the following: predivorce parental fighting and arguing, announcement of parents' decision to divorce, determination of custody and the children's roles in this decision, visiting with the nonresidential parent, parental dating, children's relationships with live-in partners and stepparents, and family life in remarriage.

Their work with groups has confirmed our finding that although many students cope well with their parents' divorce, children still benefit from psychological services that help them cope with the family changes. They note that the parental divorce is a stressor that sets in motion *a series of life events that may potentiate the stress of the divorce itself.* They report that the majority of themes introduced by the participating children were related to adjustment difficulties in a *postdivorce* and *remarried* families. Outcome data from these groups has yet to be compiled; however, preliminary analysis reveals they were viewed favorably by nearly all participants and parents.

Stolberg and Cullen (1983) and Stolberg and Garrison (1985) describe groups that are part of a multi-model prevention program designed to facilitate postdivorce adjustment of mothers and children. Their 12-session children's groups were structured to include weekly meetings of 1 hour each with small groups of students ages 7 to 13. Participants were from families who were within 33 months of parental separation. Relaxation, impulse and anger control techniques, and communication skills were taught through methods that included modeling and role playing. Outcome data indicated that the child participants attained better self-concepts at the end of 12 sessions. At the 5-month follow-up, child participants also were found to have improved social skills.

Pedro-Carroll and Cowen (1985) and Pedro-Carroll (1985) reported on children's school groups in which they used a variation of Stolberg and Cullen's (1983) strategies for teaching effective coping skills to children in the postdivorce family. Their 10-week-long groups included students from fourth to sixth grade, with widely varying lengths of time from the parental divorce.

In the first three sessions, the main goal is to build support for children by giving them opportunities to share common feelings related to the parental divorce and to help clarify common misconceptions about divorce. This process is accomplished by the use of filmstrips on parent–child reactions to marital dissolution and discussions of feelings common to children in the divorcing family.

Sessions 4 through 9 attempt to help children learn social problem-solving skills. Using role playing and discussion, leaders emphasize defining problems, thinking of ways to solve problems or recognizing that a problem cannot be solved by the child alone, and recognizing consequences of behavior.

With the acquisition of better coping skills, children feel less out of control and helpless and the tendency to impulsively act out is decreased as the sense of mastery increases. Sessions 10 and 11 are spent focusing on understanding the causes of anger and helping youngsters to express anger appropriately. The final sessions are used to help children arrive at more differentiated views of the family through discussion of various family forms, and to terminate the group.

The participants reported an increased sense of mastery as well as a decreased sense of isolation and confusion. Postitive effects of the group intervention were seen both clinically and statistically.

Setting Up the Group

This section discusses issues involved in conducting direct group interventions on the school site with elementary and junior high school students. Our experience has come from working as outside consultants in suburban public school systems in California.

Group Structure.   Groups met once weekly for 50–75 minutes over a 6- to 12-week period. Variation in duration and number of group sessions was dictated by the vagaries of the school calendar. Our preference is for a 1-hour weekly meeting, over a 10-week period. This is the general consensus of the length of session and number of weeks in the literature referred to previously.

Group Heterogeneity.   Groups have included children from families in which the initial disruption ranged from 10 years to 3 months prior to the start of the group intervention. Those children with greater distance from the initial familial disruption helped those children for whom the divorce and resulting trauma were more recent. This is a finding confirmed by Kalter and his colleagues (Kalter, 1985). In some groups, not all the children had experienced the loss of the intact family as a result of divorce. Children were also included whose parents, although never married, did live together and co-parent a youngster, subsequently terminating their living arrangements. As in most of the group interventions described in the literature, our groups were primarily mixed sex groups, with five to eight children in each. Less than five children is too few because the loss of a member due to absenteeism is a common phenomenon and more than eight children does not allow enough time for the discussion of individual concerns.

We have found that establishing same-sex groups for young adolescents has some advantages over mixed-sex groups. Because parental dating and sexuality are especially important concerns at this age, single-sex groups allow these young people to discuss their perceptions of parental sexuality without the burden of concurrently feeling strong heterosexual pulls toward others in the group.

Confidentiality.   Confidentiality, always an important issue in treatment, assumes a magnitude not easily grasped until one actually works in the school setting. Group members have a history with one another before the group starts, as do their parents and teachers. Addressing the issue of confidentiality with all concerned is vital. The extension of the group over a period of 10 to 12 weeks helps surmount the greater resistances to disclosure caused by the fact that children see and know one another in a context other than the group setting.

An example of such a problem was experienced when two young adolescents who were boyfriend and girlfriend were asked to be in the same group. Although they initially complied, their difficulty in discussing the recent divorce of their parents in front of one another was insurmountable, and eventually both left the group. Letting students know prior to the group who the participants may be is a prudent move that gives children and leaders time to assess the previously established interpersonal relationships among children. Although this raises a new question of confidentiality, on balance this seems minor in comparison with selecting a compatible group.

Pregroup Interviews.   Considerable attention was given to differentiating longstanding psychopathology from reactive responses to the familial change. Individual interviews were conducted by the group leader with each child participant, lasting between 1 and 2 hours. Utilizing Wallerstein's (1983) conceptualization of the child's resolution of divorce as a series of developmental tasks, we employed the Kinetic Family Drawing (K-F-D) (Burns, 1982) and the Coopersmith Scale of Self-Esteem (Coopersmith, 1967), along with the divorce-specific assessment technique (Wallerstein & Kelly, 1979), to gain the necessary diagnostic information for structuring group interventions.

Postgroup Interviews.   An individual interview was carried out within 1 month of the final group session. Its purpose was to evaluate the child's subjective response to the group, to offer an opportunity to discuss specific family and school problems in greater depth, and to offer the child an opportunity to request the group leader's help in dealing with significant adults in his or her life. In some cases this resulted in family sessions or conferences among school personnel, child, and parents in order to address problems that the child had reported. The vast majority of participants (95%) expressed enthusiasm over group participation, and stated that the peer support that they had gained, was critical to them.

Follow-up Interviews.   In those schools where we have worked on-site for a period of years, we have employed a follow-up with the students, their parents, and faculty participants. These interviews take place approximately 9 to 10 months after the initial group intervention. The extent of the follow-up varies with information provided either by faculty or through our own observations regarding youngsters at risk. Depending on the students' postdivorce adjustment, a variety of interventions are instituted, ranging from special class placement and referrals for psychological treatment to consultation and collaboration with parents and/or faculty and administration.

Assessing Referrals to the Group and Determining Group Content

Although the literature just reviewed describes excellent school-based group interventions, writers have not sufficiently demonstrated how such interventions address either the child's particular family situation or the stage of resolution the child has reached.

Most of the programs that have been described in the literature accept children into groups with widely varying time from divorce. However, this heterogeneity may result in groups where the crisis of coping with the actual divorce is not the primary need of the participant. Inclusion of children with many years distance from the marital rupture may shift the focus of the group from one of a crisis intervention to a model characterized by the tenets of tertiary prevention. Thus, the demands for collateral work with parents and teachers increase. In the group itself, issues involving adjustment to the postdivorce family and "working through" loss, disappointment, and anger rather than coping with crisis come to the fore.

How such a group may facilitate working through can be seen in the following example:

One group participant was a child whose father had recently returned from a vacation announcing he had remarried while away. Not only was the child not invited to the wedding, he was not even told of plans for the marriage.
During a group meeting when this child happened to be absent, the group planned a picnic. Knowing the child's struggle with feelings of being left out and powerless, the group leader met with the child individually to let him know of the proposed plan. During this meeting the group leader commented on the similarity between the two circumstances and the child was able to acknowledge his feelings.

Because of the probable mandate to provide treatment for students exhibiting problems at school, and due to the constraints of time placed on the school psychologist or counselor, it is not likely that these professionals will be able to offer group interventions to an entire school population. In screening students referred to groups and determining the actual content of group sessions, the following should be considered.

We have found that those participants who had experienced a familial change within 2 years of participation benefited most from the group. They were able to use the group to lessen confusion, increase coping skills, and gain emotional support. Children with longstanding difficulties and no recent familial change benefited less from the standardized group format. However, when individualized group sessions were combined with collateral work with parents and teachers to meet specific needs of children in the latter group, more benefit accrued.

By using historical information gained in individual interviews, we have been able to construct group sessions that differed significantly from group to group.

Group activities were "tailor-made" to address specific issues in the youngsters' histories. For example:

> In one group of students with great disparity in length of time from initial marital separation, the common themes of all sessions related to parental remarriage. Sibling rivalry and problems of having to share with stepparents were addressed through interpreting the competition among group members for attention from the leader and their response to including a new member in the group.
>
> In another group with several children from remarried families, family trees were constructed. Over half of the participants "discovered" that their grandparents had been divorced. We could then discuss the feelings that they might have in common with their parents as "children of divorce."

Some group activities lend themselves particularly well to being used with many different groups while retaining their individual nature. For instance, "Dear Abby" letters can be written by the group leader prior to meeting posing problems from the lives of the particular group members. These can then be answered as part of a group activity.

Journals can be used in many ways during a group to give a sense of privacy and individuality. For example, sketch books in which youngsters can write to the group leader between sessions and receive answers confidentially can give a sense of continuity to the group, "holding" youngsters between sessions.

In an early group session in which the idea of the journal is introduced, a Polaroid picture taken of each child and incorporated as a frontpiece can be used to talk about ways in which the child is unique. During the final session, after discussing how children can use their peer group for support, group Polaroid photos added to the journal give children a concrete group remembrance to leave with.

Parent Participation

Initial contact with the custodial parent was made by a school administrator or pupil personnel employee and almost without exception consent was given for the child's participation in a group. Following this, a letter detailing group goals and logistics was sent along with a written consent form. The custodial parent was then engaged in a face-to-face contact with the group leader either (a) in an individual pregroup interview, (b) a one-time evening meeting for parents of all participating children with individual postgroup interviews, or (c) a series of four evening group meetings designed to parallel the children's group. The choice of format evolved during the 5 years of our work in the schools and is based on availability of clinical time and the perceived needs of the parents and school.

All parents were requested to complete a questionnaire on their child which asked for school history, previous psychotherapy, description of current custody arrangements, and their view of the child's strengths and weaknesses. Parents were told that the information would be kept confidential and would not become part of the child's school record.

Included in the questionnaire was a request to contact the child's noncustodial parent. Because research (Kurdek & Berg, 1983; Wallerstein & Kelly, 1980) clearly indicates that children who have continued stable contact with both parents generally fare better in the postdivorce family, we believe that inclusion of the noncustodial parent in school-related activities is crucial to good postdivorce adjustment. We found that in most families in which both parents still resided in the same geographic area, permission to contact the noncustodial parent was readily given.

Parent group meetings were less specifically child-focused than individual consultations with parents. Group participants used the meetings primarily to relieve guilty feelings over pursuing their own needs for development in roles other than that of parent. Individual interventions tended to be more focused on problem areas within the postdivorce and the remarried family, and related more specifically to the child group members. However, both types of interventions tended to cover these focal points: rearrangement of visitation patterns; differentiation of child and parent roles; amelioration of loyalty conflicts experienced by children; and education in expectable reactions to divorce, remarriage, and normal child development.

We have found that parents of younger children and those parents who were recently divorced (within 1 year of the intervention) were more interested in a series of group meetings than were parents of older students and those who had experienced a family change years before.

Teacher Participation

Consistent involvement of teachers is an important facet of creating successful prevention models for the school system. Although direct work with families, either in group or individual interventions, must be carried out by a person with professional training in the counseling arts, it is the teacher who will have the greatest cumulative effect on the largest number of students and therefore must be a central collaborator in this process. Of major importance, as well, are administrators who make policy determinations regarding how the needs of single-parent and remarried families will be incorporated in their schools.

Our intervention thus has included a strong emphasis on consultation to teachers regarding the child participants in our groups. After discussing their referral suggestions with them, each classroom teacher involved in a child participant's education, was asked to fill out two written evaluations at the beginning and end of the group. These evaluations helped teachers to focus their attention on students in a behavior-specific way. During the course of the group, the leader was available for weekly consultations with the teachers of participating youngsters. In many instances such consultations took the form of a 5-minute check-in. In some cases, conjoint conferences among teachers, parents, and students were facilitated by the group leader in an effort to enhance communication about a student's school progress.

The cumulative effect of such consultative efforts has been considerable. At the secondary prevention level, the classroom teachers involved in this approach have come away with an informed stance vis-á-vis these families. This is reflected in their more thoughtful approach to including nonresidential parents in academic planning, in their sensitivity to the language with which they describe non-intact families, and with the skills to recognize what may be a reactive depression to the family change.

CONCLUSION

Given the prevalence of divorce in the United States, indicators that the incidence rate is rising, coupled with the clear evidence that many youngsters have resultant learning problems, school personnel must become prepared to engage in prevention strategies with this population. Evidence has mounted sufficiently to indicate that the school may well be the single most comprehensive continuing resource for children during the divorce crisis. This places the school psychologist or counselor in a unique position to intervene broadly at the systems level and develop appropriately varied and comprehensive programs to meet this community need.

An example of a preventive school-based model was provided that addresses the multiple and frequently chronic stressors of divorce affecting the lives of children and adolescents. This model emphasizes the need to assess each youngster's respective resolution of the divorce and accommodation to the post-divorce family as critical elements in planning on-site, time-limited psycho-education groups. Further, given the nature of the stressor and the resultant family disequilibrium, often continuing beyond a 2- or 3-year period, the school becomes a primary (if not exclusive) source of ongoing support and guidance for youngsters. The school psychologist has the capacity to embed short-term group interventions for students in the larger context of teacher, administrator, and parent collaboration. The effectiveness of this model lies in ongoing, but brief contacts with identified children at risk, their families and school personnel, as required.

ACKNOWLEDGMENTS

We would like to thank Andrew Lamden and Susan Zegans for their contributions of clinical case material included in this paper.

REFERENCES

Ainsworth, M. (1969). Object relations, dependency and attachment: A theoretical review of the infant-mother relationship. *Child Development*, *40*, 969–1025.

Bain, A. (1978). The capacity of families to cope with transitions. *Human Relations*, *31*(8) 675–688.

Beal, E. (1980). Separation, divorce and single-parent families. In E. Carter & M. McGoldrick (Eds.), *The family life cycle* (pp. 77–93). New York: Gardner Press.

Bloom, B. L., Asher, S. J., & White, S. W. (1978). Marital disruption as a stressor: A review and analysis. *Psychological Bulletin*, *85*, 967–894.

Bowlby, J. (1980). *Attachment and loss. Vol. 3: Loss, sadness and depression.* New York: Basic Books.

Bowlby, J. (1982). Attachment and loss: Retrospect and prospect. *American Journal of Orthopsychiatry*, *52*, 664–678.

Brown, F. B. (1980). Children from one-parent families. *Phi Delta Kappan*, *62*, 537–540.

Burns, R. (1982). *Self-growth in families.* New York: Brunner/Mazel.

Cantor, D. W. (1977). School-based groups for children of divorce. *Journal of Divorce*, *2*, 357–361.

Cantor, D. W. (1979). Divorce: A view from the children. *Journal of Divorce*, *1*, 183–187.

Caplan, G. (1981). Mastery of stress: Psychosocial aspects. *American Journal of Psychiatry*, *138*. 413–420.

Clay, P. L. (1981). *National committee for citizens in education.* 410 Wilde Lake Village Green, Dept. S.P., Columbia, Maryland 21049.

Coddington, R. D. (1972). The significance of life events as etiologic factors in the diseases of children—II. A study of a normal population. *Journal of Psychometric Research*, *16*, 205–213.

Coopersmith, S. (1967). *The antecedents of self esteem.* San Francisco: Freeman.

Drake, E. A. (1981). Helping children cope with divorce: The role of the school. In I. R. Stuart & L. E. Abt (Eds.), *Children of separation and divorce: Management and treatment* (pp. 147–172). New York: Van Nostrand Reinhold.

Drake, E. A., & Shellenberger, S. (1981). Children of separation and divorce: A review of school programs and implications for the psychologist. *School Psychology Review*, *10*, 54–61.

Elam, S., & Gough, P. (1980) Comparing lay and professional opinion on Gallup poll questions. *Phi Delta Kappan*, *62*, 33–46.

Gallup, G. (1980). The 12th annual Gallup poll of the public's attitude toward the public schools. *Phi Delta Kappan* 62 33–46.

Gardner, R. (1976). *Psychotherapy with children of divorce.* New York: Jason Aronson.

Goldman, R. K. (1981). *Teachers look at children of divorce in the classroom.* Corte Madera, CA: Center for the Family in Transition.

Goldman, R. K., & King, M. J. (1985). Counseling children of divorce. *School Psychology Review*, *14*(3), 278–290.

Goldman, R. K., King, M. J. & Lamden, A. (1983, April). *School-based interventions with children of divorce.* Paper presented at the meeting of the American Orthopsychiatric Association, Boston.

Guidubaldi, J., Perry, J. D., & Cleminshaw, H. K. (1983). *The legacy of parental divorce: A nationwide study of family status and selected variables on children's academic and social competencies.* Kent, OH: Kent State University.

Guidubaldi, J., Perry, J. D., Cleminshaw, H. K., & McLoughlin, C. S. (1983). The impact of parental divorce on children; report of a nationwide NASP study. *School Psychology Review 12*, 300–323.

Guidubaldi, J. (1984). *Differences in children's divorce adjustment across grade level and gender: A report from the NASP-Kent State Nationwide Project.* Kent, OH: Kent State University.

Guidubaldi, J., Cleminshaw, H. K., & Perry, J. (in press). The effects of parental divorce on children's and their parents' health. In J. E. Zins & I. Wagner (Eds.), *Promoting physical and emotional well-being in educational settings: Innovative approaches and practices* (thematic issue). *Special Services in the Schools*, 1.

Hess, R. D., & Camara, K. A. (1979). Postdivorce family relationships as mediating factors in the consequences of divorce from children. *Journal of Social Issues*, *35*, 79–96.

Hetherington, E. M. (1979). Divorce: A child's perspective. *American Psychologist, 34,* 851–858.

Hetherington, E. M., Cox, M., & Cox, R. (1978). Play and social interaction in children following divorce. *Journal of Social Issues, 35,* 26–49.

Hunter, J. E., & Schuman, N. (1980). Chronic reconstitution as a family style. *Social Work, 26,* 446–451.

Jacobson, D. S. (1978a). The impact of marital separation/divorce on children. *Journal of Divorce, 1,* 341–360.

Jacobson, D. S. (1978b). The impact of marital separation/divorce on children: II. Interparent hostility and child adjustment. *Journal of Divorce, 2,* 3–19.

Jacobson, D. S. (1978c). The impact of marital separation/divorce on children: III. Parent-child communication and child adjustment, and regression analysis of findings from overall study. *Journal of Divorce, 2,* 175–194.

Kalter, N. (1985) *Time-limited developmental facilitation groups for children of divorce manual.* Unpublished manuscript, University of Michigan, Ann Arbor, MI.

Kalter, N., & Rembar, J. (1981). The significance of a child's age at the time of parental divorce. *American Journal of Orthopsychiatry, 51,* 85–100.

Kalter, N., Pickar, J., & Lesowitz, M. (1984). School-based developmental facilitation groups for children of divorce: A preventative intervention. *American Journal of Orthopsychiatry, 54,* 613–623.

Kelly, J. B., & Wallerstein, J. S. (1977). Brief interventions with children in divorcing families. *American Journal of Orthopsychiatry, 47,* 23–26.

Kelly, J. B., & Wallerstein, J. S. (1979). Children of divorce. *The National Elementary Principal,* October, 52–58.

Kurdek, L. A. & Berg, B. (1983). Correlates of children's adjustment to their parents' divorce. In L. Kurdek (Ed.), *Children and divorce: New directions for child development series* (Vol. 19, pp. 47–60).

Kurdek L. A., Blisk, D., & Siesky, A. E. (1981). Correlates of children's long-term adjustment to their parent's divorce. *Developmental Psychology, 17,* 565–579.

Lindemann, E. (1944). Symptomatology and management of acute grief. *American Journal of Psychiatry, 101,* 141–148.

Mahler, M., Pine, F., & Bergman, A. (1975). *The psychological birth of the human infant.* New York: Basic Books.

Neal, J. H. (1983). Children's understanding of their parent's divorces. In L. Kurdek (Ed.), *Children and divorce: New directions for child development series* (Vol. 19, pp. 3–14).

Pedro-Carroll, J. (1985). *Children of divorce intervention program procedures manual.* Unpublished manuscript University of Rochester–Center for Community Study, Rochester, NY.

Pedro-Caroll, J. L., & Cowen, E. L. (1985). The children of divorce intervention project: an investigation of the efficacy of a school-based prevention program. *Journal of Consulting and Clinical Psychology, 53,* 603–614.

Peterson, G. W., Leigh, G. K., & Day, R. D. (1984). Family stress theory and the impact of divorce on children. *Journal of Divorce, 7*(3), 1–20.

Ricci, I. (1979). Divorce, remarraige and the schools. *Phi Delta Kappan,* March, 509–511.

Springer, C., & Wallerstein, J. S. (1983). Young adolescents' responses to their parents' divorces. In L. Kurdek (Ed.), *Children and divorce: New directions for child development series* (Vol. 19, pp. 15–27).

Stolberg, A. L., & Cullen, P. M. (1983). Preventive interventions for families of divorce: The divorce adjustment project. In L. Kurdek (Ed.), *Children and divorce: New directions for child development series* (Vol. 19, pp. 71–82).

Stolberg, A. L. & Garrison, K. M. (1985). Evaluating a primary prevention program for children of divorce: The divorce adjustment project. *American Journal of Community Psychology, 13,* 111–124.

Wallerstein, J. S. (1983). Children of divorce: The psychological tasks of the child. *American Journal of Orthopsychiatry, 53,* 230–243.

Wallerstein, J. S. (1984). Children of divorce: Ten-year follow-up of young children. *American Journal of Orthopsychiatry*, *54*, 444–458.
Wallerstein, J. S., & Kelly, J. B. (1980). *Surviving the breakup: How children and parents cope with divorce*. New York: Basic Books.
Winnicott, D. W. (1971). *Playing and reality*. London: Tavistock.

5

Maltreatment of Children

Robert B. Germain
Worthington Public Schools, Ohio

Allen was standing there sobbing and shaking, eyes bulging, nose running, and tears streaming down his face. His father was holding him tightly, holding a knife to his cheek. "This is what I'll do if you can't learn to act right," his father said. Allen could hardly listen; he'd been spanked pretty hard before, but the knife was terrifying. His mind was racing and he knew that he'd better start acting right. But he was confused; he thought he had been behaving.

Is this a scene from a soap opera or a cheap novel? It sounds like it, but such dramas may be fairly regular among the children attending any given school. How do we respond?

PERSPECTIVES ON CHILD MALTREATMENT

Definitions

Although it is most common to think of maltreatment as physical and sexual abuse, another kind of maltreatment that can lead to crisis for children is *psychological* maltreatment. Allen's situation typifies only one type of psychological maltreatment—terrorizing. Psychological maltreatment includes other acts of commission such as humiliating, exploiting, rejecting, and corrupting, as well as acts of omission such as psychological neglect and unavailability of caregiving.

The term *maltreatment* is used most often in this chapter because it includes both acts of commission (abuse) and omission (neglect). Thus, maltreatment refers to physical and psychological abuse and neglect, and to sexual abuse.

Maltreatment as a Psychological Crisis

Although there may be both physical and psychological damage from abuse, in most cases it is the psychological damage that is generally considered to be the most devastating aspect of the experience (Garbarino & Vondra, 1983). That is, in most, although certainly not all cases, bruises and broken bones heal, and sexual abuse may have little physical impact. But it is the psychological impact from these types of maltreatment that makes them particularly harmful to the child.

Relative to the categories of crises discussed by Sandoval (chapter 1), maltreatment can be viewed as an example of traumatic stress. Maltreatment is often unexpected, uncontrolled, and emotionally overwhelming. What can make psychological maltreatment even more traumatic is when there is an on-going, rational fear of reoccurrence of the maltreatment. The child is often in a primary, dependent, long-term relationship with the perpetrator, and may believe there is no recourse or escape. The child believes, and others reinforce, that caregivers (which often includes the perpetrator) must be acting in the legitimate best interests of the child.

Maltreatment does not produce results that are linked to any one diagnostic category; the outcomes are varied. Research, however, suggests that maltreatment leads to psychological maladjustment, and may predict serious emotional and behavioral disorders (Brown & Finklehor, n.d.; Faller, 1981; and Kadushin & Martin, 1981). Research in the area of sexual abuse, for example, has documented that the impact of abuse is pervasive and far-reaching. Brown and Finklehor (n.d.), on the basis of clinical and empirical studies, describe the results of sexual abuse on females. Initial impact (i.e., within 2 years of termination of abuse) include:

1. *emotional reactions*, such as *anxiety and fear* (Adams-Tucker, 1981; Anderson, Bach, & Griffith, 1981; Browning & Boatman, 1977; Gelinas, 1983; Goodwin, 1982; Justice & Justice, 1979; Peters, 1976; Summit & Kryso, 1978); *guilt and shame* (Burgess & Holstrom, 1978; DeFrancis, 1969; Finch, 1967; Kaufman, Peck & Tagiuri, 1954; Weiss, Rogers, Darwin, & Dutton, 1955); *depression and grief* (Anderson et al.; 1981; Burgess & Holstrom, 1978; de Young, 1982; Kaufman et al., 1954; Sgroi, 1978); and *decreased self-worth* (DeFrancis, 1969; Justice & Justice, 1979). In addition, children's fears may revolve around *recurrence* (of maltreatment itself), *disclosure* (not being believed or being punished for disclosure), or *resolution* (possible loss of parent). Anger may be directed not only at the perpetrator, but also at other family members and significant others who failed to provide protection.

2. *physical reactions*, such as *somatic complaints* (Adams-Tucker, 1981; Anderson et al., 1981; Browning & Boatman, 1977; Goodwin, 1982; Kaufman et al., 1954; Peters, 1976) and *direct physical consequences*, for example, internal bleeding (Goodwin, 1982; Justice & Justice, 1979). These might also include regressive physical behaviors such as thumb-sucking and bed-wetting.

3. *social behavior*, such as *difficulties in interpersonal relating* (Jehu & Gazan, 1983; Justice & Justice, 1979; Peters, 1976; Steele & Alexander, 1981; Summit

& Kryso, 1978; Tsai & Wagner, 1978), *dysfunctional sexual attitudes and behavior* (Finch, 1967; Gelinas, 1983; Justice & Justice, 1979; Rosenfeld, Nadelson, Krieger, & Backman, 1979), and *deviant behavior* (James & Meyerding, 1977; Justice & Justice, 1979; Nakashima & Zakas, 1977). For example, a child might be disruptive, attempt suicide, or be overly compliant.

Many studies have sought to determine the long-term effects of sexual abuse. The findings, in many ways, parallel those of short-term impact. The long-term outcomes include impaired functioning in the emotional, physical, and social domains. After reviewing clinical literature, Vevier and Tharinger (1986) identify four consistent sequelae of child sexual abuse. These consist of a lack of trust, low self-esteem, feelings of helplessness and depression, and self-destructive behavior. Brown and Finklehor (n.d.) point out that long-term effects have been found even among survivors who were not seeking help, although many other studies found no differences between non-abused individuals and those abused individuals who had not sought therapy. They conclude that the long-term effects may be more subtle than the immediate impact.

Theories Regarding the Causes of Maltreatment

There are three approaches to understanding why people maltreat children. These consist of a focus on the abuser, the family, and the larger context of the community and culture.

Factors Within the Child Abuser.   Research focusing on abusers document that they tend to be a heterogeneous group. Investigators have paid particular attention to physical and sexual abusers. Although some studies have found no differences in personality functioning of abusers and non-abusers (Gaines, Sandgrund, Green, & Power, 1978; Milner & Wimberly, 1980; Spinetta, 1978; Starr, 1982; Wright, 1976), others have found explicit personality characteristics. Some of these include a history of low-frustration tolerance, non-empathetic relationships, unmet dependency needs, power-authoritarianism problems, low self-esteem, depressed emotions, learned helplessness, and an adverse and traumatic experience (Smith, 1984). Main and Goldwyn (1984) describe the characteristics of abusers and controlling aggression differently and less effectively than others, tending to isolate themselves, and being unsympathetic to distress in others (see also Frodi & Lamb, 1980).

Other researchers have focused on cognitive characteristics rather than personality traits. They identify abusers as having unusually high expectations for children, distorted perceptions of a child's behavior (i.e., views behavior as a problem when others see behavior as acceptable, or makes internal and stable attributions of misbehavior), and a lack of awareness of children's needs (Larrance & Twentyman, 1983; Mash, Johnson, & Kovitz, 1983; Spinetta & Rigler,

1972; Steele & Pollock, 1968). Similarly, maltreating parents may fail to recognize improvements in a child's behavior and thus fail to modify their own punitive behavior (Bell & Harper, 1977; Egeland & Sroufe, 1981).

This body of research on abusers has emanated from the perspective that there is some personality or characterological flaw in abusers (Melnick & Hurley, 1969; Steele & Pollock, 1968) that leads to maltreatment. On-going ecological factors are secondary to the individual's cognitive, affective, motivational, and behavioral factors.

Research from this perspective has been criticized on two grounds. First, although significant differences may appear in studies, findings reveal that only about 5% of abusers show signs of significant observable disorders (Friedman, Sandler, Hernandez, & Wolfe, 1981; Kempe, 1973; Spinetta & Rigler, 1972; Starr, 1979). Second, this research approach, which emphasizes the individual, undermines efforts directed at the family and community (Garbarino, 1982; Ross & Zigler, 1980).

Factors Within the Family.   As an alternative, many experts view maltreatment to result from family dysfunction, for example from the interaction between the level of parental competence and the demands of a situation. Belsky (1984) focuses on the interaction among the personal psychological resources of the parents, characteristics of the child, and the contextual sources of stress and support. Parents not skilled in dealing with developmental characteristics associated with a young child or adolescent may experience greater stress than skilled parents.

Other research has focused on the influence of the child's behavior on the behavior of adults. Although two studies found no difference in the behavior of abused and non-abused children, several other studies found that abused children were more disruptive than those children in families without such problems (Bonsha & Twentyman, 1984; Lahey, Conger, Atkeson, & Treiber, 1984; Lorber, Felton, & Reid, 1984; Wolfe & Mosk, 1983). It should be noted that some investigators have differentiated abusing from neglecting parents. It may be that specific child behaviors are important contributors to parental behavior in abusing families, but not in neglecting families. Rather, neglecting parents tend to be coping inadequately, failing to assume basic responsibilities and to meet their own emotional needs (Aragona & Eyberg, 1981; Gaines et al., 1978; Herenkohl, Herenkohl, & Egolf, 1983). Although neglecting parents interacted less frequently with their family than did abusers (Bonsha & Twentyman, 1984), the two groups did not differ with respect to either their child-rearing knowledge (Larrance & Twentyman, 1983; Spinetta, 1978) or the aversiveness of their interactions—aversiveness was highly prevalent in both groups (Burgess & Conger, 1978).

In addition to personal psychological resources of parents and characteristics of children, sources of stress within the family system has been identified as related to the incidence of abuse. Some of the endogenous factors include: (a) the presence of multiple problems without accompanying coping skills; (b) characteristics of enmeshed families, or where there is a great dependence on family relationships yet little support within the family; (c) individuals who are disengaged from family responsibilities; (d) power that is centered in one adult only, typically the male; and (e) marital stress (Emery, 1982; Straus, 1980). There sometimes appears to be a pattern of escalating power and coercion (Burgess & Richardson, 1984; Patterson, 1982; Reid, Taplin & Lorber, 1981) and/or inappropriate disciplinary techniques (ineffective contingencies and consistencies) that eventuate in harm to the child (Kelly, 1983; Wolfe & Sandler, 1981). Wolfe (1985) concludes that abusive mothers and abused children seem to interact in a fashion that actively maintains aversive behavior.

In addition to factors within the family, exogenous factors that increase family stress might also contribute to the incidence of maltreatment. These factors include poverty, blue-collar (vs. white-collar) employment, unemployment (Gelles & Straus, 1979; Straus, 1980), and change in residence, income, or work schedules (Justice & Duncan, 1976).

However, some researchers suggest that abusers may not be subjected to significantly more economic disadvantage than non-abusers (Gaines et al., 1978; Starr, 1982), but that any such disadvantage is perceived as more unpleasant and debilitating (Conger, Burgess, & Barrett, 1979; Mash et al., 1983; Rosenberg & Reppucci, 1983). Similarly, abusers may not have fewer social supports available, but may more typically fail to use these supports (Garbarino, 1976, 1982). Thus, maltreatment may not spring from a psychological disorder or an unusually stressful environment, but an interaction of psychological functioning and coping skills with stressful life events.

Factors Within the Context of the Community and Culture. Whereas Garbarino (Garbarino & Vondra, 1983), for example, views economic stress and social isolation within the community as being associated with maltreatment, others have focused on more pervasive aspects of the culture, attempting to identify factors that lead to a greater number of individuals at-risk to be perpetrators of maltreatment. Some of these community-cultural factors include:

1. cultural endorsement of domestic violence and corporal punishment, e.g., spanking and demeaning children are viewed as an acceptable way to enhance character and promote learning (Hyman, 1983);

2. socialization of men to view sex as gratification only, to objectify sexual partners, to seek partners inferior in size and age, to be dominant in sex (Finklehor, 1979, 1984); and

3. institutional (e.g., schools) disrespect for culture, lifestyle, language, and cognitive style of minorities (Jones & Jones, 1983).

Gil (1971, 1983), for example, has identified a number of realities of the current socioeconomic–political system as leading to maltreatment. He believes maltreatment results from a failure to meet an adult's developmental needs. When certain individuals are necessarily excluded from a basic standard of living, or from making meaningful economic contributions through their work, maltreatment is inevitable. Basically, Gil believes that any economic–political system based on inequality, such as patriarchy, slavery, feudalism, capitalism, imperialism, or totalitarianism, will lead to a significant portion of the population with unmet developmental needs. Therefore, such societies would be likely to have a high prevalence of maltreatment. Similarly, any society where children are viewed as parental property, and do not possess fundamental human rights, is guaranteed to have significant levels of maltreatment. Any culture where force and coercion are viewed as a legitimate means to an end is guaranteed to have significant maltreatment. These conditions create a large number of families with high levels of stress, and individuals who have learned to use violence as a coping strategy.

Incidence of Maltreatment

The incidence and prevalence of maltreatment varies not only with the type of maltreatment under consideration, but also with the specific definitions and methodology used in any particular study.

Sexual Abuse. Compiling the results of several studies, it appears that between 10% and 35% of women have had childhood sexual encounters with an adult male, and approximately one half to one fourth as many men have had childhood sexual encounters with an adult. In considering female victims, approximately 75% to 93% are abused by someone within their extended family. Of the female victims, 4% of the cases involve sexual intercourse (Finklehor, 1984). The perpetrators are overwhelmingly, but not quite exclusively, males. In the 1981 National Study by the U.S. Department of Health and Human Services, the incidence of sexual exploitation was reported at .7 per 1,000 individuals.

Physical Maltreatment. The estimated incidence of physical maltreatment varies between 200,000 and 2 million, with 1.4 to 1.9 million children at high risk for physical abuse (Gelles & Straus, 1979). There are approximately 60,000 cases reported nationwide per year. The 1981 National Study reported an incidence of 3.4 per 1,000 and physical neglect at 1.7 per 1,000.

Psychological Maltreatment. In the 1981 National Study, emotional abuse was reported at a rate of 2.2 per 1,000 children and emotional neglect at 1.0 per 1,000 children. Psychological maltreatment constituted the primary problem identified in about 39% of the abuse cases and 18% of the neglect cases.

Individuals at Risk for Encountering Maltreatment

As in many other areas of study, determination of risk levels rests with statistically significant correlations between demographic or other descriptive variables and the behavior one is trying to predict. Given the data presently available, the following characteristics are associated with a higher incidence of maltreatment: poverty, blue-collar (vs. white-collar) employment, unemployment, families with two children as contrasted with one child (no other size effect), families where parents experienced violence as a child (Gelles & Straus, 1979), families going through acute periods of change (e.g., residence, income, composition, work schedules, health, marital relations) (Justice & Duncan, 1976), chaotic and enmeshed families, families with stepparents (Russell, 1984) and families who are more punishing and less supportive (Garbarino, Sebes, & Schellenbach, 1984).

The purpose of determining risk levels is typically to provide differential treatment to those at risk. This might involve anything from closer monitoring of behavior to specially designed programs. The question, then, is not whether there is a statistically significant correlation, but whether the data just cited lend themselves to dichotomizing populations (i.e., classifying children as at-risk, or not-at-risk) and providing differential treatment. Often, they do not. For example, for unemployed individuals the incidence of physical abuse is 22% as compared to 14% for employed individuals (Gelles & Straus, 1979). If one were to just monitor children of unemployed parents, there would be little improvement over a random selection procedure, and much to be lost with the maltreated children of employed individuals. Even an equation adding together multiple factors in order to predict level of risk may not be useful with the present data. In a study of a test for predicting abusive behavior using several different estimators, the majority of subjects earning scores above the cutoff (predicting abuse) did not abuse (Milner, Gold, Ayoub, & Jacewitz, 1984). Also, when one considers psychological, and not just physical and sexual maltreatment, virtually all children are at risk of being abused.

However, there are two groups of children that can be considered at risk and helped by differential service. The first are children whose families are experiencing significant stress, under conditions of isolation from social support networks and a deficit in coping skills. The second are children who have been maltreated previously. It is fairly clear that when the perpetrator has not received significant help, and is still in contact with the child, or where other family members are likely to respond to the still-high level of stress, maltreatment is likely to recur. Of reported maltreatment cases, only 6% involve a single incident; 94% involve multiple incidents of maltreatment before detection (Gelles & Straus, 1979). Although there are some children that may be monitored more closely than others, it is still more appropriate to consider all children at risk when it comes to designing school-based prevention activities.

PRIMARY PREVENTION ACTIVITIES

Society and Culture

Gil (1971, 1983) and Giovannoni (1971) believe that without a substantial change in our socioeconomic–political system, there will always be maltreatment. Therefore, any primary prevention activity aimed at individuals or families will fail to prevent maltreatment totally unless and until substantial sociocultural changes are made. Specifically, Gil maintains that we must put and end to poverty, change to an egalitarian and cooperative society, make work a meaningful experience, and change our culture to one where children are highly valued and violence and coercion are seen as illegitimate. School personnel must continue to work for changes in societal conditions that create a world that is safe for children.

Institutions

Garbarino (1982) believes that efforts at levels less broad than the society and culture can be effective. Efforts aimed at legal, educational, and community institutions will have important payoffs.

Legal. In balancing the rights of parents and schools with the rights of children, the basic constitutional rights of children have been curtailed. A number of existing statutes related to punishment of children, medical treatment of children, and legal rights of children, both reflect and create attitudes toward children that encourage maltreatment. For example, many rights, such as "privileged communication" relate only to adults unless specifically designated as applicable to children. Many states do not have such a designation. The creation of laws that respect the rights of children could be an important part of primary prevention.

In the absence of laws that include appropriate definitions of maltreatment, and allow for effective prosecution of perpetrators of physical, sexual, and psychological maltreatment, there are few legal remedies against a perpetrator and little protection for the child against future occurrences.

Educational. It seems plausible that courses in family planning, family life education, child development, and lifelong coping skills would prevent some stressors and provide some skills for parents and thus reduce the incidence of maltreatment. To date, no direct evidence exists as to the long-term outcomes of such educational programs.

Communities. A neighborhood-based national health service would reduce one aspect of family stress. Within communities, there would need to be publicized means of obtaining help for a wide variety of problems. Collaborative efforts among social agencies, church groups, industry, and schools could more effectively safeguard the well-being of individuals (Garbarino & Vondra, 1983). Because the school is the one system, other than family, to which all children belong, schools can take a leadership role in the identification, prevention, and treatment of maltreatment. School psychologists can provide education about maltreatment and reporting laws to school staff, as well as provide consultation when staff or parents want to talk about their observations or experiences with certain children.

Individuals

Adults. Adults need to be given training in parenting skills, dealing with emotions (particularly anger), differentiating appropriate from inappropriate methods of disciplining, developing social skills, and developing supports to deal with life-stress (Forehand & McMahon 1981; Wolfe & Sandler, 1981). Jaffe, Thompson, and Wolfe (1984) suggest focusing on the dysfunctional family, reducing their distress.

Children. Some primary prevention activities aimed at children run the risk of seeming to "blame the victim." Although some theories presented earlier identify child characteristics that may positively correlate with incidence of maltreatment, it is nevertheless reasonable to conclude that children are not responsible for maltreatment. However, all children can be helped to identify some behaviors of maltreatment and to learn how to seek assistance.

WORKING WITH CLIENTS AT RISK

For the purpose of this section, *adults at risk* are defined as those individuals who are going through significant stress in their lives or who have committed acts of maltreatment previously. Because any child might come into contact with potentially maltreating caregivers in family, educational, or recreational settings, *children at risk* are defined as all children.

Parents and Other Caregivers

The main purpose of intervention with parents and other caregivers is to decrease the likelihood of them maltreating children. As part of this goal, the purpose would be to increase their self-esteem or ego strength, and thus decrease the likelihood of impulsive acting-out behavior when frustrated. A social worker, or some other mental health professional, can provide a variety of services in this regard. Such services include an evaluation of the safety of the home, intervention with and support of parents, and provision of on-going family treatment. To relieve family stress, community services such as daycare, homemaker services, home helpers, and respite care could be effective.

Professionals can play an important role in decreasing the likelihood of psychological maltreatment and corporal punishment occurring in schools. For example, they can provide emotional support for teachers and help them with classroom management and advocate for policies and procedures that reduce teacher stress. For example, an uncomfortable physical environment, inappropriate class size, and limited discipline options, might be factors that could be changed to reduce stress.

For both parents and teachers, the development of empathy, behavior management skills, and skills for coping with life stress are likely to be crucial in reducing the incidence of maltreatment. School psychologists or other school personnel can play important roles in direct and indirect service to teachers and parents. School psychologists can educate these groups concerning what constitutes maltreatment, when to suspect it, and how to report it (which may include contacting professionals such as the school psychologist).

Children

The purpose of intervention with at-risk children is primarily to decrease the negative impact of maltreatment, should it occur, and whenever feasible, to decrease the likelihood of its occurrence. There are three fundamental aspects to minimizing the psychological damage of maltreatment. The first is to build and to develop a positive self-concept in the child. Children need to trust and to feel good about themselves. Children who have a solid and positive image of themselves can deal effectively, in the context of support, with the confusion and doubts created by maltreatment. Also, as part of self-respect, children need to be able to communicate clearly when an individual violates them or is bordering on violating them in any way, sexually, physically, and psychologically. That is, self-respect is part of the appropriate training that would lead to a child being able to say, "No," or "Stop," to effectively communicate their sense of violation. This intervention could be part of a larger program in assertiveness training.

Second, a child needs to have one positive, stable, intimate relationship. With open lines of communication, it makes it more likely that the child will be willing to confront the feelings, beliefs, and behavior resulting from maltreatment, rather than accepting any intimidation and/or engaging in long-term repression, denial, guilt, and so forth. This relationship also would provide an all important positive model of a relationship in contrast to the one in which the maltreatment occurred. There is no reason to think that this positive, stable, intimate relationship could not be with an adult in the school or other agency. As part of providing for the psychological well-being of all children, a school or agency professional might have as a goal to insure that each child have such a relationship with one adult.

Third, children need information on what is acceptable caregiver behavior. For example, they need to know what differentiates an appropriate from an inappropriate touch (Brassard, Tyler, & Kehle, 1983), and appropriate from inappropriate physical and psychological treatment. Thus, a child will be able to identify maltreatment behavior, and will therefore be less likely to see it as legitimate and deserved, and be more likely to take action to put an end to it. All of these may be accomplished by involved and accessible school personnel.

In summary, if a child has a positive self-concept, one positive relationship with a significant adult, and adequate information about appropriate and inappropriate treatment, should maltreatment occur, the child will be more likely to seek help, to seek the help more quickly, and to use the help more effectively.

INTERVENING WITH ABUSED CHILDREN AND THEIR PARENTS

Although the purpose of this chapter is not to present an exhaustive review of services and programs available, several programmatic interventions, dealing with prevention and treatment, are presented in the Appendix.

Intervening with and on Behalf of Children

Legal Interventions. Two of the principles of crisis counseling, mentioned by Sandoval (chapter 1) are to take action quickly and to be directive rather than having the client assume most or all of the responsibility. One of the most important ways to do this in dealing with a child who has been maltreated is to provide legal interventions.

There is a child protection unit in every county. If maltreatment is suspected, the school psychologist should contact this agency, and then can maintain a liaison with them if it is appropriate for the case. A social worker can inspect the state child abuse registry to note any previously reported incidents. Every state has a mandatory reporting law for helping professionals when they suspect sexual or physical abuse. No state requires proof of maltreatment, just a statement about the condition of the child. Helping professionals have immunity from civil liability and criminal penalty as long as the report was made in good faith, even if maltreatment did not occur. On the other hand, there can be civil action brought against school personnel who knew of, but did not report abuse.

Although legal actions are important, they are often avoided or not fully implemented. Often state statutes do not define maltreatment effectively, and few have provisions for psychological maltreatment (Corson, 1983). Additionally, Berliner and Barbieri (1984) cite four reasons why it is difficult to prosecute cases of sexual assault against children, many of which apply to all forms of maltreatment: (a) adults are skeptical that the incident took place; (b) adults believe that perpetrators are mentally disturbed and are better handled by the mental health rather than the legal system; (c) adults believe children will be traumatized by the legal proceedings, adding to the damage done by the maltreatment itself; and (d) prosecutors fear that the child will not perform adequately as a witness. Berliner and Barbieri (1984) state that, in reality, "there is little or no evidence indicating that children's reports are unreliable, and none at all to support the fear that children make false accusations of sexual assault or misunderstood innocent behavior by adults" (p. 127).

Identification and Diagnosis.   School personnel can help, and must legally help, by identifying children who have been abused. Through observation of the behavior of all children, certain children will come to the attention of school staff. For many children, direct questionning may elicit a direct and honest answer. Often, children are relieved to share their "secret" with someone they trust. With adolescents, one may ask, "Have you or anyone in your family ever been sexually molested? (or been physically hurt by another person)." Simpler questions may be asked of younger children, such as "How do people in your family give hugs to show love?" or "If someone in your family is angry at someone else, what do they do?"

Sometimes a child gives verbal cues such as, "I don't want to be alone with _____," They may have bizarre, sophisticated, or unusual sexual knowledge or behavior.

For a young child, play techniques, such as general dollhouse play, may serve as both a diagnostic and therapeutic technique. For sexual abuse, demonstration or play with anatomically correct dolls can serve both as an effective diagnostic and therapeutic technique. Often, there are clues in other projective techniques, such as drawings of family or self (Sgroi, Porter, & Black, 1982).

In order to identify victims, one possibility is to have self-identification through a drop-in center. However, although drop-in centers work well for children who feel comfortable with the setting and personnel, not every maltreated child will "drop-in." Therefore, an out-reach program should be developed as well.

Individual Counseling.   In the absence of psychological support, the child's most likely adjustment, that of accommodation to the maltreatment, may be to develop chronically low self-esteem. Therefore, some form of counseling is imperative.

As mentioned earlier, a helping professional may take responsible and directive action by immediately proceeding with legal actions. Sometimes, however, concern for the legal facts may get in the way of asking a child, "How do you feel?" One survivor reported feeling intimidated by being "put in a chair bigger than me," and by having everything that she said tape recorded. Thus, it is important to consider simultaneously the legal needs of the case and the emotional needs of the child.

When a maltreated child is identified, an interview with the child should take place in a private setting. The reasons for this should be explained to child. Counseling should be an on-going process from the point at which the child is identified as having been maltreated.

There are four strategies in counseling that have been identified (Germain, Brassard, & Hart, 1985):

1. Ventilation of feelings. Survivors typically need consistent and substantial compassion and nurturance, in addition to help in labeling the various reactions to their experience.

2. Repeated replaying of experience through verbal means, role plays, or puppets. Often there is a need for a repetitive recounting of events.

3. Cognitive and emotional re-appraisal of the experience. Often, even when they know about the maltreatment, peers and significant others in the child's life err in one of two ways. They urge the child to forget it all and "return to normal" or they never facilitate the child's acceptance that the experience occurred and the need to move on. Cognitive restructuring, involving the ideas presented here, and emotional re-working, through techniques such as systematic desensitization, are seen as crucial in facilitating the child's acceptance of the experience.

4. Strategies for dealing with the potential of continued maltreatment. Because of problems with the legal and social systems and the protection of the rights of parents, often a child who has been maltreated will be given no protection in the home; that is, the perpetrator will still be in the home with the child. When maltreatment is possibly going to reoccur, the goal is for the child to keep a vigilant awareness of the possibility of threats rather than dealing with this possibility by avoidance, denial, or anxious preoccupation of pending disaster. Vigilant awareness would involve the child determining the warning cues (e.g., verbal and nonverbal behavior prior to more escalated maltreatment, alcohol consumption), and selecting among alternative strategies when warning cues are present (e.g., leaving the situation, calling a specific person for help).

There are five issues in the cognitive restructuring of individuals who have been maltreated, issues that are assumed to be crucial in minimizing the impact of maltreatment:

1. You are not responsible for the family break-up; the perpetrator is. Not all cases of maltreatment lead to break-up of the family, but many do. Very often, the victims see themselves as the betrayer of the family, because it is their actions that may have immediately precipitated the break-up of the family.

2. You did nothing wrong; you are not to blame. Children often believe that they are responsible for the maltreatment, that they behaved badly and deserve the maltreatment. They need to be told that the perpetrator's behavior was inappropriate and be told why it was inappropriate.

3. You are not the only one to whom this has happened. Children may feel alone, different, and isolated, and as a result be unsure about whether their peers would ever accept them. Realizing that they are one of many children to whom this happens can help them feel less "different."

4. You have another person to care about you. In view of the loss of trust in a significant other, the child especially needs to feel protected from maltreatment in other settings, such as school. It therefore can be important for some professional in the school to take responsibility for being this child's "significant other."

5. The perpetrator's behavior was inappropriate, but the person may still love you. This is probably the most complex aspect of the counseling; these are two

feelings that are very difficult to reconcile. But it is important to recognize that even parents who maltreat are vitally important to their children.

Group Counseling. Groups can be particularly important for the maltreated child of elementary school age or beyond. A group can help a child realize:

1. "I am not alone";
2. "Someone really understands what it feels like, because they've been through it, too";
3. "Maybe it's not my fault, because other good kids have been abused";
4. "I can work out my problem individually, with the support of others"; and
5. "If others can survive the experience effectively, so can I."

There are community-based groups for abused adolescents that have been established in many communities. For example, "Sons and Daughters United," for incest victims, uses group techniques to decrease social isolation, and to re-establish self-control and self-respect (Giaretto, 1981). School psychologists with appropriate training can start or help facilitate the starting of such groups.

Intervening with Abusers

For the purpose of this section, it is assumed that it is the parents who are suspected of having maltreated the child. Sometimes, it might be during a parent conference that a school psychologist crystallizes a suspicion that a child has been maltreated. Under these circumstances, it might be helpful to have a private setting, inform parents about the report and your legal responsibility, and not try to "prove abuse" (Broadhurst, 1979).

At times, the issue of whether the client is the child or the parent may arise, nevertheless it is my professional opinion that the primary perspective would be to do what is in the best interest of the child. The secondary perspective would be to provide therapeutic processes rather than punishment for the perpetrators. In this regard, Kempe and Kempe (1978) estimate that only 10%–20% of the families who abuse are beyond the conventional rehabilitation and treatment models. These are parents who cannot or will not provide adequate care for children. In these instances, in the best interest of the child, immediate action to terminate parental rights should be started.

However, for the other 80%–90%, alternative programs may be warranted. When maltreatment is discovered, generally a bad family situation is exacerbated. Often, there are severe negative consequences, in addition to those to the victim, for an offender and the family as a result of the identification and investigation of maltreatment. There may be job loss with accompanying economic pressures, marital or family separation, and there may be a loss of whatever social support had been available from friends of the family. Diversion of court-ordered therapy programs, rather than imprisonment, would allow for a possibly lower recidivism rate, avoidance of welfare, less reliance on foster care, and would possibly keep the family intact (Tyler & Brassard, 1984).

Parents who have maltreated may need help in acquiring appropriate developmental expectations, skills in empathy, skills in dealing with anger, frustration, and dependency, and strategies for alternative disciplinary techniques. Community resources can be mobilized for parents in order to decrease their stress.

Parents can be helped through agencies that provide group treatment by and for child abusers, for example "Parents United" or "Parents Anonymous." This not only provides a parent with models of other individuals who have overcome acting abusively, but also with a much-needed social support network.

CONCLUSION

Helping professionals have a vital role to play in the identification of maltreated students, and in working with them, their parents, the community, and the society as a whole. The school often is cited as an institution that has the potential for great impact in the area of maltreatment. Garbarino (1976, 1982) believes that the school must serve not only as an academic specialist, but also as a community support system. Schools can help in the identification of maltreated children, provide support, refer to appropriate agencies, assist children and the foster/adoptive parents. School personnel can help in the provision of a stable, nurturant, interpersonal relationship. There needs to be an active policy and program to assess the quality of life for the school's families, in cooperation with other agencies. Schools need to join with other agencies in helping parents deal with the stresses of everyday life, and school professionals can stimulate the community to assume this responsibility as well.

APPENDIX: RESOURCES

The National Committee for the Prevention of Child Abuse (NCPCA/ 332 South Michigan Avenue/ Suite 1250/ Chicago, IL 60604-4357; phone: 312 663-3520) has a variety of catalogs and brochures identifying resources for use with survivors, potential victims, and those who maltreat. These catalogs and brochures are available free upon request from the NCPCA Publishing Department. Because of the continual development of new materials in this area, these listings tend to become non-exhaustive very quickly. However, these NCPCA brochures and catalogs are continually updated, and, in my opinion, are outstanding in their usefulness. Three of these are worth mentioning in particular.

1. The NCPCA has a brochure (1985) entitled *Child Sexual Abuse Prevention Resources* that provides descriptions, addresses, and phone numbers to order

materials including: audiovisual materials; live performances and theater groups; curricula; games, dolls, puppets, cards, posters; programs; organizations; printed materials for children and teenagers; printed materials for adults; and further resources.

2. *Selected Child Abuse Information and Resources* (NCPCA, April, 1984) includes a listing of chapters of the national committee, "other ways to get involved" (including Parents Anonymous, Social service departments, Volunteer clearinghouses), "innovative approaches to intervention" (including Adults Molested as Children United, Formerly Abused Children Emerging in Society, and I'm in Charge), "support for parents" (including Big Brothers/Big Sisters of America, National Institute of Mental Health, National Coalition Against Domestic Violence, Parents Anonymous, Parents United/Daughters and Sons United, and Salvation Army), "support for children and youth" (including National Network of Runaway and Youth Services, National Runaway Switchboard, and Parents Anonymous), "children's rights and advocacy," "child abuse statistics," "support for families," "parenting education," "adoption," "foster care," "self-help groups," "disabled," "missing children," "legal assistance," "locating community resources," "directories," "audiovisuals," and "organizations." Each section includes a description of the organization and services as well as the appropriate address and phone number.

3. The NCPCA Catalog includes a variety of resources, not all of which are mentioned in the *Child Sexual Abuse Prevention Resources*, but does include those that can be ordered directly from NCPCA. It also includes research findings and public awareness materials, as well as some materials which are translated into Spanish.

REFERENCES

Adams-Tucker, C. (1981). A sociological overview of 28 abused children. *Child Abuse and Neglect, 5*, 361–367.

Anderson, S. C., Bach, C. M., & Griffith, S. (1981, August). *Psychosocial sequelae in intrafamilial victims of sexual assault and abuse.* Paper presented at the Third International Conference on Child Abuse and Neglect, Amsterdam, The Netherlands.

Aragona, J. A., & Eyberg, S. M. (1981). Neglected children: Mothers' report of child behavior problems and observed verbal behavior. *Child Development, 52*, 596–602.

Bell, R. Q., & Harper, L. (1977). *Child effects on adults.* Hillsdale, NJ: Lawrence Erlbaum Associates.

Belsky, J. (1984). The determinants of parenting: A process model. *Child Development, 55*, 83–96.

Berliner, L., & Barbieri, M. K. (1984). The testimony of the child victim of sexual assault. *Journal of Social Issues, 40*, 125–137.

Bonsha, D. M., & Twentyman, C. T. (1984). Mother-child interactional style in abuse, neglect, and control groups: Naturalistic observations in the home. *Journal of Abnormal Psychology, 93*, 106–114.

Brassard, M. R., Tyler, A. H., & Kehle, T. J. (1983). School programs to prevent intrafamilial child sexual abuse. *Child Abuse and Neglect, 7*, 241–245.

Broadhurst, D. (1979). *The educator's role in the prevention and treatment of child abuse and neglect* (DHEW Publication No. OHDS-79-30172). Washington, DC: DHEW.

Brown, A., & Finklehor, D. (no date). *The impact of child sexual abuse: A review of the research.* Durham, NH: Family Violence Research Program.

Browning, D. H., & Boatman, B. (1977). Incest: Children at risk. *American Journal of Psychiatry, 134,* 69-72.

Burgess, A. W. & Holstrom, L. L. (1978). Accessory to sex: Pressure, sex, and secrecy. In A. W. Burgess, A. N. Groth, L. L. Holstrom & S. M. Sgroi (Eds.), *Sexual assault of children and adolescents* (pp. 85-98). Lexington, MA: Lexington Books.

Burgess, R. L., & Conger, R. (1978). Family interactions in abusive, neglectful, and normal families. *Child Development, 49,* 1163-1173.

Burgess, R. L., & Richardson, R. A. (1984). Coercive interpersonal contingencies as determinants of child abuse: Implications for treatment and prevention. In R. F. Dangel & R. A. Polster (Eds.), *Behavioral parent training: Issues in research and practice* (pp. 239-259). New York: Guilford.

Conger, R., Burgess, R., & Barrett, C. (1979). Child abuse related to life change and perceptions of illness: Some preliminary findings. *Family Coordinator, 28,* 73-78.

Corson, J. (1983, August). *A survey of the states' statutes: Do they include "emotional abuse" in their definitions of child abuse and/or neglect?* Paper presented at The International Conference on Psychological Abuse of Children and Youth. University of Indiana, Indianapolis, Indiana.

DeFrancis, V. (1969). *Protecting the child victim of sex crimes committed by adults.* Denver: American Humane Association.

de Young, M. (1982). *The sexual victimization of children.* Jefferson, NC: McFarland.

Egeland, B., & Sroufe, L. A. (1981). Attachment and early maltreatment. *Child Development, 52,* 44-52.

Emery, R. E. (1982). Interparental conflict and the children of discord and divorce. *Psychological Bulletin, 92,* 310-330.

Faller, K. (Ed.), (1981). *Social work with abused and neglected children.* New York: The Free Press.

Finch, S. M. (1967). Sexual activity of children with other children and adults. *Clinical Pediatrics, 3,* 1-2.

Finklehor, D. (1979). *Sexually victimized children.* New York: The Free Press.

Finklehor, D. (1984). *Child sexual abuse: New theory and research.* New York: The Free Press.

Forehand, R. L., & McMahon, R. J. (1981). *Helping the noncompliant child: A clinician's guide to parent training.* New York: Guilford.

Friedman, R., Sandler, J., Hernandez, M., & Wolfe, D. (1981). Child Abuse. In E. Mash & L. Terdal (Eds.), *Behavior assessment of childhood disorders* (pp. 221-255). New York: Guilford.

Frodi, A. M., & Lamb, M. E. (1980). Child abusers' responses to infant smiles and cries. *Child Development, 51,* 238-241.

Gaines, R., Sandgrund, A., Green, A. H., & Power, E. (1978). Etiological factors in child maltreatment: A multivariate study of abusing, neglecting, and normal mothers. *Journal of Abnormal Psychology, 87,* 531-540.

Garbarino, J. (1976). The family: A school for living. *National Elementary Principal, 55,* 66-70.

Garbarino, J. (1982). *Children and families in the social environment.* Hawthorne, NY: Aldine.

Garbarino, J., Sebes, J., & Schellenbach, C. (1984). Families at risk for destructive parent-child relations in adolescence. *Child Development, 55,* 174-183.

Garbarino J., & Vondra, J. (1983, August). *Psychological maltreatment of children and youth.* Paper presented at The International Conference on Psychological Abuse of Children and Youth, University of Indiana, Indianapolis, Indiana.

Gelinas, D. J. (1983). The persisting negative effects of incest. *Psychiatry, 46,* 312-332.

Gelles, R. J., & Straus, M. A. (1979). Violence in the American family. *Journal of Social Issues, 35,* 15-39.

Germain, R. B., Brassard, M. R., & Hart, S. N. (1985). Crisis intervention for maltreated children. *School Psychology Review, 14,* 291-299.

Giaretto, H. (1981). A comprehensive child sexual abuse treatment program. In P. B. Mrazek & C. H. Kempe (Eds.), *Sexually abused children and their families* (pp. 179-189). New York: Pergamon Press.

Gil, D. G. (1971), A sociocultural perspective on physical child abuse. *Child Welfare, 50*, 380–395.

Gil D. G. (1983, August). *Institutional abuse: Dynamics and prevention.* Paper presented at The International Conference on Psychological Abuse of Children and Youth. University of Indiana, Indianapolis, Indiana.

Giovannoni, J. M. (1971). Parental mistreatment: Perpetrators and victims. *Journal of Marriage and the Family, 33*, 649–657.

Goodwin, J. (1982). *Sexual abuse: Incest victims and their families.* Boston: John Wright.

Herenkohl, R. C., Herenkohl, E. C., & Egolf, B. P. (1983). Circumstances surrounding the occurrence of child maltreatment. *Journal of Consulting and Clinical Psychology, 51*, 424–431.

Hyman, I. (1983, August). *Psychological correlates of corporal punishment and physical abuse.* Paper presented at The International Conference on the Psychological Abuse of Children and Youth, University of Indiana, Indianapolis, Indiana.

Jaffe, P., Thompson, J., & Wolfe, D. A. (1984). Evaluating the impact of a specialized civilian family crisis unit within a police force on the resolution of family conflict. *Journal of Preventive Psychiatry, 2*, 63–69.

James, J., & Meyerding, J. (1977). Early sexual experiences and prostitution. *American Journal of Psychiatry, 134*, 1381–1385.

Jehu, D., & Gazan, M. (1983). Psychosocial adjustment of women who were sexually victimized in childhood or adolescence. *Canadian Journal of Community Mental Health, 2*, 71–81.

Jones, R. & Jones, J. (1983, August). *Institutional abuse.* Paper presented at The International Conference on the Psychological Abuse of Children and Youth, University of Indiana, Indianapolis, Indiana.

Justice, B., & Duncan, D. F. (1976). Life crisis as a precursor to child abuse. *Public Health Reports, 91*, 110–115.

Justice, B., & Justice, R. (1979). *The broken taboo.* New York: Human Sciences Press.

Kadushin, A., & Martin, J. (1981). *Child abuse: An interactional event.* New York: Columbia University Press.

Kaufman, I., Peck, A., Tagiuri, C. (1954). The family constellation and overt incestuous relations between father and daughter. *American Journal of Orthopsychiatry, 24*, 266–279.

Kelly, J. A. (1983). *Training child abusive families: Intervention based on skills training principles.* New York: Plenum.

Kempe, C. H. (1973). A practical approach to the protection of the abused child and the rehabilitation of the abusing parent. *Pediatrics, 51*, 804–812.

Kempe, R. S., & Kempe, C. H. (1978). *Child abuse.* Cambridge, MA: Harvard University Press.

Lahey, B. B., Conger, R. D., Atkeson, B. M., & Treiber, F. A. (1984). Parenting behavior and emotional status of physically abusive mothers. *Journal of Consulting and Clinical Psychology, 52*, 1062–1071.

Larrance, D. T., & Twentyman, C. T. (1983). Maternal attributions and child abuse. *Journal of Abnormal Psychology, 92*, 449–457.

Lorber, R., Felton, D. K., & Reid, J. B. (1984). A social learning approach to the reduction of coercive processes in child abusive families: A molecular analysis. *Advances in Behavior Research and Therapy, 6*, 29–45.

Main, M. & Goldwyn, R. (1984). Predicting rejection of her infant from mother's representation of her own experience: Implications for the abused-abusing intergenerational cycle. *Child Abuse and Neglect, 8*, 203–217.

Mash, E. J., Johnston, C., & Kovitz, K. (1983). A comparison of the mother-child interactions of physically abused and non-abused children during play and task situations. *Journal of Clinical Child Psychology, 12*, 337–346.

Melnick, B., & Hurley, J. R. (1969). Distinctive personality attributes of child-abusing mothers. *Journal of Consulting and Clinical Psychology, 33*, 746–749.

Milner, J. S., Gold, R. G., Ayoub, C., & Jacewitz, M. M. (1984). Predictive validity of the Child Abuse Potential Inventory. *Journal of Consulting and Clinical Psychology, 52*, 879–884.

Milner, J. S., & Wimberly, R. C. (1980). Prediction and explanation of child abuse. *Journal of Clinical Psychology, 35,* 875–884.

Nakashima, I. I., & Zakas, G. E. (1977) Incest: Review and clinical experience. *Pediatrics, 60,* 696–701.

Patterson, G. R. (1982). *Coercive family processes.* Eugene, OR: Castilia.

Peters, J. J. (1976). Children who are victims of sexual abuse and the psychology of offenders. *American Journal of Psychotherapy, 30,* 398–421.

Reid, J. B., Taplin, P. S., & Lorber, R. (1981). A social interactional approach to the treatment of abusive families. In R. B. Stuart (Ed.), *Violent behavior: Social learning approaches to prediction, management, and treatment* (pp. 83–101). New York: Bruner/Mazel.

Rosenberg, M. S., & Reppucci, N. D. (1983). Abusive mothers: Perceptions of their own children's behavior. *Journal of Consulting and Clinical Psychology, 51,* 674–682.

Rosenfeld, A., Nadelson, C., Krieger, M., & Backman, J. (1979). Incest and sexual abuse of children. *Journal of the American Academy of Child Psychiatry, 16,* 327–339.

Ross, C. J., & Zigler, E. (1980). An agenda for action. In G. Gerbner, C. J. Ross, & E. Zigler (Eds.), *Child abuse: An agenda for action* (pp. 293–304). New York: Oxford.

Russell, D. E. H. (1984). The prevalence and seriousness of incestuous abuse: Stepfathers vs. biological fathers. *Child Abuse and Neglect, 8,* 15–22.

Sgroi, S. M. (1978). Child sexual assault: Some guidelines for intervention and assessment. In A. Burgess. A. Groth, L. Holstrom, & S. Sgroi (Eds.), *Sexual assault of children and adolescents* (pp. 129–142). Lexington, MA: Lexington Books.

Sgroi, S. M., Porter, F. S., & Black, L. C. (1982). Validation of child abuse. In S. M. Sgroi (Ed.), *Handbook of clinical intervention in child sexual abuse* (pp. 39–79). Lexington, MA: D. C. Heath.

Smith, S. L. (1984, June). Significant research findings in the etiology of child abuse. *Social casework. The Journal of Contemporary Social Work,* 337–346.

Spinetta, J. J. (1978). Parental personality factors in child abuse. *Journal of Consulting and Clinical Psychology, 46,* 1409–1414.

Spinetta, J. J., & Rigler, D. (1972). The child-abusing parent: A psychological review. *Psychological Bulletin, 77,* 296–304.

Starr, R. H., Jr. (1979). Child abuse. *American Psychologist, 34,* 872–878.

Starr, R. H. Jr. (1982). A research-based approach to the prediction of child abuse. In R. H. Starr, Jr. (Ed.), *Child abuse prediction: Policy implications* (pp. 105–134). Cambridge, MA: Ballinger.

Steele, B., & Alexander, H. (1981). Long-term effects of sexual abuse in childhood. In P. B. Mrazek & C. H. Kempe (Eds.), *Sexually abused children and their families* (pp. 223–234). New York: Pergamon Press.

Steele, B. F., & Pollock, C. (1968). A psychiatric study of parents who abuse infants and small children. In R. E. Helfer & C. Kempe (Eds.), *The battered child* (pp. 89–133). Chicago: University of Chicago Press.

Straus, M. A. (1980). Stress and child abuse. In C. H. Kempe & R. E. Helfer (Eds.), *The battered child* (3rd ed., pp. 86–102). Chicago: University of Chicago Press.

Summit, R., & Kryso, J. (1978). Sexual abuse of children: A clinical spectrum. *American Journal of Orthospsychiatry, 48,* 237–251.

Tsai, M., & Wagner, N. (1978). Therapy groups for women sexually molested as children. *Archives of Sexual Behavior, 7,* 417–429.

Tyler, A. H., & Brassard, M. R. (1984). Abuse in the investigation and treatment of intrafamilial child abuse. *Child Abuse and Neglect, 8,* 47–53.

U.S. Department of Health and Human Services (1981). *National study of the incidence and severity of child abuse and neglect: Study findings* (Publication, No. OHDS-81-30325). Washington DC: Author.

Vevier, E. & Tharinger, D. J. (1986). Child sexual abuse: A review and intervention framework for the school psychologist. *Journal of School Psychology, 24,* 293–311.

Weiss, M. D., Rogers, M. D., Darwin, M. R., & Dutton, C. E. (1955). A study of girl sex victims. *Psychiatric Quarterly, 29,* 1–27.

Wolfe, D. A. (1985). Abusive parents: An empirical review. *Psychological Bulletin, 97,* 462–482.

Wolfe, D. A., & Mosk, M. D. (1983). Behavioral comparisons of children from abusive and distressed families. *Journal of Consulting and Clinical Psychology, 51,* 702–708.

Wolfe, D. A., & Sandler, J. (1981). Training abusive parents in effective child management. *Behavior Modification, 5,* 320–335.

Wright, L. (1976). The "sick but slick" syndrome as a personality component of parents of battered children. *Journal of Clinical Psychology, 32,* 41–45.

6

Children with Handicapped Parents

Mari Griffiths Irvin
University of the Pacific

The passage of Public Law 94-142, The Education for All Handicapped Children Act, has brought increasing attention not only to the needs of handicapped children but to the needs of their parents and siblings as well. Discussions of the various needs of members of the "handicapped family" are frequently found at professional conferences and in the literature. School personnel often take the lead in providing interventions designed to attend to the specific needs of children adversely affected by a particular handicapping condition in the family.

The needs of many such children remain more hidden, however, as the handicapping condition within the family is less visible to school personnel. These children, the children of handicapped parents, are not a homogeneous group, as the disabilities incurred by their parents and their family situations are varied. But in each instance the child lives a life in relationship to a parent who has incurred a significant impairment or disability. Who among these children needs supportive intervention?

The purpose of this chapter is to (a) help the school pupil personnel services practitioner develop an awareness of this particular population of children; (b) provide preliminary information about the critical variables that must be considered in the determination of the needs of these children; and (c) suggest ways in which the school pupil personnel services staff might serve these children and their parents.

WHO ARE HANDICAPPED PARENTS?

Disabled or *Handicapped*?

Many professionals do not uniformly distinguish between the use of the adjec-

93

tives *disabled* and *handicapped*. The United Nations "Declaration on the Rights of Disabled Persons" (1975) defined a *disabled person* as "any person unable to ensure by himself or herself wholly or partly the necessities of a normal individual and/or social life, as a result of a deficiency, either congenital or not, in his or her physical or mental capabilities." Hamilton (1950) stated that the actual limitations of the individual, the disability, does not necessarily handicap the individual. English (1971a), using Goffman's (1963) definition of *stigma* as an attribute that is highly disturbing to others and suggestive of less than human or normal, summarized a body of literature that indicated that most physically disabled persons are stigmatized to some extent. English (1971b) also noted that stigma implied human devaluation and depreciation and included "the negative perceptions and behaviors of so-called normal people to all individuals who are different from themselves" (p. 1).

Battle (1974) went beyond the disability/handicap distinction and cited Susser and Watson as distinguishing among three components of handicap: organic, functional, and social.

"Impairment" is the organic component, a static condition of the process of disease. "Disability" is the functional component, or the limitation of function imposed by the impairment and the individual's psychologic reaction to it. "Handicap" is the social component, the manner and degree in which the primary impairment and functional disability limit the performance of social roles and relations with others. (Battle, 1974, p. 131)

For the purposes of this chapter, the Susser and Watson definition cited in Battle is useful. Physical impairment and disability may result from a variety of causes and always are interactive with the personality dynamics of the disabled individual. Thus, great care should be taken to avoid stereotyped descriptions or prognostic statements about either disabled persons or the significant others in their lives. However, because of the stigma effect resulting in attributions directed toward the disabled person by a society that highly values the "normal," it is highly probable that most disabled persons must struggle with the question of their self-worth at some point in their lives (Geis, 1977). Thus, it is that the "handicapping condition" is likely to result from a combined effect of the actual impairing condition, societal attributions about that condition, and the subsequent psychological effects on all involved persons.

Types of Handicapping Conditions

Handicaps may have their basis in a variety of impairing or disabling conditions to an individual. Perhaps the individual with a *physical* anomaly or *sensory deficit* is most readily associated with the term *handicap* as it is within the life experience of most adults to have had personal interaction with an individual with significant physical, visual, or hearing deficit. *Mental retardation* and *mental illness* are also commonly perceived as handicapping conditions, especially when the degree of impairment is sufficient to be readily observable behaviorally. Less immediately observable may be those individuals who are handicapped as a result of *substance abuse*. Individuals whose lives are seriously affected by the use of alcohol or drugs may often appear normal to the casual observer, although members of their immediate families or close work associates are likely to experience the negative effects of their addiction. Perhaps most invisible to the life experience of the majority of persons are those individuals whose physical health is seriously impaired through *chronic illness*. The invisibility of the illness may be related to one of two conditions. Either the individual with a chronic illness may be in the early state of a debilitative disease process in which the individual appears relatively normal, or the chronically ill person may be so impaired as to be only in social contact with members of the immediate family.

It is probable that every public school serves children who have parents with at least some, if not all, of the handicapping conditions identified. It is also likely that school instructional, administrative, and support personnel are not aware of the total number of children attending any given school who have handicapped parents. It may be argued that it is not necessary, nor perhaps even desirable, to identify those children who have parents with handicapping conditions unless the behavior of the children commands the attention of school personnel. However, it is reasonable to hypothesize that some unidentified children with handicapped parents are at-risk children who will have difficulty learning to their potential in school. Preventive interventions for such children cannot be made unless these children can be identified prior to "problem referral" for school special services.

WHO ARE AT-RISK CHILDREN OF HANDICAPPED PARENTS?

The professional literature is sparse regarding children of handicapped parents. The effects of physical disability and chronic illness upon the individual have had a longer history of study (Garrett & Levine, 1973; Marinelli & Dell Orto, 1977; Schonz, 1975; Wright, 1960) and have provided some insight into the variables that must be considered if the needs of children of handicapped parents are to be well recognized. In addition, the study of the ability of the family to cope with the experience of major illness (Hill & Hansen, 1964) resulted in the identification of factors that were grouped into four categories: (a) characteristics of the disabling event; (b) the perceived threat of the disability to family relationships, status, and goals; (c) resources available to the family; and (d) the past experience of the family in dealing with the same or similar situation.

However, the publication of S. Kenneth Thurman's (1986) *Children of Handicapped Parents: Research and Clinical Perspectives*, represents a significant contribution to both the practitioner and the researcher in that it explicitly sets forth the complexity of the potential impact of parental handicap in the lives of children. In the Thurman book, Coates, Vietze, and Gray (1986) discuss the methodological issues specifically involved in the study of children of disabled parents. This chapter has heuristic value for the school practitioner who is concerned about children of handicapped parents both at the problem prevention and problem resolution levels. The authors present a systematic discussion of the variables that must be considered in determining the impact of parental handicapping condition upon a given child.

Coates et al. (1986) identify the onset of the disabling condition of the parent (i.e., is the condition congenital or "adventitious") as the first question that must be answered. If the parental disability is not congenital, the time relationship of the disability and the arrival of the child must then be considered a critical question. Other variables of importance—type of disability, family status, child status, and family process—assume differing relationships to each other, dependent on the time of onset of the disabling condition in the life of the child under consideration.

Significance of Time of Onset of Parental Disability

It may seem obvious that the time of the onset of a disability in the life of an individual would play a large role in the determination of the personal self-awareness and the manner in which the disabled person is able to relate to others and to fulfill social roles. Individuals who have congenital disabilities develop self-awareness with the impairment or disability as a "given" in their lives. That is not to say that there may not be "grieving" for what might have been. But such individuals have experienced themselves in no other way and the process of self-development in some way includes the reality of the disability. Similarly, the significant others in the lives of congenitally disabled persons have known the individual in no other way.

Although the developmental process of congenitally disabled persons proceeds with the disability woven into the fabric of the lives of both the disabled person and the persons of significance in his or her life, the stigma referred to earlier by Goffman (1963) and English (1971b) is likely to transform the impairment or disability into handicap to a greater or lesser degree. The point here, however, is that the ability of the disabled person to take on the social roles of spouse and parent is "negotiated" with the perceived handicapping condition already present as a part of the "life space" of the involved parties. For congenitally disabled persons who become parents, the disability and how it is perceived by all parties involved operates more as an independent variable that directly affects both family process and child outcomes as dependent variables.

In contrast, in the case of non-congenital disabilities, regardless of the time of onset, the disability is experienced by the self and significant others as an assault, an intrusion to which there must be coping and adaptation. The loss, or continuing loss in the case of individuals with degenerative disease process, of function brought about by the disabling condition represents a type of "death" that needs to be acknowledged and truly grieved if subsequent optimal living is to occur (Keleman, 1974; Kubler-Ross, 1969; Matson & Brooks, 1974).

The person who has incurred the impairment or disability is not the only individual who is experiencing loss and needs to grieve. Family members who have strong emotional ties to the person with the disability, especially when dependency or interdependency of some type is involved, are likely also to experience traumatic loss (Cole, 1978; Feldman, 1974). Family members go through a period of emotional turbulence subsequent to the disabling event as each seeks to accommodate the reality of the personal loss experienced (Shellhase & Shellhase, 1972). The five-stage developmental sequence (denial, bargaining, anger, depression, and acceptance) used by Kubler-Ross (1969) to characterize personal reactions of the individual to dying is also applicable to the process each parent must undergo in dealing with the reality of a handicapped child. This model may also have utility in understanding the behavior and needs of children of handicapped persons. Behavior of family members can easily be misinterpreted during this indefinite period of "coping" (Duncan as cited in Seligman, 1979). Unfortunately, the needs of family members are often overlooked or ignored as energy is directed toward the person who is impaired or disabled. This exclusive focus on the injured is sometimes true even when "family" is involved in the rehabilitative process (Lindenberg, 1977).

Regretfully, there can be no hard and fast rules to guide school personnel in the determination of whether a specific parental disability necessarily results in a negative outcome for a given child. Nonetheless, the precipitous onset of parental disability is more likely to have a negative impact upon the child, at least temporarily, until the family has the opportunity to reorganize itself with the parental disability as a component of the family's reality. This is surely a time when school personnel need to demonstrate sensitivity to the varied and multiple needs of the child and the family.

Significance of Parental Disability Variables

Do specific parental disabilities result in specific outcomes for children or are children likely to be affected simply by the fact that they have a disabled parent? Coates et al. (1986) raised this question that they claim has not been adequately dealt with in the research that has been done on children of handicapped parents. Nonetheless, the literature does contain a number of studies that point to certain outcomes for children based upon a specific parental disability variable. There is, for example, a growing body of primarily descriptive and self-report data on children of alcoholic parents that suggests some very strong and predictable child outcome effects (Brenner, 1984). This literature is particularly important because of the large number of children affected by alcohol abuse, a number estimated to be between 16% and 24% of school-age children (Deutsch, DiCicco, & Mills as cited in Brenner, 1984).

Glass (1986) concluded her review of the literature relating to the impact of parental disability on the child and the family by citing Bucks and Hohmann's (1981) conclusion that little objective research is available. She also referred to Romano's (1984) observation that "much of what appears in the literature indicates that able-bodied health professionals project their own negative fantasies onto families where there is a disabled parent, as if it were fact" (p.151). Glass (1986) then went on to state:

> Much of the available literature depends on highly selected and biased samples, anecdotal case descriptions, or opinion based on personal experience. . . . There is a great need for well-developed and well-grounded research using sound, scientific methods with application of standardized measurement and adequate controls. Of great interest and value would be cooperative longitudinal studies of families with a disabled parent, using a systematic and uniform method of obtaining data; controlled empirical studies of effects of parental disability on children of different ages and stages; comparison of the responses and adjustment of children to an already-disabled parent with the responses of children to a parent who later acquired a disability; study of children of families with one disabled parent compared with children in families where both parents are disabled, and comparison of the characteristics of coping and noncoping families. (p. 153)

It is possible that there are critical factors cutting across parental disabling conditions that could have effects upon children. Although little research exists that isolates these specific variables, practitioners working with children of handicapped parents should be sensitive to the possible effects of these factors on children.

Severity. The severity of the parental handicapping condition, the degree to which the parent has independent living skills, is likely to affect the child. How the handicapped parent is cared for, the amount of family energy, both financial and emotional, which must go toward providing direct care for the disabled member, may have decided implications for the needs of other family members, particularly children. The severity of the parental handicap is also likely to be related directly to the amount and kind of nurturance that the child is able-to receive from the handicapped parent.

Stability. Certain disabling conditions, regardless of the severity of the condition, are relatively stable throughout the lifetime of the person. That is not to say that the disability may not have different significance for the person at various times throughout the individual's lifetime; rather, the condition does not itself result in deterioration of function over time. For example, the individual who loses a leg as the result of an automobile accident can be contrasted with an individual who has multiple sclerosis (MS). Although both disabilities are for the lifetime of the persons involved, the amputee has incurred a one-time "assault" whereas the person with MS is likely to experience an unpredictable disease pattern with episodic loss of various types of physical function and the possibility of gradual physical deterioration resulting in total or near-total physical dependency. The accident amputee has incurred a sudden loss for which there has not been an opportunity to prepare. However, the rehabilitative task is usually one with good prognosis as the disability is not degenerative. In contrast, the person with MS is likely to experience continual adjustment and readjustment to the physical losses resulting from a characteristically erratic disease process. It seems likely that children growing up in families with a handicapped parent who experiences periodic, major negative changes as the result of disabling or gradual deterioration of function might be living in a more stressful home environment than children who grow up in families wherein the parental handicapping condition is a one-time event.

Such children will need support in school, particularly during times of disruption, but school personnel need also to be aware that the child who is experiencing the slow death of a parent may be undergoing a continuous grieving process over a period of months or even years. In such a situation, the child is likely to experience many "little deaths" as the disease process continues and the limitations of the parent with their attendant implications for child–parent interaction become more global. The actual death of such a parent may at last provide closure for the child, so that the grieving can be completed.

Similarly, the spouse of a person with a debilitating disease will be experiencing a series of losses as well as increases in family and, more than likely, economic responsibilities. It is possible that some of the priorities of school personnel may become less urgent in such a family situation given this increase in parental responsibility and the very real limitations of parental time and energy. What may appear to be lack of parental concern in response to a given perceived need of the child by school personnel may in reality be a reflection of the cumulative effects of parental stress. Sensitivity to the less apparent, more subtle variables operating upon the family experiencing a parental debilitative disease process may be a major contribution to the ability of such a family to cope with its various problems and stresses.

Chronicity.   Related to the stability variable in handicapping conditions is chronicity; that is, how long has the parent been disabled and for how long is it anticipated that the parent will be disabled? Some handicapping conditions are "forever," but some "forevers" are longer than others. For example, the life expectancy for individuals with major diseases may vary from a few weeks to several decades. Support may be more available for individuals in "acute" rather than "chronic" situations because of the ability and willingness of many individuals to respond to "emergencies" that require an immediate and focused response.

Less energy may be available for the sustained support both of the handicapped individual and members of the family if there is no immediate resolution of the problem. Thus, it is probable that the effects of parental handicap in the lives of children may vary based upon the length of time the parent is afflicted with the disability. School personnel should not, however, make any assumptions about the specific effects of this time variable upon a given child or family; rather, each instance needs to be reviewed carefully with attention given both to the child's various needs and to sources of ongoing support available to the child and the family.

Involved Processes.   What functions are affected by the handicapping condition? Is the disabled person primarily restricted in physical movement but mental processing remains unimpaired? Is cognitive processing affected? Is the primary handicapping condition a mental illness or are emotional responses such as depression secondary to a physical disease or disability? Does the handicapping condition result in mood changes or volatile behavior? Answer to these questions may have definite implications for the risk status of children of handicapped parents.

Visibility.   How visible, literally, is the handicapping condition? The degree of impairment resulting from some handicapping conditions is signaled by a commonly understood aid (e.g., white cane or wheelchair). In contrast, some handicapped individuals use supports that alert the observer to a problem but provide much less information about the extent of the handicapping condition (e.g., a hearing aid). It is difficult to state globally whether handicap visibility serves to help or hinder handicapped individuals relate to nonhandicapped persons. The visibility of the handicapping condition, on one hand, may serve as a stigma in that it alerts observers to the differences between such individuals and the so-called normal persons. As such, the handicapped individual may experience stereotypic behavior as relational responses from persons. On the other hand, the visibility of the handicapping condition may prevent misinterpretation of certain behaviors of the handicapped person. As an example, a person with MS who is experiencing problems with gait while walking might be perceived as intoxicated or on drugs by unaware observers.

Societal Acceptance.   Because of the stigma assigned to disability and impairment (Goffman, 1963), it is probable that the impaired person will experience questioning of self-worth subsequent to the awareness of the disabling condition. "Depression, self-blame and self-hatred, blocked motivation, slowed behavior or pathological compensatory activity, and difficulties progressing on the rehabilitation program and in community adjustment—these are all concomitants of feelings of low worth" (Geis, 1977, p. 131). Thus, it is possible that the primary variable for affected children of handicapped parents, at least for those with adventitious handicaps, relates to the living in a family situation that is struggling with the emotional sequella of the experiencing of handicap.

In addition, some disabling conditions are more readily acceptable societally. For example, an individual impaired by heart disease is usually afforded more understanding and acceptance than an individual who is battling AIDS or recovering from an accidental overdose of an illegal addictive substance. It is possible that the type of handicapping condition of the parent will have implications for the sensitivity of the school community to the child's needs, but it is difficult to predict whether more or less support will be afforded the child dependent on the values placed on the parental handicapping condition. The existing perception of the child by the teacher may be a critical variable in determining the degree of support given the child. Particularly vulnerable, then, may be the child whose behavior is already disturbing to the teacher. Conversely, knowledge of the parental condition may be useful to the teacher in "understanding" the problematic behavior of a child. Clearly, in each instance of a child with a disabled parent, school personnel should accept the child's needs for in-school support independent of their evaluation of the handicapping condition of the disabled parent.

Family Status Variables

Family status variables, background information about the family, are assumed to contribute to child outcome behavior. The answers to specific contextual family questions can be helpful in ascertaining the diverse needs of family members, especially children. Does the child have two parents or is the handicapped parent a "single parent"? If the child lives within an extended family unit, does this family pattern represent internal family support or is it an additional source of stress? Does the family have external support through close friends or religious affiliation? Does the community in which the family lives provide support to the family through the provision of needed medical or social services? Is the economic status of the family stable? Have roles within the family changed as the result of parental disability; are roles presently stable or does the nature of the disability result in ongoing change in role function that must continuously be assimilated by family members?

Child Status Variables

The assumption should not be made that all children in a family with a handicapped parent will experience similar effects. In such families, the age and birth order of children may be critical variables in assessing the impact of the effect of the handicapping condition upon a given child. The gender of the disabled parent, particularly in combination with the gender/age of the child, may also have a differential effect. Child status variables may be particularly important when the onset of the handicapping condition is adventitious, when the disability serves as an unwelcome intrusion in the family's developmental pattern.

Family Process Variables

Coates et al. (1986) summarized family process or interaction variables as falling into three general categories: (a) power-decision-making style, (b) communication, and (c) problem-solving effectiveness. Again, the time of disability onset, congenital or adventitious, tends to determine whether independent or dependent variable status is assigned to the parental handicapping condition in relation to these processes and the effects of the handicapping condition on the child.

ROLE OF SCHOOL PUPIL PERSONNEL SERVICES STAFF

Specifically, what can and should be done in schools for at-risk children of handicapped parents? Who should provide those services?

Use of a Team Model

Perhaps the best vehicle for potential use in identifying at-risk children of handicapped parents is the Multidisciplinary Team (MDT). Since the passage of Public Law 94–142 and its mandate of the team approach to the identification of handicapped children, MDTs have assumed a primary coordinational responsibility in schools for the identification of children with special needs. Although the literature points to limitations in team effectiveness (Abelson & Woodman, 1983; Yosida, 1983), it can be argued that some of the difficulties experienced in using the team model are a function of the relative inexperience of team members in using a collaborative process for problem identification and resolution. The model offers considerable potential for usage beyond that of decision-making for handicapped children.

Pfeiffer and Tittler (1983) have presented a model of team functioning based on a family systems orientation. This model appears to have particular utility in serving children of handicapped parents in that it assumes that school and family are "intimately interrelated and reciprocally influential" (p. 168). The determination of risk status of any given child with handicapped parents cannot be done by relying on existing research outcomes, but there is ample evidence of critical variables that need to be considered. This exploration can only be done if school personnel and family members are able to share information systematically. A school–family systems orientation is needed to provide for the generation of the kind of data needed to make appropriate child-specific recommendations for children of handicapped parents.

Identification of At-Risk Children

A two-fold approach is recommended for the determination of at-risk children of handicapped parents—specific child referral and school screening.

Specific Child Referral.   Follow-up to each child problem referral to the MDT should include sufficient family and health information to determine whether either of the child's parents or immediate caregivers is, in fact, impaired or disabled. This task may not be as easy as it may appear, given the variety of conditions, some more invisible than others, that may constitute a parental handicap. School personnel who have had contact with the family over time should be interviewed, and the contact with the family subsequent to the referral of the child should be made by personnel who are sensitive to the presence of handicapping conditions in families. Pfeiffer and Tittler (1983) recommended that the focus of any formal assessment extend beyond the child and include data regarding the family. Ideally the involvement with the family should begin before the time of a "problem referral" on a child.

School Screening.   When screening occurs in a school, for whatever purpose, the intention is to identify those students for whom preventive intervention may be appropriate. Thus, it is hoped that the number of problem referrals can be reduced or, more ideally, eliminated. The objective is to prevent times of school crisis by anticipating need rather than reacting to it. In such a model, data are gathered on all children so that a determination might be made as to which children are in need of more extensive follow-up and services.

A "family interview" would be one means by which such screening could occur to identify children of handicapped parents. The child's first teacher within a given school system could be a primary person in arranging for such a home or school contact. The logistics of an every-child family interview are significant, given contemporary working patterns both of parents and school professionals. It is unrealistic to expect that such an opportunity for interaction between family and school representatives will occur without the use of released time specifically designated for such a purpose. Only those administrators who regard the use of time for this purpose as a long-term investment in successful child outcomes are likely to implement such an approach.

A second, less-ideal approach to screening for the purposes of identifying children of handicapped parents would be to include some critical questions about the family in the data-gathering done by the school for other purposes, such as vision and hearing screening. The disadvantage to this approach is that it relies heavily on "hearsay" information and does not necessarily include the interviewer as an observer. However, even limited data gathered in such a way, if reliable, would afford the opportunity to determine whether additional involvement with the family is warranted for the purposes of identifying at-risk children of handicapped parents.

What Next?   Gathering data on families about the possible presence of a handicapped parent in the family unit should not be seen as an end unto itself. The mere fact that a child has a handicapped parent does not necessarily warrant "unusual" services by the school district to that family or to the child. Rather, it is one "bit" of data that must be integrated with other known information about the child and then used for decision-making in determining whatever "appropriate" educational services are for that child.

INTERVENTION STRATEGIES

Prevention of Crisis Situations

Sandoval (chapter 1, this volume) identified several strategies that can be used in schools to prevent crises. One of them, anticipatory guidance, has much possibility for use with children of handicapped parents. Such guidance provides the opportunity for children to prepare for events that are likely to occur in their future. School personnel, especially if working together with family members, can on a child-specific basis help a given child prepare for events and situations that have the potential for disruption for the child. Similarly, teachers who work regularly with the child can be provided information so that they might also prepare for specific changes in the child's life. If, for example, school personnel can be alerted to the absence of a parent from the home for an extended period of rehabilitation, school personnel can help the child deal with this event both factually and emotionally. The focus in such guidance is to provide the child with the emotional resources needed to cope well with the necessary life changes that are occurring for the large part outside of the child's control.

Such guidance can be more easily provided when there is a collaborative school-home relationship. However, some parental handicapping conditions do not as easily lend themselves to such collaboration. If both parents are addicted to alcohol, for example, the child cannot depend on the parents to work collaboratively with school personnel, as denial may be a component of their disease process. In such instances, school personnel may need to work directly and only with the child, to the degree that the parents will support such involvement. Similarly, when the parental handicapping condition involves the possibility of child abuse and child protective services need to be involved, school personnel will be limited in their choices. However, in most situations throughout the period of the child's public school enrollment, parents have the right to be advised, even if they need not consent, before supportive services can be provided to the child.

The Developmental Variable

Generally speaking, the younger the child the more probable that significant others will be needed to provide support. The provider of support services to the child needs to attend carefully to the child's level of understanding of the parental handicap. What feelings are elicited by this experience? How are they different, if they are, from the feelings expressed by other children of comparable chronological age in regard to their parents? Is the child developmentally ready to relate to other children in a group situation designed to strengthen coping skills? How much "information" can the child handle about the parental handicap?

Persons who work with the children of handicapped persons need to be sensitive to the ways in which the child receives information about the parent's disability. It is quite possible that the individual child is experiencing difficulty in decoding parental behavior. One cannot assume that the child has specific information about the parent's impairment. Often children in the family are "protected" from knowledge about the parental handicap. Even when the condition is signaled in some visible manner, the child may not have the life experiences to enable appropriate interpretation.

When the behavior of a child of handicapped parents suggests that the child is receiving mixed messages about the parental handicap or when the child gives evidence of confusion or concern about the parental condition, school personnel may find it helpful to discuss this matter explicitly with one or both of the parents. It is possible that the parents may not be aware of the child's particular understanding of the parental handicap.

It is also possible that the parents may need help in deciding what the child should be told or how to discuss with the child what may be a particularly painful topic for them. Again, no assumptions that are not checked out carefully should be made about the feelings or the needs of the parents in this matter. Rather, school personnel should attempt to work as supportive partners with the parents in the process of helping the child acquire the information, emotionally loaded that it is, about the parental handicap appropriate for the child's developmental level. In addition, school personnel may be able to serve as resources to the child as the child makes decisions about what or how to share information about the parental condition with friends.

Support for the Supporters

A parental handicapping condition is usually a long-term experience in the lives of children. The passage of time does result in changes within the family unit, many of which may reflect the adaptation and adjustment that alleviate certain types of stress. But it is possible that family helpers may need their own support resources to enable them to continue to work well with persons undergoing a chronic type of stressful condition. When energy is put into helping people deal with crisis, there may be an expectation, recognized or not, that change will occur in a relatively short period of time. The problems affecting many families with handicapped parents tend to be slow to resolve in a satisfactory manner.

Teachers who work for a limited period of time, usually one academic year, with a given child may be able to receive adequate support from the school pupil personnel services staff, support that will enable them to work productively with a child and parents who are experiencing significant difficulty related to parental handicap. But school pupil personnel services staff may find themselves working for several years with a given family that is experiencing chronic stress related to parental disability. It may indeed be a frustrating and painful experience to "watch" a family struggle with the ongoing effects of disability over time. Such school staff need to be particularly aware of the possibility of "blaming the victim" for lack of satisfactory resolution of difficult problems. Staff support groups may be one vehicle for the "working through" of issues related to serving as providers of services to families experiencing chronic and difficult problems related to parental handicap.

CONCLUSION

As the number of children affected by similar adverse conditions are recognized societally, interventions have been designed to attend to the needs of these children. The needs of other children, however, remain more hidden because the source of their stress is not as apparent. One such group of children are those with handicapped parents. Although not a homogeneous group, many of these children experience significant loss or distortion of parenting care as the result of the disability incurred by one of their parents. School pupil personnel services staff are encouraged to work with teachers and administrators in the identification of families incurring stress as the result of parental handicap. Interventions should be designed for such children and families that will provide for ongoing support. School personnel need to be sensitive to their own needs in working with families whose problem situations continue over time.

REFERENCES

Abelson, M. A., & Woodman, R. W. (1983). Review of research on team effectiveness: Implications for teams in schools. *School Psychology Review, 12*, 125–136.

Battle, C. U. (1974). Disruptions in the socialization of a young, severely handicapped child. *Rehabilitation Literature, 35*, 130–140.

Brenner, A. (1984). *Helping children cope with stress.* Lexington, MA: Lexington Books.

Bucks, F. M., & Hohmann, G. W. (1981). Personality and behavior of children of disabled and non-disabled fathers. *Archives of Physical Medicine and Rehabilitation, 62*, 432–438.

Coates, D. L., Vietze, P. M., & Gray, D. B. (1986). Methodological issues in studying children of disabled parents. In S. K. Thurman (Ed.), *Children of handicapped parents: Research and clinical perspectives* (pp. 155–180). Orlando, FL: Academic Press.

Cole, C. M. (1978). The role of brief family therapy in medical rehabilitation. *Journal of Rehabilitation, 44*, 29–42.

English, R. W. (1971a). Combating stigma toward physically disabled persons. *Rehabilitation Research and Practice Review, 2*, 19–27.

English, R. W. (1971b). Correlates of stigma toward physically disabled persons. *Rehabilitation Research and Practice Review, 2*, 1–17.

Feldman, D. J. (1974). Chronic disabling illness: A holistic view. *Journal of Chronic Diseases, 27,* 287–291.

Garrett, J., & Levine, E. (Eds.). (1973). *Rehabilitation practices with the physically disabled.* New York: Columbia University Press.

Geis, H. J. (1977). The problem of personal worth in the physically disabled patient. In R. P. Marinelli & A. E. Dell Orto (Eds.), *The psychological and social impact of physical disability* (pp. 130–140). New York: Springer.

Glass, D. D. (1986). Onset of disability in a parent: Impact on child and family. In S. K. Thurman (Ed.), *Children of handicapped parents: Research and clinical perspectives* (pp. 145–154). Orlando, Fl: Academic Press.

Goffman, E. (1963). *Stigma.* Englewood Cliffs, NJ: Prentice-Hall.

Hamilton, K. W. (1950). *Counseling the handicapped in the rehabilitation process.* New York: Ronald Press.

Hill, R., & Hansen, D. A. (1964). Families under stress. In H. T. Christensen (Ed.), *Handbook of marriage and the family* (pp. 782–819). Chicago: Rand McNally.

Keleman, S. (1974). *Living your dying.* New York: The Free Press.

Kubler-Ross, E. (1969). *On death and dying.* New York: Macmillan.

Lindenberg, R. (1977). Work with families in rehabilitation. *Rehabilitation Counseling Bulletin, 21,* 67–76.

Marinelli, R. P., & Dell Orto, A. E. (1977). *The psychological and social impact of physical disability.* New York: Springer.

Matson, R. R., & Brooks, N. A. (1974). Adjusting to multiple sclerosis: An exploratory study. *Social Science and Medicine, 11,* 245–250.

Pfeiffer, S. I., & Tittler, B. I. (1983). Utilizing the multidisciplinary team to facilitate a school-family systems orientation. *School Psychology Review, 12,* 168–173.

Romano, M. (1984). Impact of disability on family and society. In J. V. Basmajian & R. L. Kirby (Eds.), *Medical rehabilitation* (pp. 273–276). Baltimore, MD: Williams & Wilkins.

Schonz, F. C. (1975). *The psychological aspects of physical illness and disability.* New York: Macmillan.

Seligman, M. (1979). *Strategies for helping parents of exceptional children: A guide for teachers.* New York: The Free Press.

Shellhase, L., & Shellhase, F. (1972). Role of the family in rehabilitation. *Social Casework, 53,* 544–550.

Thurman, S. K. (Ed.). (1986). *Children of handicapped parents: Research and clinical perspectives.* Orlando, FL: Academic Press.

United Nations. (1975, December 9). Declaration on the Rights of Disabled Persons, General Assembly Resolution 3447 [XXX]. New York.

Wright, B. A. (1960). *Physical disability—A psychological approach.* New York: Harper & Row.

Yosida, R. K. (1983). Are multidisciplinary teams worth the investment? *School Psychology Review, 12,* 139–143.

Illness: A Crisis for Children

Margaret S. Steward
University of California, Davis

Recently, I got a call from a second-grade teacher who asked me about the wisdom of putting Billy into a small reading group. I started to ask about his reading skills, but the teacher interrupted me saying, "No, you don't understand, Dr. Steward, Billy has diabetes, and I don't want the rest of the children to catch it!". That phone call was an indirect result of three events: the enactment of Public Law 94142 that guarantees children like Billy a place in a public school classroom, important advances in modern medical practice such that with regular medication Billy has sufficient health and energy to cope with school, and gradual public acceptance of persons with disabilities (Walker & Jacobs, 1985). It is likely that in these changing times school personnel need to make a concerted effort to understand the physical capacities and limitations, and medical needs of each chronically ill child in their midst. At the same time, medical personnel need to know more about the educational demands and opportunities of the specific classroom into which their young patient is going/returning, and we all need to be brought up to running speed with respect to what it means for a child to cope with illness.

Unfortunately the teacher who called me was not quite ready for Billy in her class. Once I understood her concerns, there were a number of avenues to explore. One obvious issue was the teacher's need for accurate information to quell her concern that Billy's metabolic disease might be contagious and therefore that the children (and possibly she herself) might be vulnerable. Of course, there were other issues. For example, did she have a feel for how Billy's diabetes might influence his behavior during the school day to interrupt or compromise his learning? Had she learned to scan for behavioral clues such as uncharacteristic irritability and uncooperativeness that might suggest that his blood sugar is too low, or understand that increased requests for drinks of water and trips to the bathroom suggest that his blood sugar is too high? Had his parents told her that he might need special supervision at lunch or snacktime? Could Billy's physician be invited to conduct an inservice session so that the whole staff would know how to identify a medical emergency, which for Billy might mean seizures or a coma, and what to do about it?

We know that it is also important to understand what Billy thinks is wrong with him. Does he believe, as some young children with that disease have told us, that he got the disease by eating too much candy, or that he will die because he has "die-a-beasties"? What does he tell classmates who ask? His disease— chronic, at times life-threatening, but for all practical purposes "invisible"— can be a source of much confusion, misapprehension, and anxiety. If he is being treated with the latest medical technology, he will be involved in testing his own blood sugar level, and making judgments about what to do about the fluctuations he finds. His experiences will change as he moves from middle childhood into adolescence, and to the astonishment and dismay of his parents and physician, he may become less rather than more reliable in "managing" his illness. The increased cognitive flexibility of adolescence will make the uncertainty of his disease more starkly clear. The temptations of "teenage" food, activities, and the strong pull for identification with his healthy classmates will make him even more painfully aware of his differentness, and dangerously vulnerable to peer pressure.

As the laws are implemented and new medical treatments are discovered, there will be more and more Billys in our classrooms. The classroom may be "the only place where I'm normal". The response of school personnel can be pivotal. The teacher's understanding or misunderstanding of childhood cancer will be transmitted to the rest of the students in the classroom. A principal, with the best intentions in the world, may warn students not to touch a hemophilic child, leaving the child not only "untouchable" but also feeling powerless and humiliated (Massie, 1985). A school nurse can support an asthmatic child's immature dependency on adults for heath care, or can encourage independent observations and judgments about necessary medical intervention (Lewis, Lewis, & Palmer, 1977). A school psychologist can passively listen as a child retells his or her story about a painful medical procedure or can actively teach that child strategies to cope with the almost inevitable teasing from peers (Ross & Ross, 1984). Informed, compassionate personnel can insure that school is one of the child's best experiences, or can create an atmosphere that may contribute to a child's low self-esteem and may stimulate troubling or avoidant coping strategies such as school phobia or school failure.

In this chapter, I present information on the current estimates of the childhood disease in our country. Next, I have selected two research issues in behavioral medicine to give the reader a context for relating to sick children. This is followed by a section on children and illness, which discusses children's experiences of acute and chronic illness, and hospitalization. Next developmental models of children's understanding of illness, and medical procedure will be presented. Finally, some useful resources for planning crises intervention are given.

INCIDENCE AND PREVALENCE OF DISEASE IN CHILDHOOD AND ADOLESCENCE

Nearly 20 years ago, Wolff (1970) identified illness as the universal stress of childhood, and although advances in medical research and technology have changed the face of pediatric illness, it still may be a fair assumption that every child has direct experience with brief, acute disease. The frequency of acute illnesses such as colds, flu, and respiratory diseases, recurrent events in children's lives, is dependent in part on family size and inevitable sequential spreading of infection through a family, or a classroom (Parmelee, 1985). In the United States, the typical child is absent as a result of illness about 5 school days a year. Although the incidence of "common childhood diseases" is dropping, the accident rate is climbing and children under 15 years are the most likely victims of accidental

TABLE 7.1
Prevalence Estimates for Eleven Childhood Chronic Diseases
Ages Birth to 20 Years, United States, 1980

Disease	Estimated Percentage Surviving to Age 20*	1980 Prevalence Estimated per 1,000**
Asthma (moderate and severe)	98	10.00
Congenital heart disease	65	7.00
Diabetes mellitus	95	1.80
Cleft lip/palate	92	1.50
Spina bifida	50	.40
Sickle cell anemia	90	.28
Cystic fibrosis	60	.20
Hemophilia	90	.15
Acute lymphocytic leukemia	40	.11
Chronic renal failure	25	.08
Muscular dystrophy	25	.06
Estimated Total (assuming no overlap)		21.58

* Estimate refers to the survival expected of a birth cohort to age 20, given current treatments
** Estimates are from population prevalence data or are derived from estimates of incidence (or prevalence at birth) and survival data.
Source: Hobbs, Perrin, and Ireys (1985).

injury, disability, and death. It is striking to note that currently in adolescence the leading causes of mortality and morbidity are accidents, homicide, suicide, drug abuse, venereal disease, and teenage pregnancy—all behaviorally determined. As a result of disease or injury, one person in two will require hospitalization during childhood or adolescence.

Of the children and adolescents in America 10%–15% have a chronic health condition; 1%–2% have a condition severe enough to interfere with their daily activities (Hobbs, Perrin, & Ireys, 1985). It is estimated that an elementary school teacher will have six chronically ill children in her classes over a 10-year period, while the typical high school teacher will have approximately 30 chronically ill youngsters over the same 10-year period. Given the current prevalence of chronic diseases (see Table 7.1), half of these children will have asthma, while the other half will have one of a dozen other chronic diseases such as diabetes, hemophilia, congenital heart disease, or cancer.

CURRENT RESEARCH IN BEHAVIORAL MEDICINE

There are two current issues in the growing field of behavioral medicine that should interest school personnel. Each provides a different perspective from which to understand the experiences of sick children. The first issue deals with the important differentiation between disease and illness. The second issue provides examples of how the introduction of behavioral strategies has empowered patients to a more active role in management of their own diseases.

Disease versus Illness

The current literature in behavioral medicine differentiates *disease* from *illness* (Eisenberg, 1977). The former designates biological pathophysiology that results in symptoms and signs that are commonly recognizable in everyone who is diagnosed with the disease. The latter refers to the experience of the individual. Put more simply, *disease* is a term that belongs to the medical system, whereas *illness* belongs to the personal, family, and social systems. In the case of an individual child in the classroom, both disease and illness must be dealt with.

Parmelee (1985) has pointed out that one can have a disease without feeling ill, as well as feeling ill without having a disease. Koocher (1985) has noted that the research and clinical literature on sick children is generally of two types: categorical and generic. The categorical work focuses on a single disease entity, such as cancer, diabetes, asthma, or cystic fibrosis discussing etiology, treatment, and psychological adaptation. Generic investigations focus on physical, emotional, and social burdens associated with children's illness and often link those issues to important developmental milestones. This movement parallels the disease versus illness motifs previously discussed.

Although a compelling argument can be made that the school personnel must understand each child's medical diagnosis in order to understand as much as possible about the specific disease process that the child is undergoing, it is also critical that the child's experience or illness be understood. Two simple generic matrices are presented that focus on the child's perspective: one of children's experience of illness, and a second of children's experience of medical procedures.

Matrix I: Dimensions of Illness. In this matrix there are two intersecting dimensions: (a) duration of illness (ranging from acute to chronic), and (b) relative visibility of the disease/treatment process (ranging from invisible to clearly visible). As noted in Fig. 7.1, any particular quadrant can have diseases of quite different etiologies. However, we believe that children within the same quadrant will share many common illness experiences, struggle with some of the same demons, and may benefit from similar interventions.

Our clinical experience with children suggests that the quadrants can be rank ordered with respect to the stressfulness of the illness experience (all other things being equal—which, of course they never really are). Children in quadrant #1 who experience a brief illness that gives visible clues that change as recovery occurs will have the least difficulty explaining the experience to themselves and others. They will be given the most validation in the patient role by peers, teachers, and parents (because everyone can see for themselves that the child is sick) and they will have the easiest time monitoring their own healing process. Thus, measles with spots that recede, and the skin rash of poison oak fit this descriptive experience. So too does a broken bone, complete with cast, traction, and so on. Therapeutic intervention with children in this quadrant could include opportunities for replaying the experience, and assurance of the body's power to heal.

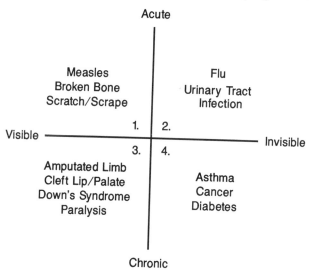

FIG. 7.1. Dimensions of illness.

Children in quadrant #4 who must live with chronic, invisible disease find the experience that results from this kind of disease very confusing. Many, diagnosed in infancy have lived with the disease "from forever," and have never experienced life without it. However, outside the medical setting it is hard to retain the patient role because "you don't look sick to me!". Children often have difficulty complying with medical regimes because it is sometimes impossible to tell when they are getting better, or even getting control of the invisible symptoms. Children often create or select clues that are irrelevant to the actual disease process and act in response to them. Therapeutic intervention activities using such expressive techniques as story, drawing, and free play can usefully focus on a child's theories of casuality, and beliefs about treatment. It is also useful to consult with medical personnel to check out the accuracy of the child's understanding, and to identify sensory clues that accurately monitor fluctuating disease process.

Of the two remaining quadrants, children in quadrant #2 with invisible but brief illness, tend to experience more initial cognitive and affective disruption than children in quadrant #3 who can see what is going on. Many children with quadrant #2 symptoms feel like they have been "tricked" by their bodies and are quite angry. Yet the time-limited nature of their experience rarely strains the coping capacity of most children. Some develop strange little rituals for a brief time after they are well to protect themselves from reoccurrence. However, especially younger children who have found the experience, for example of vomiting with the flu, particularly distasteful make strong resolve "never to do that again." Should the child's reaction reach crises proportions, focus on the self-healing power of the body can be helpful.

The difficult assignment for children is quadrant #3 with visible, but chronic conditions is not only that they must live everyday with the debilitating condition but they must also transform their understanding of their disease as their minds and bodies grow. However, we are beginning to find that many physically handicapped children cope exceptionally well developing an accurate body image, and satisfactory compensatory strategies and move through childhood and adolescence with their self-esteem intact (Harter, 1985). But Massie (1985) reminds us, that when a disability is visible to a child and to others, the child "must endure the frightened looks that mark every initial encounter" (p. 17). Strategies for coping with other people's reaction to the child with visible, chronically disabling conditions becomes increasingly important in the elementary school years. Reverse role play—with the child playing the critical, embarrassed, gawking stranger—often generates some marvelous possible responses.

Matrix II: Dimensions of Medical Procedure.   This matrix has three intersecting dimensions that we have identified from the clinical literature and from our observation of children in hospitals: (a) relative painfulness (ranging from no pain to excruciating pain); (b) proximity to body (ranging from treatments that do not touch the body to those that penetrate body boundaries, e.g., breaking the skin or penetrating an orifice); and (c) cognitive congruence with child's understand-

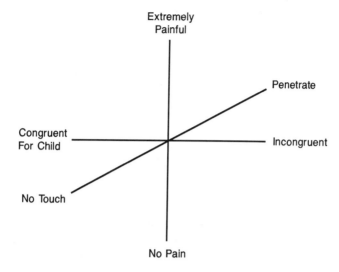

FIG. 7.2   Dimensions of medical procedure

ing of need for treatment (ranging from consonant with child's understanding to totally incongruent and incomprehensibile to the child; see Fig. 7.2).

Using this matrix we would predict that any procedure that could be described as painful, breaking body boundaries, and incongruent or unnecessary from the child's perspective would be maximally disruptive both cognitively and emotionally for a child. "The needle" fits that description, and indeed clinical experience and survey research confirm that children fear/dislike needles more than any other experience during hospitalization. It is a common theme in hospital playrooms as children give their dolls hundreds of shots, reversing roles and replaying what has happened with a vengeance.

Any procedure that falls at the extreme of any of the three variables will probably cause a child emotional and/or behavioral disruption. Thus an X-ray or CT Scan, which does not hurt, and does not touch the body can still be traumatic to a child who believes that the purpose of the procedure is so that "the doctors can read the bad thoughts in my mind." We found that the stethoscope was not feared because its touch is cold, but because the doctor might find out "that I be dead" (Steward & Regalbuto, 1975). Children do not adapt to pain—some procedures hurt everytime they are administered.

School psychologists and other nonmedical school personnel can use this matrix to help prepare children for medical procedures, ranging from routine vision and hearing screening usually completed on school sites to more rare, dramatic, usually painful procedures that often repeatedly accompany the treatment of chronic disease. To use this model, one must understand exactly what will be happening to the child, so that you can answer the questions: will it hurt? what will it feel like? and why are they doing it to me? Given this information, such coping strategies as "thought-stopping" can effectively reduce anticipatory anxiety (Ross, 1984). The matrix may also be useful in the emotional debriefing of a child returning to school following medical procedures.

Use of Behavioral Strategies with Children

Behavioral therapy and behavioral strategies, initially limited to the use of biofeedback to induce relaxation, were used first with adult patients in the 1960s and 1970s (Agras, 1982). Increasingly, a broad range of behavioral approaches are being introduced in the treatment of pediatric patients as well (Russo & Varni, 1982; Schaefer, Millman, & Levine, 1979; Wright, Schaefer, & Solomons, 1979). Strategies such as operant and social-learning procedures, cognitive and behavioral self-regulation procedures, as well as biofeedback and physiological self-regulation procedures are now being employed with children. The result is that sick children are encouraged to participate more actively in the management of the symptoms of their disease, and hopefully—in the language of the previous discussion—will experience less illness. By tapping into a child's emotional and cognitive resources and capacity to learn, a child will experience less needless emotional trauma, less pain, and a more competent sense of self.

The current pediatric literature is full of examples. For inflants and young children, Schwartz (1984) recommends the use of operant–instrumental learning theory, in which direct control over the autonomic responses is sought—without the need for verbal instruction or understanding on the part of the child. He gives the example of teaching a 3-year-old first to lower EMG levels and raise the temperature of his hands (with contingent snack reinforcers) in order to control migraine headaches, and then teaching him to detect the subjective precursors and prevent his headaches.

Melamed, Robbins, and Graves (1982) have been successful in using same-sex peer modeling in preparing children for hospitalization. We now know that children are easily hypnotized, and responsive to self-hypnosis so that in the clinic or hospital setting those strategies may be used to reduce fear and pain during necessary medical procedures (Hilgard & Le Baron, 1984). Another behavioral technique, systematic desensitization, has been used to reduce anticipatory nausea and vomiting prior to chemotherapy in pediatric cancer patients (Dahlquist, Cox, & Fernbach, 1986).

As already noted, childhood asthma is by far the most common chronic condition that school personnel will deal with. Therefore, the series of steps developed by Creer (1980; Creer, Renne, & Chai, 1982) for helping children discriminate early symptoms of asthma may be of special interest. Children with asthma need no longer be victims of the frightening spector of an inevitable asthma attack, but can learn that they can initiate several possible strategies to abort an asthma attack. A child's teachers and playground supervisors could work with the child's physician and family to learn the intervention schedule, thus supporting the child.

The imagery of illness has become of interest to a number of clinicians (Simonton, Matthews-Simonton, & Creighton, 1978; Zeltzer & LeBaron, 1986) and behavioral researchers. Images are uniquely constructed by a person from the ideas, feelings, attitudes, and beliefs the person holds and are powerful forces in dealing with illness. Viney (1983) found distressing images of illness such as helplessness, isolation, and uncertainty tend to make people more vulnerable to illness and work against rehabilitation and recovery. In contrast when anxiety, anger, and depression—also typical negative reactions to illness and injury—are identified and expressed it promotes rehabilitation and recovery. The positive images of happiness, a sense of personal competence and control, and supportive relationships with family and friends have been found to enhance health and aid in rehabilitation and recovery from illness.

It is inviting to focus on the role that positive emotions play in the recovery of ill children. Humor is especially effective with children—and easy to tap. A 10-year-old child at our medical center with muscular dystrophy described and drew her "perfect wheelchair" complete with propellers, a rearview mirror, and a stereo disc player. Humor involves using two sets of images at once, as in a metaphor, so that the slow, low budget wheelchair is transformed into a luxury model that can fly (Gordon, 1978). Viney cautions that joking about illness can "fall flat" if it is done without understanding and gentleness. In contrast, humor can allow distance from reality, and can cut into the inherent inflexibility of some of the negative imagery by offering a wider choice of imagery, and the laughter creates bonds between people.

J. K. Whitt (personal communication, July, 1986) and his colleagues at the University of North Carolina School of Medicine are working to create metaphors for disease processes that are accurate, but nonviolent, on the assumption that some of the negative imagery introduced to children as a means of explanation is unnecessarily frightening to them. For example, an epileptic seizure that is likened to getting a wrong number when you dial a phone carries far more positive tone than does "an electrical storm in your brain."

CHILDREN AND ILLNESS

This section examines children's experience of acute and chronic illness, and hospitalization.

Acute Illness: An Average Expectable Crisis for Children

Anna Freud (1952) described the dramatic withdrawal of some children who had only harmless sore throats, upset stomachs, raised temperatures, or common infectious diseases of childhood. She rightly observed that, as with adults, there is not a direct correlation for children between the severity of the physical disease and the intensity of the child's emotional response. It is the transformation of a typically active and alert child into a quiet, withdrawn one that is often the first clue to an adult that a child is sick. The psychoanalytic interpretation of this behavior defines a change in libidinal distribution during which cathexis is withdrawn from the object world and concentrated on the body and its immediate needs. This affective process is believed to be a beneficial one, serving the purpose of recovery.

Coping with disease, in addition to the eliciting of an affective response, usually demands the exercise of cognitively based skills as well. The intellectual accommodation that a child must make to mild illness meets the Piagetian criteria of ''moderate novelty'' that facilitates cognitive growth and development (Snyder & Feldman, 1977). Vernon, Foley, Sipowicz and Schulman (1965) found that although some mothers reported that their children demonstrated troublesome behaviors during and following illness, others reported that the behavior of their children actually improved.

Parmelee (1985) asserts that there are real cognitive, social, and emotional benefits in the natural ebb and flow of a child's experience with his or her own brief illness, and in the participation of caretaking when siblings and/or parents are ill. He suggests that recurring illnesses of short duration provide children with expanded experiences of their physical selves and with associated mood changes, feelings of distress, and loss of vigor. Our own longitudinal research on children's drawings of the body (Steward, in press; Steward, Furuya, Steward, & Ikeda, 1982) demonstrates the point that during illness their usual sense of self is altered and then restored; although physical recovery precedes psychological recovery for some children by as much as a month. It is believed that a successful voyage through a time-limited illness in childhood acts as a psychological innoculation against ''learned helplessness'' when the wear and tear of adulthood increases our vulnerability to the illness role (Reich, Steward, Rosenblatt, & Tupin, 1985; Seligman, 1975).

In the school setting, as in the family, children not only experience their own illness, but also see teachers, staff, and other children move through illness and back into health. Children can test their own and their family's explanatory models (Campbell, 1975) on classmates, teachers, and school staff. This often gives them the opportunity to develop an appreciation for the multiple potential causes of feeling ill, and enables some to differentiate the ''math headache'' (Lewis, 1986) from virus induced symptoms with great accuracy.

Chronic Illness: A Randomly Cyclic Crisis

Perrin (1985) suggests that severely chronically ill children share a number of characteristics and experiences, regardless of the specific disease, an observation made earlier by Koocher. Perrin reports that most chronic diseases of childhood are costly to treat, require care over an extended period of time, and require medical services intermittently. The daily burden of care falls on the family and the child. Most chronic diseases are painful, and require treatments that are also painful. Many chronic diseases entail slow degeneration, and although children's lives are being extended through vigorous treatment, most children with chronic illness—even if they live into young adulthood—face a premature death.

Today, for children, their classmates, and their teachers, chronic disease means something different than it did even as recently as 10 years ago. At that time, a diagnosis—especially one of the childhood cancers—meant swift withdrawal from school, hospitalization, and inevitable death. Schooling was seen as relatively unimportant because children often did not survive to graduate. By contrast, to-day a child with that same diagnosis may well be back in his or her own second-grade classroom, post-chemotherapy, struggling with an arithmetic assignment wearing a T-shirt proclaiming that "Bald is Beautiful." There is no doubt that the presence of the child with chronic disease in the classroom is frightening to teachers, parents, and peers. The most prominent fear is fired by "contagion" (Kister & Patterson, 1980); a close second is the often unspoken fear that a child might die during the year; and the third is that the child's symptoms might erupt in the midst of class and require instant and competent care.

Most chronically ill children can be and are being mainstreamed, as their diseases do not impair intelligence. Many, however, experience interference in academic achievement as a direct result of limited stamina and attention, indirectly through medication, and/or as a result of lowered self-esteem, self-assurance. Some also have limited social skills for relating to peers and teachers (Walker & Jacobs, 1985). Sometimes, children's performance is lowered by protective stances of their physicians, their parents, or teachers who inadvertently ask for less, and therefore get less.

One way to think about what it means to carry around the burden of a diagnosis of a chronic illness, is that a child is living with a series of acute illness events that are especially troublesome because they are inevitable but randomly occur-ring, and may be life-threatening. A tumble on the stairs at school may or may not begin the dreadful internal bleeding in the ankle joint of a child with hemophilia; even the most conscientious diabetic child watching every bit of food that goes into his or her mouth may still suddenly be thrown into ketoacidosis, a diabetic coma, and the hospital; the epileptic child who is "well-controlled" on medication, may still experience a seizure state observed by peers on the playground. If the hemophiliac child is pushed or chased down the stairs, the diabetic child taunted into snacking on forbidden foods at a birthday party, or the epileptic child is mimicked later in the afternoon—the more complex psychosocial burden of the child with chronic illness becomes evident.

Because chronically ill children are more likely to be in school than in the hospital, relationships with teachers and peers are important. The world of the hospital gives them more intimate contact with more adults than most children

have. Their unique socialization leaves them more skilled at relating and/or complying with adults than negotiating with peers. Peer acceptance may be dependent on two factors: (a) how obvious a child's symptoms are, and (b) how much
the disease interferes with a child's participation in the regular school activites
(Healey, McAreavey, Saaz von Hippel, & Jones, 1978). The more visibly symptomatic and impaired the child, the more difficult it will be to gain peer acceptance, and the more likely the child will experience discrimination. For the
chronically ill child, frequent, brief absences from school are the rule, causing
interruptions not only in classwork, but also in friendships and serve as a source
of curiosity/speculation about whether the child is still alive.

How a child's classmates are prepared to see what they see, may also make
a critical difference. School psychologists are often asked by parents and teachers
about the best way to prepare a class before a child returns. Potter and Roberts
(1984) have recently explored children's perceptions of two chronic diseases—
diabetes and epilepsy. First graders who pretested as preoperational thinkers, and
third and fourth graders who pretested as concrete operational thinkers, were
presented with one of two vignettes that either described the symptoms of a child
with the disease, or described the child's symptoms and then went on to explain
the disease process with a metaphor (developed by Whitt). Children were interviewed about such things as their own sense of vulnerability, their ability to comprehend and remember the new information, and their judgment about the attrac-
tiveness of the ill child described.

Potter and Roberts (1984) found that preoperational children, and concrete
operational children who received only the description of the symptoms believed
themselves to be more vulnerable to the disease that did the concrete operational
children who received the metaphorical explanation. Children with diabetes were
seen as more attractive than those with epilepsy, a finding that supports Healey's
work. Children's understanding of illnesses can be improved significantly with
the provision of explanatory information. As would be expected developmentally, concrete operational children could comprehend and remember the new information better than the preoperational children. The provision of information
about the nature of epilepsy, a disease with highly observable and often rather
frightening symptoms, tended to decrease rather than increase attraction.

The results of this research suggests different strategies should be employed
with younger versus older children, and especially suggests some caution in preparing younger children. It is probably best to let younger children become acquainted
with a chronically ill child before launching into an explanation—rather than introducing the explanation before the child. Also, because chronically ill children
are themselves increasingly well-informed about their disease, actively involved
in monitoring their own symptoms and initiating treatment, it seems appropriate
to consult with them about how they wish their classmates to be informed, and
what they want them to know. We often see chronically ill children, during periods
of hospitalization, essentially practicing their story on other children in the hospital,

or on siblings. This rehearsal enables them to better tell peers when they get back to school.

Hospitalization

There is no doubt that hospital admission, especially for preschool children is likely to be an emotionally expensive experience (Goslin, 1978). Rutter (1981) claims that "The two key observations . . . with respect to hospital admission are (1) that one admission during the preschool years has *no* association at all with psychiatric disorder some years later, and (2) that the experience of two hospital admissions *is* associated with a markedly increased risk of subsequent disorder" (p. 31).

Plank (1971) is the pioneer in the clinical preparation of children for hospitalization in the United States, and Beuf (1979) has provided the best description of the realities of the "child–patient role." Melamed et al. (1982) have utilized both psychological and physiological parameters in judging preparation strategies. Their work demonstrates the efficacy of film/video modeling of coping with medical and surgical procedures by same sex peers, and suggests that the timing of hospital preparation should be based on the age of the child. Young children, under the age of 7, become more anxious with preparation too far in advance of the actual hospitalization, and ideally should be prepared the day of the procedure, whereas children 7 years and older can "worry well" and use 7 to 10 days notice effectively.

At our own university medical center, and at other large urban hospitals, over 75% of the children are brought in on an emergency basis, with no opportunity for elegant and timely preparation. With trends to brief hospitalization because of third party payment, the federal push for cost containment, and out-patient/1-day surgery, the usefulness of general preparation of well-children via hospital tours, is of questionable value.

Once hospitalized, the child who has been in school has special needs that can be met in part by sensitive liaison work by school personnel. Children who require a long-term stay usually continue to work on school assignments under the special tutelage of a hospital teacher; a practice, incidentally, that Beuf (1979) feels is discriminatory against children—as we rarely require the hospitalized adult patient to continue working. What some children miss the most is not the intellectual stimulation and exercise of the classroom, but rather the social interaction with friends, teachers, and counsellors at school. Many classmates and even teachers drop the communication ball because they do not know what to say/write/send to the hospitalized child. Fear, embarrassment, and sometimes even guilt for feeling healthy often stop people from reaching out to the child. It is worth the effort to keep that link between the child and the classroom alive, and to encourage a wide range of contact by visit, phone, notes, audiotape, and so forth.

CHILDREN'S UNDERSTANDING OF ILLNESS: DEVELOPMENTAL MODELS

Increasingly, there has been interest in illness as a cognitive and social construct that develops through childhood and adolescence—and quite possibly throughout the entire life cycle. The first clinical study of developmental characteristics of well children's theories of illness was an investigation by Nagy (1951). Gellert (1962) followed with interviews of hospitalized children. Most of the research studies completed within the past 10 years with healthy and hospitalized children have relied on a Piagetian framework to explore the linkages between children's cognitive developmental level and their experience of illness (see Burback & Peterson, 1986; Perrin & Gerrity, 1984; Whitt, 1982, for reviews of this literature).

School personnel who work with ill children and their classmates may find the work of Bibace and Walsh (1979) especially useful. They have spelled out six qualitatively different stages of children's explanations of illness, which are ordered developmentally and drawn from the structural work of Piaget and Werner. During the preoperational stage, characteristic of most preschoolers and some first and second graders, there are two categories of illness explanation: phenomenism and contagion. During the concrete operational stage, characteristic of most elementary school children, they describe contamination and internalization. During the formal operational stage, characteristic of some junior and senior high school students, they describe physiological and psychophysiological explanations. Their strategies are briefly described as follows:

1. *Phenomenism.* During this stage, children conceptualize the cause of illness as a single external, usually, sensory, phenomenon. Egocentrically the child believes that all illness is caused by some sight, sound, or smell that the child uniquely has associated with illness in his or her past experience. The sensory stimulus may co-occur with the illness but is spatially and/or temporally remote (e.g., people get heart attacks from "the sun"; colds from "the wind", etc.).

2. *Contagion.* In this stage, the cause of illness (and the source of cure) is located in objects or people who are proximate to, but not touching, the child. The link between cause and illness is contagion, conceptualized in "magical" terms (e.g., people get colds/measles "when you walk near them"). There is still a single, external cause, but the explanations are less idiosyncratic.

3. *Contamination.* At this stage of development, children acknowledge multiple physical symptoms. The source is still external but touches the child (e.g., cures are rubbed on the surface of the body). Because mind and body are not well differentiated, illness can be caused by a person, object, or action external to the child, which is "bad" or "harmful" for the body (e.g., bad or immoral behavior, dirt, and germs are equally likely sources of illness).

4. *Internalization.* The focus at this stage is the process by which external sources of illness (and medicines) get into the body (swallowing, breathing). There

is some understanding of the presence and functioning of internal organs. With reversible thought, the child can understand that a sick person can become well, also there is a developing awareness of both preventive behaviors and self-curative powers of the body.

5. *Physiological.* The focus at this stage is the malfunctioning of "invisible" internal physiological structures or process. There is understanding of external triggers, and resulting symptoms. There can be multiple causes and multiple cures, and the creation of hypotheses about the relationship between environment and body.

6. *Psychophysiological.* A functioning biopsychosocial model is possible with the fuller understanding of the role of psychological causes in physical illness and recovery (people get heart attacks by being "nerve-wracked").

There is general agreement that the sequence of development of illness-related concepts is predictable and parallels cognitive development in other content areas. Experience and the affect associated with it contributes to children's understanding of illness as well. For example, there are some data to suggest that there is a lag in the rate of acquisition of illness concepts for healthy children, when compared to their understanding of physical causality (Perrin & Gerrity, 1981). We found that healthy children with chronically ill siblings performed at a lower development level with respect to illness causality and treatment than peers with healthy siblings (Carandang, Folkins, Hines, & Steward, 1979)—a finding compatible with the relative emotional and cognitive isolation of healthy siblings who must compete with an ill child for parental attention and affection. Moss (1985) found that children accidentally injured who were causal thinkers displayed fewer post-accident behavior problems, better social competence, and more advanced self-help skills than their precausal peers.

Ill children often experience a reoccurrence of egocentric or magical thinking that challenges more sophisticated modes of thinking. Brewster (1982) gives the example of a troubled 12-year-old who said, "I know that my doctor told me that my illness is caused by too many white cells, but I still wonder if it was caused by something that I did" (p. 361). Schowalter (1977) reminds us that when children are sick "regression is the rule," and thus some discrepancy between children's general cognitive capacities, and their ability to cope with illness might well be expected (Myers-Vando, Steward, Folkins, & Hines, 1979). Although neither sex of child, nor specific disease seems to affect a child's response to illness, personality factors such as internal versus external locus of control (Neuhauser, Amsterdam, Hines, & Steward, 1978) and information-seeking versus avoidant coping strategies (Peterson & Toler, 1986) do modify a child's experience and therefore contribute to a child's understanding.

Children's understanding of medical procedures done for diagnostic and therapeutic purposes also seems to follow a developmental progression. Our own epigenetic model, derived from the pediatric literature, examines the child's perception of three interrelated components across the six Piagetian stages: the instrument–body interaction, the relationship between the medical staff and the patient, and the purpose of the procedure (Steward & Steward, 1981). Brewster identified three general stages in the experience with medical procedures of chronically ill 5- to 12-year-olds who were hospitalized: (a) the preoperational children believed that the medical procedure was invoked as a punishment; (b) the concrete operational children perceived the procedures correctly but believed that the staff's empathy depended on the child expressing pain; and (c) the formal operational children could infer both intention and empathy from the staff. There is an implied relationship between age and stage in both of these models, but in the real world, even adults often carry with them very primitive understandings of the etiology and treatment of their illnesses as a quick look at TV commercials and the range of over-the-counter self-medications suggests.

EFFECTIVE INTERVENTIONS

Bibliotherapy

Books can be effective tools to help children, their classmates and teachers understand and cope with illness. In *Health, Illness and Disability: A Guide to Books for Children and Young Adults* Azarnoff (1983) has categorized and annotated 1,000+ fiction and nonfiction books that describe children's experiences with their bodies and with disabilities, hospitalization, and medical treatments. An earlier annotated collection of children's books by Fassler (1978) entitled, *Helping Children Cope*, includes a chapter on Hospitalization and Illness, and another on Death, as well as other stress-producing events for children. One value of her book is the careful review of the contents of children's books for accuracy. In addition, she discusses sound and sophisticated ways in which stories can be used to prepare children for medical experiences, to elicit thoughts and feelings such as loneliness and anger. There is nearly a full page of books that deal with "nighttime in the hospital."

Preparing for Intervention

For school psychologists who have not had personal or professional experience in contemporary pediatric procedures, Petrillo and Sanger (1980) provide a fine, step by step description of the critical issues in the hospitalization of a child, response to family and staff, and verbatim explanations that can be used with children to prepare them for specific diagnostic and surgical procedures. In *Biting off the Bracelet*, Beuf (1979) provides an empathetic description of the hospital setting from a child's perspective.

   The single best resource book for school personnel on the medical, social, and political issues that are related to chronic illness is the book that has resulted from the work of Nicholas Hobbs and James Perrin (1985), *Issues in the Care of Children with Chronic Illness*. In addition to specific information on 13 chronic diseases, chapters on family experiences, professional and interprofessional issues, educational and vocational issues, and economic and political considerations are included.

In response to the requests of parents, school personnel, and health-care professionals, I anticipate that we will see an increasing number of publications from the national organizations that support research and educational efforts with respect to individual diseases. For example, the Leukemia Society of America has developed a wonderful workbook for children: *What it is that I have, don't want, didn't ask for, can't give back and how I feel about it*. The American Cancer Society booklets, *What Happened to You Happened to Me*, written by children from 6 to 19 years who have had cancer, and *When you have a student with cancer* are useful. Some hospitals have developed their own booklets, often using a coloring book format, to orient children to special hospital units.

School psychologists may want to tap into the computer search capabilities that are now revolutionizing access to the research and clinical literature. One such is The Illness Behavior Bibliography (IBB), developed at the University of Wisconsin Medical Center by Dr. Barry Blackwell (Blackwell, Gutmann, & Geenen, 1985). The IBB is updated every 6 months and includes references organized by subject content (e.g., pain, biological, psychological, and social environment factors in illness behavior, therapy/outcomes, etc.) and type of article/study (review, descriptive, single case study, cartoon, etc.). In addition to the IBB (which can be purchased), individualized computer searches can be ordered.

A recent study (Iannotti, 1986) demonstrated that elementary school children are bringing far more "medicine" to school than their mothers know about. Thus, this final recommendation for a book that should be available at every school is *Children's Medicine* by Kepler and Kepler (1985). The heart of the book is the medication profile of 27 prescription drugs and 17 drugs that can be purchased over-the-counter. Critical issues like dosage form and strength, side effects, effects of long-term use, and the effects of missing a dose are clearly discussed for each drug. It is not meant to be a substitute for a pharmacist or a physician, but should be a very useful companion piece in a school setting.

Listening Well

Most researchers in clinical settings agree with Brewster's recommendation that adults who work with ill children should put "information gathering before information giving," and that we approach any distorted ideas that a child might have with some appreciation that they may serve important defensive needs. However, when discrepancies do exist, it is possible to intervene with great effectiveness to increase a child's cognitive and behavioral control of an illness experience. It has been demonstrated that children can learn best when the material presented is no more than one step above their present level of cognitive understanding (Turiel, 1969). We believe that children are most vulnerable to emotional disruption and concommittant behavioral problems in the management of illness when they are at transitional point, for example, between preoperational and concrete operational thinking, or between concrete and formal operations. That is also when they are most open to new learning.

REFERENCES

Agras, W. S. (1982). Behavioral medicine in the 1980s: Nonrandom connections. *Journal of Consulting and Clinical Psychology, 50*, 797–803.

American Cancer Society. (1980). *When you have a student with cancer.* New York: Author.

American Cancer Society. (1984). *What happened to you happened to me.* New York: Author.

Azarnoff, P. (1983) *Health, illness and disability: A guide to books for children and young adults.* NY: R. R. Bowker.

Beuf, A. H. (1979). *Biting off the bracelet: A study of children in hospitals.* Philadelphia, PA: University of Pennsylvania Press.

Bibace, R., & Walsh M. E. (1979). Developmental stages in children's conceptions of illness. In G. C. Stone, F. Cohen, & N. E. Adler (Eds.), *Health psychology* (pp. 285–302). San Francisco, CA: Jossey-Bass.

Blackwell, B., Gutmann, M. C., & Geenen, P. R. (1985). *Illness behavior bibliography.* Milwaukee, WI: Mount Sinai Medical Center.

Brewster, A. B. (1982). Chronically ill hospitalized children's concepts of their illness. *Pediatrics, 69*, 355–362.

Burback, D. J., & Peterson, L. (1986). Children's concepts of physical illness: A review and critique of the cognitive-developmental literature. *Health Psychology, 5*, 307–325.

Campbell, J. D. (1975). Illness is a point of view: The development of children's concepts of illness. *Child Development, 46* 92–100.

Carandang, M. L. A., Folkins, C. H., Hines, P. A., & Steward, M. S. (1979). The role of cognitive level and sibling illness in children's conceptualizations of illness. *American Journal of Orthopsychiatry, 49*, 474–481.

Creer, T. L. (1980). Self-management behavioral strategies for asthmatics. *Behavioral Medicine, 7*, 14–24.

Creer, T. L., Renne, C. M., & Chai, H. (1982). The application of behavioral techniques to childhood asthma. In D. C. Russo & J. W. Varni (Eds.), *Behavioral pediatrics: Research and practice* (pp. 27–66). New York: Plenum Press.

Dahlquist, L. M., Cox, C. N., & Fernbach, D. J. (1986, March). *Correlates of anticipatory nausea in pediatric cancer patients.* Paper presented at the Society for Behavioral Medicine, San Francisco, CA.

Eisenberg, L. (1977). Disease and illness. *Culture, Medicine and Psychiatry, 1*, 9–23.

Fassler, J. (1978). *Helping children cope.* New York: The Free Press.

Freud, A. (1952). The role of bodily illness in the mental life of children. *Psychoanalytic Study of the Child, 7*, 69–80.

Gellert, E. (1962). Children's conceptions of the contents and function of the human body. *Genetic Psychology Monograph, 65*, 293–450.

Gordon, D. (1978). *Therapeutic metaphors.* Cupertino, CA: Meta.

Goslin, E. R. (1978). Hospitalization as a life crises for the preschool child: a critical review. *Journal of Community Health, 3*, 321–346.

Harter, S. (1985). Processes underlying the construction, maintenance and enhancement of the self concept in children. In J. Suls & A. Greenwald (Eds.), *Psychological perspectives on the self* (Vol. 3, pp. 137–181). Hillsdale, NJ: Lawrence Erlbaum Associates.

Healey, A., McAreavey, P., Saaz von Hippel, C., & Jones, F. H. (1978). *Mainstreaming preschoolers: Children with health impairments.* Washington, DC: U.S. Department of Health, Education and Welfare.

Hilgard, J. R., & Le Baron, S. (1984). *Hypnotherapy of pain in children with cancer.* Los Altos, CA: William Kaufman.

Hobbs, N., & Perrin, J. M. (Eds.). (1985). *Issues in the care of children with chronic disease.* San Francisco, CA: Jossey-Bass.

Hobbs, N., Perrin, J. M., & Ireys, H. T. (1985). *Chronically ill children and their families.* San Francisco, CA: Jossey-Bass.

Iannotti, R. (1986, March). *The early development of health behaviors and attitudes: Implications for intervention.* Paper presented at the society for Behavioral Medicine, San Francisco, CA.

Kepler, A., & Kepler, J. (1985). *Children's medicine.* Chicago: Contemporary Books.

Kister, M. C., & Patterson, C. J. (1980). Children's conceptions of the causes of illness: Understanding of contagion and use of immanent justice. *Child Development, 51,* 839–846.

Koocher, G. P. (1985). Promoting coping with illness in childhood. In J. C. Rosen & L. J. Solomon (Eds.), *Prevention in health psychology* (pp. 311–327). Hanover, VT: University Press of New England.

Leukemia Society of America. (1983). *What it is that I have, don't want, didn't ask for, can't give back, and how I feel about it.* New York: Author.

Lewis, C. (1986, March). *Improving the health behavior of children and adolescents: Some conceptual and developmental issues.* Paper presented at the Society for Behavioral Medicine, San Francisco, CA.

Lewis, C., Lewis, M. A., & Palmer, B. (1977). Child-initiated care: the use of school nursing services by children in an "adult free" system. *Pediatrics, 60,* 499–507.

Massie, R. K. (1985). The constant shadow: reflections on the life of a chronically ill child. In N. Hobbs & J. M. Perrin (Eds.), *Issues in the care of children with chronic illness* (pp. 13–23). San Francisco: Jossey-Bass.

Melamed, B. G., Robbins, R. L., & Graves, S. (1982). Preparation for surgery and medical procedures. In D. C. Russo & J. W. Varni (Eds.), *Behavioral pediatrics* (pp. 225–267). New York: Plenum Press.

Moss, N. E. (1985). *Attributions of causality and recovery among pediatric accident victims.* Unpublished doctoral dissertation, University of California, Davis, CA.

Myers-Vando, R., Steward, M. S., Folkins, C. H., & Hines, P. A. (1979). The effects of congenital heart disease on cognitive development, illness, causality concepts, and vulnerability. *American Journal of Orthopsychiatry, 49,* 617–625.

Nagy, M. H. (1951). Children's ideas of the origin of illness. *Health Education Journal, 9,* 6–13.

Neuhauser, C., Amsterdam, B., Hines, P., & Steward, M. S. (1978). Children's concepts of healing: Cognitive development and locus of control. *American Journal of Orthopsychiatry, 48,* 325–341.

Parmelee, A. H. (1985, April). *Children's illnesses: Their beneficial effects on behavioral development.* Paper presented at the meeting of the Society for Research in Child Development, Toronto, Canada.

Perrin, E. C., & Gerrity, P. S. (1981). There's a demon in your belly: children's understanding of illness. *Pediatrics, 67,* 841–849.

Perrin, E. C., & Gerrity, P. S. (1984). Development of children with chronic illness. *Pediatric Clinics of North America, 31,* 19–31.

Perrin, J. M. (1985). Introduction. In N. Hobbs & J. M. Perrin (Eds.). (1985). *Issues in the care of children with chronic disease* (pp. 1–10). San Francisco, CA: Jossey-Bass.

Peterson, L., & Toler, S. M. (1986). An information seeking disposition in child surgery patients. *Health Psychology*, *5*, 343-358.

Petrillo, M., & Sanger, S. (1980). *Emotional care of hospitalized children* (2nd ed.). Philadelphia, PA: J. B. Lippincott.

Plank, E. N. (1971). *Working with children in hospitals: A guide for the professional team* (2nd ed.). Cleveland: Press of Case Western Reserve University.

Potter, P. C., & Roberts, M. C. (1984). Children's perceptions of chronic illness: The roles of disease symptoms, cognitive development and information. *Journal of Pediatric Psychology*, *9*, 13-27.

Reich, J. H., Steward, M. S., Rosenblatt, R., & Tupin, J. P. (1985). Prediction of response to treatment in chronic pain patients. *Journal of Clinical Psychiatry*, *46*, 425-427.

Ross, D. M., (1984). Thought-stopping: A coping strategy for impending feared events. *Issues in Comprehensive Pediatric Nursing*, *7*, 83-89.

Ross, D. M., & Ross, S. A. (1984). Teaching the child with leukemia to cope with teasing. *Issues in Comprehensive Pediatric Nursing*, *7*, 59-66.

Russo, D. C., & Varni, J. W. (1982). *Behavioral pediatrics*. New York: Plenum Press.

Rutter, M. (1981). Stress, coping and development: Some issues and some questions. *Journal of Child Psychology and Psychiatry*, *22*, 323-356.

Schaefer, C. E., Millman, H. L., & Levine, G. E. (1979). *Therapies for psychosomatic disorders in children*. San Francisco, CA: Jossey-Bass.

Schowalter, J. E. (1977). Psychological reactions to physical illness and hospitalization in adolescents: A survey. *Journal of the American Academy of Child Psychiatry*, *16*, 500-516.

Schwartz, G. E. (1984). Toward a comprehensive theory of clinical biofeedback: A systems perspective. In C. Van Dyke, L. Temoshok, & L. S. Zegans (Eds.), *Emotions in health and illness* (pp. 97-115). New York: Grune & Stratton.

Seligman, M. E. P. (1975). *Learned helplessness: On depression, development, and death*. San Francisco: Freeman.

Simonton, D. C., Matthews-Simonton, S., & Creighton, J. (1978). *Getting well again*. Los Angeles: Tarcher.

Snyder, S. S., & Feldman, D. H. (1977). Internal and external influences on cognitive-developmental change. *Child Development*, *49*, 937-943.

Steward, M. S. (in press). Affective and cognitive impact of illness on children's body image. *Psychiatric Medicine*.

Steward, M. S., Furuya, T., Steward, D. S., & Ikeda, A. (1982). Japanese and American children's drawings of the outside and inside of their bodies. *Journal of Cross Cultural Psychology*, *13*, 87-104.

Steward, M. S., & Regalbuto, G. (1975). Do doctors know what children know? *American Journal of Orthopsychiatry*, *45*, 146-149.

Steward, M. S., & Steward, D. S. (1981). Children's conceptions of medical procedures. In R. Bibace & M. E. Walsh (Eds.), *Children's conceptions of health, illness, and bodily functions* (pp. 67-84). San Francisco, CA: Jossey-Bass.

Turiel, E. (1969). Developmental processes in the child's moral thinking. In P. Mussen, J. Langer, & M. Covington (Eds.), *New directions in developmental psychology*. New York: Holt, Rinehart & Winston.

Vernon, D. T., Foley, J. M., Sipowicz, R. R., & Schulman, J. L. (1965). *The psychological responses of children to hospitalization and illness*. Springfield, IL: Charles C. Thomas.

Viney, L. L. (1983). *Images of illness*. Malabar, FL: Robert E. Krieger.

Walker, D. K., & Jacobs, F. H. (1985). Public school programs for chronically ill children. In N. Hobbs & J. M. Perrin (Eds.), *Issues in the care of children with chronic disease* (pp. 615-655). San Francisco, CA: Jossey-Bass.

Whitt, J. K. (1982). Children's understanding of illness: developmental considerations and pediatric intervention. In M. Wolraich & D. Routh (Eds.), *Advances in Developmental and Behavioral Pediatrics*, *3*, 163-201.

Wolff, S. (1970). *Children under stress*. London: Penguin Press.

Wright, L., Schaefer, A., & Solomons, G. (1979). *Encyclopedia of pediatric psychology*. Baltimore, MD: University Park Press.

Zeltzer, L. K. & Le Baron, S. (1986). Fantasy in children and adolescents with chronic illness. *Developmental and Behavioral Pediatrics, 7*, 195–198.

8

Helping Children Cope
with Death

Pamela G. H. Wilson
Private Practice, San Rafael, California
Reed School District, California

This chapter addresses the role of the school mental health professional when a child's life has been touched by death. Because of an increased interest in issues related to death and dying since the 1960s, there is now a greater understanding of the bereavement process in general. Much consideration has been given to the special needs and problems faced by children in mourning. Special attention to their conceptions of death and how they relate to the resolution of grief has provided both prevention and intervention strategies for a variety of circumstances. In addition, attention to the role of available support systems has suggested the potential significance of the social context of the school. An informed professional can effectively use the school environment to offer understanding, stability, and support to a child in mourning and can monitor and respond to the progress of the grieving process.

Although people have been going through the grieving process for thousands of years, special circumstances of our present culture place an extra burden on the resolution of the process. We are acutely aware of the high price in mental distress and illness paid by those individuals with unresolved grief. Numerous retrospective studies and many anecdotal records relate bereavement to various physical and psychological stresses and impairments. The empirical evidence suggests that increasingly people seek help with grieving and turn to mental health professionals. Whether because of the secularization of the age or the increased mobility of the population, people less often look to religious leaders or institutions for healing or to extended family for support and guidance. The sense of community—spiritual, secular, and familial—has diminished for the individual and family, for the adult and the child. Therefore, people turn more and more to health-care and social systems for assistance. As a primary caretaking institution, the school can offer significant predictability, stability, and guidance for many children and families, solely or in conjunction with other support systems.

Sadly, every child is vulnerable to the loss through death of someone close. It is not possible to predict which child will be faced with such a loss. Statistics are not available for the numbers of children who experience the loss of a mother, father, both parents, or a sibling. Nor are such figures available for the loss of extended family members, friends, teachers, or other significant people in a child's life. Nevertheless, because the worries and fears engendered by death are also stirred in the friends, classmates, families, and community members close to a mourning child, it is clear that a very large, undetermined group of individuals can be variously affected by a single death.

Bereavement is a very complex issue, and people experience and respond to death in predictable as well as idiosyncratic ways. Grieving children are especially at risk of being misunderstood or overlooked. In order to employ meaningful prevention strategies and to respond effectively with direct and institutional interventions, it is necessary to understand the tasks of the mourning process and how children respond to their understanding of death.

TASKS OF MOURNING

An integral component of the study of death and dying is the nature of human attachments, both what they are and how they develop. Bowlby (1960), a British psychiatrist, has been a central figure in the development of attachment theory. His conceptualization of the human tendency to make strong emotional bonds credits a need for security and safety that develops early in life. These attachments are usually directed toward a small number of specific people and tend to last throughout most of the life cycle. The early availability of these attachment figures provides a foundation of basic trust (in the Eriksonian sense) and a source of strength from which to venture and explore the world outside the relationship (Erikson, 1950). The patterns established with these attachment figures provide a basis for relationships later in life. When the early attachment is disrupted or threatened or severed, the child's response is one of intense anxiety. The greater the attachment and the vulnerability without it, the greater the distress when it is threatened or lost. Others (notably Engel, 1961) have suggested that injury to affectional bonds is traumatic in a way similar to physical injuries and that comparable healing processes must follow both wounds. Healing requires attention, corrective action, and time. It follows that the mourning process—the adaptation to loss—is necessary to the restoration of the bonding process (Worden, 1982). When considered developmentally, it is essential that the entire process of mourning be completed before an individual can be free to re-attach and to continue growing. When the process is incomplete, future bonds will be anxiety-laden, tenuous, or nonexistent. At the same time, the grieving process is "work," and difficult work. Often, it cannot be accomplished alone and is left partially undone. It can be especially difficult for children.

A number of models have been proposed to describe the mourning process. Kubler-Ross (1969), Matz (1979), Bugen (1977), and Parkes (1972) have each used a succession of stages or emotions to define the process. Although conceptually helpful, these approaches do not translate clearly to individual bereavement. A more clinically useful conceptualization is that offered by Worden (1982).

Worden has postulated four tasks of mourning. The first task is to accept the reality of the loss, to face directly the reality that the person is dead, is gone, and will not return. The initial response to death, even when it is expected, is centered on the sense that it has not happened. Denial can take many forms. It can be manifested in a belief that reunion is possible, if not in this life, then in an afterlife. Thus, the meaning of the loss can be dismissed through focusing on its reversibility or the reunification. The meaning can also be denied by dismissing the significance of the dead person. For example, "Oh, well, he wasn't such a good father anyway." Others minimize the loss by removing any tangible reminders of the person or will not tolerate mention of the person in their presence; the person no longer exists physically or psychologically. An opposite phenomenon, labeled *mummification* by psychiatrist Gorer (1965), denies the death by keeping the person alive through having the deceased's possessions ready and waiting for his or her return and more generally acting as if the deceased would reappear. Certainly, it is normal to wish for a reunion or that one had been misinformed about the death; however, if such spiritual, magical, or distorted responses are maintained, the bereaved will be unable to progress to the second stage of grieving.

The second task is to experience the pain of grief. If the emotional and behavioral pain is not acknowledged or experienced, it will be manifested through some physical symptom, aberrant thinking, or behavior. Often, there is considerable tension between social norms and the nature of this task. There can be subtle and overt pressure not to feel and not to express the sadness, anguish, and pain following death. Often, people try to distract themselves or use thought-censoring devices. Friends often act out this role for a mourner, either in the best interest of their friend or because they cannot tolerate such strong feelings. Some people focus only on positive feelings or memories and thereby both idealize the deceased and deny their negative or painful feelings. Although a temporary flight from the pain is normal, prolonged denial will be accompanied by psychological or behavioral maladaptations. The sooner the pain can be faced and felt, the sooner and more easily its effects can be worked through and movement can proceed to the next task.

Once the pain of the death has been experienced, it is possible to adjust to a new environment that does not include the deceased. This third task may mean learning to function more independently, or learning new skills, or otherwise coming to terms with living differently. Not adapting to the loss means remaining immobilized, helpless, withdrawing from the world and its requirements.

The final task of mourning is to withdraw emotional energy from the deceased and to reinvest it in another relationship. People are often troubled by the prospect of reinvolvement because they fear another loss and consider that the risk is too great. Others feel that attachment to a new person would be disloyal to the deceased, a betrayal, or somehow dishonor his or her memory. Thus, by not loving and by instead holding onto the past attachment rather than forming new ones, one does not complete the tasks of mourning.

There is no definitive measure of the end of mourning. Worden (1982) contends that it is reached when the tasks of mourning are accomplished and when the person is able to think of the deceased without pain. Although one can always expect a sense of sadness when thinking about the loss of a loved one, it is also expected that such thoughts will not have a wrenching quality and will not cause physical manifestations of anguish such as intense crying or stomach pains. At the same time, one will be able to reinvest emotions in present and future relationships without guilt or remorse and with an acknowledged awareness of the loss.

There has been considerable controversy throughout the years stemming from the psychoanalytic schools, as to whether children are capable of mourning. Working from the adult model of grieving are those (Wolfenstein, 1966) who contend that it is not possible to mourn without the complete identity formation that comes at the end of adolescence. On the other hand, others (Furman, 1974) believe that children can mourn at the age when object constancy is achieved: as early as 3 years of age. Bowlby (1960) cites mourning behaviors as early as 6 months of age. A third view (Worden, 1982) builds a model of mourning to conform to the cognitive development and understanding of the child.

A child's ability to proceed through the grieving process is dependent on a number of factors. His or her response will vary according to developmental level because that will largely determine the conceptualization of death. It also will be affected by the relationship to the deceased and by the nature of the death. The structure and the stability of the family before and after the death will be significant determinants in the grieving process and its outcome.

CHILDREN'S CONCEPTS OF DEATH

Knowing how children conceive of death can help adults to understand their behavior and to respond in a supportive manner following the loss of a significant person. Most research on bereaved children accepts the theory that there are three stages to their understanding of death. These parallel Piaget's stages of cognitive development and focus on children's ability to grasp the concept that some things cannot be reversed. Their understanding of causality is also significant to their reaction to a death (Piaget & Inhelder, 1969).

Empirical studies have examined the behavioral responses of infants following the death of a significant caretaker, usually the mother, and have demonstrated visible distress, considered by some to be mourning. However, in the current understanding of child development, children who are under 18-24 months form intense subjective images of objects, not concepts. They do not fully understand that an object has no existence apart from their sensory perception (Flavell, 1977). Thus, although infants do respond to the absence of a caretaker, it does not follow that they comprehend death.

Three to 5-year-olds tend to think that dead people live on "under changed circumstances" (Lonetto, 1980). Their reasoning includes four types of causality that are particularly relevant to understanding their concept of death. Their animistic thinking assumes that the whole world and everything in it is alive. Because inanimate objects can move, think, feel, and be at rest, it follows that people too are always alive. Death is likened to a deep sleep, a hibernation, loss of mobility, or departure. Children are concerned about the comfort and physical care of dead persons; they might be hungry, need a doctor, or some fresh air. Their magical thinking imparts a power to everyone and everything to command at will. This kind of causal thinking allows anything to happen—mountains open upon command, pears tell secrets, princes turn into frogs. Within this system, people can die because of another's wish and can return to life just as readily; just as the bite of an apple can induce sleep for a 100 years, a kiss can revive one. Artificialistic thinking is the belief that things exist for people's convenience. Because toys can be fixed upon request, so, too can dead people. Finally, children of this age ascribe personal motives to certain events. Bad dreams are brought on by misbehavior; bad falls are brought on by eating too much candy; death can also be caused by wrong thoughts or deeds.

As a result of understanding death to be temporary, reversible, and caused magically, children at this stage tend to respond in varied, often contradictory and unpredictable ways. The dead person is missing, and when he or she does not return, not only are children hurt and angry at being abandoned, they are also anxious that others might abandon them. They are frequently convinced that some thought or action of their own caused the death and so experience tremendous guilt. This can also lead to fears that "bad" wishes or actions will be punished by the child's own death. Children at this stage of development, while they are frequently able to play happily, tend to experience brief, intense outbreaks of anxiety or distress.

From about age 6 to 8, children frequently conceive of death as a person (Lonetto, 1980). As a result, Death can be fought and mastered if one's magic is strong enough. Young and healthy people do not die; only the old and sick are too weak to hold Death off. Many fears are associated with the fate of the corpse, for the dead are still invested with the ability to see, hear, and receive messages, as well as to eat and breathe. Thus, many children worry about being trapped in coffins. They are fascinated by what happens to bodies after death, and tend to be preoccupied with decomposition and decay.

During the years from 9 to 12 the earlier modes of causal thinking are being replaced by logical and naturalistic thinking. The child's objective observation of objects and events, their concrete physical and mechanistic operations and the laws governing them become the basis of their logic. By their observations they now know that plants, animals, and people are alive and that what lives also dies. Death is understood as final and irreversible. Nevertheless, it still has a capricious quality and is something they do not expect to happen to them until they are very old. If one is lucky, it is possible to escape death. Although children at this stage still mention external forces such as physical violence, disasters, or accidents as causes of death, they more frequently understand internal bodily causes. They list illness and old age, or give careful descriptions of the physiological details they have heard (Lonetto, 1980).

Anxieties related to separation and loss are still experienced in children at this stage. However, fears are not so much related to abandonment and retribution as they are to the physical consequences of death. Because thinking processes at the developmental level are concerned with physical causality and the laws of nature, many fears are focused on bodily mutilation, being buried alive, and on the physiological process of death. Limericks and rhymes about these processes ("the worms crawl in, the worms crawl out . . .") are perennial favorites of children at this age and may be understood as attempts to release anxieties. Another source of anxiety at this stage is the belief that life and death is a matter of luck. Death is capricious and can happen if you are unlucky. This is an age filled with superstitions to prevent such bad luck: holding one's breath passing a cemetery, not stepping on cracks in the sidewalk, knocking on wood. Because children can understand the irreversibility of death, they are able to consider possibilities after death. Beliefs about immortality and life after death and reincarnation become meaningful and can offer comfort. However, some children have difficulty reconciling the physiological aspects of death with religious teachings; if a body is in the grave forever, how can it go to Heaven (Grollman, 1976; Lonetto, 1980)?

During adolescence, children come to understand that death is not only final and irreversible, it is also both universal and personal. They are now capable of grasping, adopting, and formulating abstract conceptualizations. Concerns about life after death are no longer about the physical state of the body and whether it can be in the ground and in Heaven simultaneously, but rather focus on abstract theological beliefs or explanations. Rather than concrete and physical, death is remote and spiritual. It is inevitable, but not immediate. They are concerned with their present life and plans and deny the possibility that death could interfere with their fulfillment. Thus, with the comprehension of personal death comes an emotional and cognitive distancing that protects against the personal threat and anxiety. Their concerns are frequently about how others might respond. For example, they might attend to the appearance or the physical dignity of the dead person; they might glorify or idolize the event or the person when a peer dies (Grollman, 1976).

Thus, children's conceptions of death move from an initial understanding that is magical, reversible, and personified, which evokes fears of abandonment, personal responsibility, and guilt. The next state accepts the finality of death but attributes it to chance despite an increased awareness and understanding of the physical causes and effects of death. Finally, the adolescent is capable of comprehending personal death but distances the possibility, focusing instead on immediate life and aspirations. A child's particular concept of death is one of the major factors involved in his or her response to death. Another significant element is his or her relationship to the deceased.

THE CHILD'S RELATIONSHIP WITH THE DECEASED

Among the most significant determinants of grief are the relationship between the mourner and the deceased, who the person was, and the nature of their attachment. Certain relationships are especially significant to children. A child's dependent, vulnerable state necessarily means that the loss of caretaking people, whether parents, grandparents, or teachers—will have special weight and meanings. The loss of sibling or peer will have comparable noticeable effects. Moreover, the nature of the attachment has several relevant components.

The strength of the attachment is directly related to the intensity of the grief. The security of the attachment is a factor in the child's sense of continued well-being and self-esteem. In addition, the degree of ambivalent feelings, the manner in which they were expressed or manifested, and the way they were handled will affect the grieving process.

Death of a Parent

The death of a parent is one of the greatest catastrophies that can befall a child. It is a unique and shocking experience, especially to a young child who has no background for coping with such a situation or the range of strong emotions it evokes. The child's dependence on a parent leaves him or her with an overpowering sense of despair, helplessness, abandonment, and threat that is not always recognized. Children are not equipped with the cognitive or psychological understanding of death to cope alone with a crisis of such magnitude. When a parent dies, there are manifold increases in the child's needs. Among those most essential are continued love, comfort, and support from family members and others, as well as reassurance of continued care. Tragically, the remaining parent is often unable to care adequately for the grieving child as a result of his or her own grief, especially in the early period of bereavement. This is a time when other available caretaking adults can "adopt" the child until the surviving parent is able to cope and respond. In addition, the child needs the stability and security of a familiar environment. All too often, the death of a parent means relocating, possibly for financial reasons, to be closer to other family members, or to avoid painful memories. Whatever the reason, relocating the home necessitates even more losses as well as the stress of making new friends, meeting new teachers, and neighbors (see chapter 9).

The death of either parent is a shattering event for a child of any age, evoking a host of emotions. The child feels shocked, stunned, bewildered, overwhelmed, frightened, abandoned, desolate, helpless, hurt, angry, and guilty. Not all children experience all these feelings or with the same degree of intensity. To a great extent, the response is a function of the child's developmental level. Infants perceive a parent's death as a separation and loss; they respond with anxiety, anger, and apathy. First described by Spitz (1945) as *hospitalism*, this syndrome originally applied to orphaned infants who reacted to separation from their mother first with anger and then with a kind of quiet, resigned despair. Some refused nourishment and eventually died. Further studies have demonstrated that infants and young children can recover from this primary loss if another caretaker will provide a quality of nurturing comparable to that of the mother.

Preschool children consciously experience feelings of abandonment and frequently verbalize them. They are hurt and angry at being left. They are afraid they might also lose the other parent and be completely abandoned. Their magical thinking may lead to irrational guilt for the death and to fears of punishment. If these fears are not addressed and the child is not reassured and helped with the guilt and anger, the child's development may well be seriously impeded.

Young elementary aged children may still feel a deep sense of abandonment, but more commonly are overwhelmed by sadness and loneliness. Some children withdraw both physically and emotionally from their families and peers. Their isolation is sometimes interpreted as a plea for privacy, but more often is a flight from anger or guilt. Their thoughts and fears need attention and understanding and reassurance (Furman, 1974).

Older children and adolescents often feel extremely angry with the parent for dying and for leaving them bereft. Sometimes they are angry with the surviving parent for "allowing" or "not preventing" the death, or for being alive instead of the parent who has died. They are sometimes angry with other children because they have not lost a parent, or with God for letting it happen. Often, they feel unworthy or diminished, less valued by their peers, and have lower self-esteem. Quite frequently they feel embarrassed and ashamed. The sense of being different and not understood can lead to a variety of behaviors that likely will exacerbate their isolation and frustration. Opportunities to exchange common grief reactions with others, whether adults or peers, who have experienced a recent death can be especially healing (Zeligs, 1974).

Death of a parent carries special significance to children in other ways. The extent to which the parent is seen as responsible for the financial support of the family will affect the child's sense of immediate and future security. If the parent is of the same sex as the child, there is a greater likelihood of identification with the fate of a similar early death. The death of any family member will alter the roles and alliances of other members, but they are most powerfully affected by the death of a parent. Frequently, the process of realignment is itself painful and confusing for children. And finally, completion of the grieving tasks can be impeded by the fact that the child may have no control over, or limited access to, a replacement for a dead parent. The remaining parent may or may not remarry; that parent's choice may or may not be accepted by the child; the child may reinvest in a relationship outside the family (Bowen, 1978).

Death of a Sibling

The task of childhood mourning over a sibling is also related to the child's age and his or her perception and awareness of the meaning of death. In addition, it is very much affected by the ways in which the parents cope with the loss and the nature of the sibling relationship before the death (Brenner, 1984). A child's bereavement over a dead sibling is often overshadowed by the parent's intense reaction. The loss of a child is such a trauma to the parents that they can be so overwhelmed and depleted that there is little strength left to attend to the living child. Frequently, the attention and resources of other family and friends are directed to the parents as well, so the surviving child is overlooked or an afterthought while the parents are intensely fragile. Thus, to protect the parents, childhood mourning often goes underground. It can remain suppressed forever, or until a time when it can be dealt with without fear that it will further hurt the parents.

Parents often attempt to protect surviving siblings from the realities of death. Family members might use religious or philosophical speeches or posturing to obscure or deny the death. Children might be denied the opportunity to view the body in the belief that it would be too painful or would cause nightmares. They might be told an incomplete or distorted story of the death. Such attempts to shield the surviving child usually fail to protect and instead cause other problems for the children. The vacuum of information is easily filled with fantasies about how the death occurred, and usually intensifies whatever sense of guilt or responsibility they may have about their role in the death.

A number of studies of children's disturbed reactions to a sibling loss (Cain, Fast, & Erickson, 1963; Rosen & Cohen, 1981) indicate that avoidance is exactly the wrong thing to do. Krell and Rabkin (1979) hypothesized that three profiles of children emerged from families who participated in conspiracies of silence.

Haunted children are those who live in fear of what may happen to them or what feelings they may arouse in their parents. These children are the caretakers of their parents' feelings and are constantly vigilant lest they remind their parents of the dead child. Although they are constrained and on guard at home, they often misbehave at school or develop phobias or somatic symptoms.

Bound children are overprotected because their parents live in fear that they may lose another child. As a result of the parents' real and imagined fears, they develop a new family system that is closed, guarded, overprotective, and restrictive. In this system, children are prevented from being inquisitive and risk-taking and often withdraw into a constrained household occupied by their fearful parents, the ghost of their dead sibling, and themselves. A common outcome is initial angry behavior outside the family and, ultimately, rejection of the parents.

Resurrected children are seen as substitutes for their dead sibling. They are treated as though they were the dead child with a limited chance of establishing their own identity. The more the parents undermine their attempts to develop a unique personality, the greater the risk of psychological disturbance.

Preschool children often experience the death of a sibling as the loss of a best friend and companion, an abandonment that is puzzling and hurtful. They often are guilty for wishes they had to eliminate their competitor or rival or because they did not share their toys. Young elementary aged children are often overwhelmed with sadness and loneliness and tend to withdraw from social interactions at home and at school. Frequently, to compensate for their sense of responsibility in the sibling's death, or because of a historically conflict-ridden relationship, the surviving child will misbehave and, thus, be punished. Older children and adolescents often feel extreme discomfort with their friends. They feel different, misunderstood, rejected, isolated, and often freakish. They may avoid their peers and, thus, school can become a painful experience to be avoided as well (Schumacher, 1984).

The circumstances of the death are relevant to the surviving child's response. In the case of prolonged illness, the death is somewhat easier for the parents to cope with than a sudden death because of the period of ''anticipatory grief.'' For the surviving child, however, this period may well be one of prolonged anguish, of feeling neglected, rejected, and increasingly resentful of the dying sibling. They may feel relieved and glad at the actual death, emotions that often are misunderstood, considered unacceptable, and punished. In the case of a sudden death, the surviving child is often left with an incredible sense of guilt because he or she has not had the opportunity to resolve old issues. The guilt, fear, and self-blame that may result from any of these dynamics can be expressed through misbehavior, depression, overly solicitous behavior, overeating, and other forms of self-destructive behavior (Bank & Kahn, 1982).

Death of a Grandparent

There is often a special affinity between grandchildren and grandparents. In many cases, both live outside the mainstream of productive society. Grandparents do not carry the responsibility of raising the child and so are not sources of frustration or targets of rebellion. Both parties have everything to gain and nothing to lose; this can allow for a relatively carefree and mutually satisfying relationship that can be a profound loss to a child when the grandparent dies. Additionally, a grandparent represents a sense of continuity and tradition that are central to a child's construction of an ordered world, especially in today's transient culture.

The older the child at the time of the loss, the more meaning the death will potentially have. It can be a personal loss and a symbolic loss as mentioned. Additionally, it can be an opportunity to observe the relationship between parent and grandparent, to learn from the parent's grieving how to acknowledge and resolve losses.

Death of a Friend

The effects of the death of a close peer on a child have not been systematically studied and are not often reported in the literature. One can assume that children will react much as they might to the death of a sibling, with a great sadness and loneliness, with a sense of abandonment and hurt. They are not so likely to experience intense guilt because it is unlikely that they would have the same comparable conflict ridden history or the sense of responsibility that a sibling would. However, should these factors be central to the pre-death relationship, then the bereaved child could experience profound guilt and could exhibit disturbed thinking and/or behavior.

The Dying Child

Terminally ill children of all ages need love, care, comfort, and the assurance that they will not be left to die alone. This reassurance, as well as the consistent nurturing and attention that will confirm it, are essential to the alleviation of the major fears of dying children. Natterson and Knudsen (1960) studied the fear of death in hospitalized fatally ill children and their mothers and found that the predominant causes of fear and distress were related to the child's developmental age.

Children younger than 5 were most afraid of separation from their mother, of being alone, abandoned, or lost. Frequently, these young children respond by becoming extremely clinging, with demands for the constant physical presence of an adult, and often with an intense fear of going to sleep, yet another form of separation.

Terminally ill preschool children often experience the abandonment of hospital placement, the pain and physical changes in their bodies, and the medical procedures as punishment for being bad. Their frantic attempts to ''be good'' to avoid further punishment are difficult to sustain, only making them more vulnerable to feelings of guilt and more punishment. Children from age 5 to 10 had the strongest reaction to the medical procedures. At this stage of development, children can understand the relationships between the disease and its effects on the body, as well as the specific purposes of various medical procedures. They usually become quite knowledgeable about the disease and become experts on its effects and treatments. Consistent with their developmental level, they have concerns about bodily functions and malfunctions and so are filled with anxieties about disfigurement in life and the processes of death and decay after death.

Children usually use their age-appropriate interest in concrete information to help master their fears of death. Denial is a common defense of children under the age of 10. These children need extra reassurance and support that they will not be alone without taking away their defensive stand. In such instances, health professionals are needed most by the parents so that they can meet their child's desperate need.

Terminally ill adolescents share the same fears of abandonment and physical disfigurement as do younger age groups. Unlike younger children, however, they have a greater awareness of the enormity of their impending loss. They have a sense of their own future and plans to fulfill it. As a result, their anger and bitterness are much stronger and tend to overshadow their sadness and sense of loss. They, also, consider their death to be a punishment, but they see it as cruel and undeserved. At a time when independence is central to emotional and cognitive development, a terminally ill adolescent is increasingly dependent on the old world, parents and home, and increasingly isolated from what should be the new world of friends and school. It is not surprising that the dying adolescent is so often bitter and enraged, loses self-esteem and self-assurance, and alienates him or herself from those closest as a desperate attempt to prove independence. Parents need considerable support to deal with the massive despair, rejection, and rage of these adolescents.

MANIFESTATIONS OF GRIEF

Since the first systematic study of normal grief reactions done by Lindemann (1944), an extensive and varied list of behaviors have become associated with the grieving process. Worden (1982) has grouped them in the four general categories of feelings, physical sensations, cognitions, and behaviors. Although his work was not limited to children, most of the phenomena included apply to the responses of grieving children.

Among those feelings most common to the grief process, sadness is the most pervasive. It is often expressed through crying, but the absence of tears does not mean that these feelings are being denied. Young children especially have difficulty sustaining intense sad feelings and often experience brief intermittent times of sadness. Anger is very commonly felt and generally comes from one of two sources: either from a sense of frustration that one was powerless to prevent the death or from the anxiety associated with the loss. In either case, it is essential that the anger be appropriately identified and directed toward appropriate external objects, including, at times, the deceased so that it is not turned against the self. Anger turned inward can lead to depression and to suicidal behavior.

Guilt and self-reproach are also commonly experienced. Guilt can be related to past misbehaviors or omitted expressions of care, or can be related to a specific event related to the death. Most often, the guilt is irrational and will be mitigated through continued reality testing. Anxiety usually stems either from the fear that the child will not be able to take care of him or herself or from heightened awareness of one's own mortality. The first source of anxiety is common to children of all ages; the second is more common among adolescents. Feelings of loneliness, helplessness, and numbness are often experienced by children of all ages. Yearning is particularly associated with younger children's searching behavior, but is also connected to the more passive pining of older children. A sense of emancipation or relief may be felt by some older children or adolescents, especially after a long or painful illness or a death that can allow for a dramatic, healthy shift in family structure or dynamics.

Children quite often report physical sensations and somatic complaints during the grieving process. These sensations may be stomach aches, lethargy, short-ness of breath, oversensitivity to noise, or weakness in general. They may also take the form of constipation or bedwetting, vomiting, or loss of appetite. Children will often report symptoms related to the cause of death, both from anxiety and from identification with the deceased.

Certain thought patterns are commonly experienced during the grieving pro-cess, especially in the early stages. Disbelief is often the first response to news of a death. For children, the disbelief is easily reexperienced upon awakening or when first exposed to a new situation. Children are often very confused, can-not seem to keep track of things or maintain the order of the day, and have trouble concentrating. They are frequently preoccupied with thoughts about the deceased, including fantasies of recovering the lost person. Sometimes, children report feel-ing the presence of the deceased watching over them or helping them with a dif-ficult task or experience. Occasionally, children report auditory or visual hallucina-tions, particularly a short time after the death.

The following behaviors are commonly reported among grieving children and usually correct themselves over time. Children frequently experience sleep disorders, especially during the early stages of grief. They may have difficulty falling asleep, may wake frequently, or may wake very early in the morning. Changes in eating patterns are also common. Although appetite disturbances can be manifested in either overeating or undereating, undereating is more often reported. Confused and preoccupied thinking can lead to absent-minded behavior. Among children, this is more often a source of irritation or an inconvenience than problematic, as it can be among adults. Children can respond by withdraw-ing from involvements with others or by sustained, restless activity. Both are efforts to avoid painful feelings, as are efforts to avoid any reminders or mention of the deceased. On the other hand, some children try to maintain the deceased by focusing on mementos or treasured memories or through searching behavior. Crying and sighing are very common responses for children of all ages, as are dreams of the dead person. Both normal dreams and nightmares frequently serve a number of purposes psychologically for the child in mastering the tasks of griev-ing and can be instructive to adults by providing clues to the course of the bereave-ment process.

The aforementioned manifestations of grief are considered to be within the normal responses of children immediately following a death and during the grieving process. The line of separation between normal and dysfunctional mourning reactions is not in symptom, but intensity and duration. It is the continued denial of reality even many months after the funeral that indicates a disturbed reaction. Similarly, prolonged bodily distress or persistent frenzy, unceasing apathy, consistent self-condemnation, or hostility are all indications of a distorted grief reaction. Although the intensity and duration of any of these reactions is idiosyncratic, professional consultation is advisable when there is any question. Other signals that indicate the need for professional advice include delinquency, unwillingness to attend school, difficulties in learning, sexual perversion, unreasonable withdrawal, friendlessness, excessive anger, or intense suspicion (Grollman, 1976).

Those children who would be expected to be most vulnerable during bereavement share one or more of the following experiences or characteristics. Children who have experienced previous losses, whether through death or divorce, are especially likely to be devastated and overwhelmed by another loss. Children without reliable, available support from their immediate or extended family will have greater difficulty moving through the bereavement process. Socially isolated children and those with dysfunctional peer relations will also most likely have a more difficult time. A child experiencing any of the other stresses of childhood—such as a recent move, academic difficulties, birth of a sibling—will be especially vulnerable at the death of someone close. These children may all be considered at risk and potential recipients of secondary prevention efforts.

INTERVENTION STRATEGIES

Based on understanding of children's conceptions of death and on the tasks of grieving, there is considerable agreement on strategies to help children cope with death (Brenner, 1984). For the most part, these have been developed by clinicians to be used by the adults in the child's home or school environment. There is general consensus that children should receive clear, honest information about the death. Responses to questions should be direct, brief, and repeated only when the child seems ready for more. It is important for adults to take the time to understand how the child understands what has happened in order to confirm, clarify, or correct his or her views. Children gain from preparation for a participation in those rituals or ceremonies associated with the death. These events, although difficult, offer opportunities for shared grief, public confirmation and acknowledgment of the deceased's life and death, and closure to the physical presence of that person. Adults can be helpful by encouraging children to express and share the whole range of feelings stirred by the death as well as by being available to console and comfort. Support and assistance to the other bereaving family members can provide indirect help to a child. When parents are themselves so overwhelmed that they are unable to be available to their child, other adults can often provide more direct "surrogate parenting."

The following is a review of typical ways in which children attempt to deal with their grief and a synthesis of recommendations for therapeutic responses (Bank & Kahn, 1982; Bowlby, 1960; Cain et al., 1964; Grollman, 1976; Jewett, 1982; Lonetto, 1980). Although not all of these behaviors will be evidenced directly at school, the child may talk about them. They may also be of concern to other students or to school personnel.

In working on the first task of bereavement, accepting the reality of the loss, it is not uncommon for children to act dazed upon learning of a death or to appear as if they have not heard or understood. In such cases, it is helpful for the adult to repeat the news of the death later in the day, to answer questions clearly and honestly when they arise, and to wait for the news to "sink in." Some children flatly deny that the death has occurred and sustain an unusually high activity level to avoid thinking about it. It is generally agreed to accept this denial initially, but, if it persists, consultation with a therapist is recommended (Jewett, 1982). Sometimes, children will insist on being the one to tell everyone else the news; usually their need to be the center of attention in this way will not last long and can be allowed without causing a problem for the child.

Dreams and nightmares are frequent after hearing of a death and are instrumental in accepting the loss. Nevertheless, many children panic at the dreams, are afraid of being alone and of going to sleep. In such cases, it is helpful to maintain usual routines as far as possible and to review any changes with the child frequently. Their fears of abandonment add to the terrors of the dreams, so children need reassurance that they will be cared for as well as comforted for the dreams or nightmares. It is often comforting to hear music or the sounds of life and activity during the night.

The consistency and predictability of the school routine is usually a source of comfort to children. Here, too, changes should be anticipated and reviewed to reinforce the predictable component of school life. School personnel can be very helpful to families by continued communication around the child's behavior and interactions at school related to accepting the reality of the death.

A variety of behaviors can be associated with the task of experiencing the pain of grief. Children are helped with their sadness and tears, their longing and loneliness, by sharing their feelings with adults and hearing of the adults' sadness. It is also helpful to review memories, both pleasant and unpleasant, of the dead person. Joint projects such as scrapbooks or collections of writings help to concretize shared and personal memories and experiences. When a death is close to an entire class of children (for example, one of the students or a highly involved parent), such projects serve to support the grieving needs of all the children and often the teacher, too. It is not uncommon for children to regress to earlier behavior after a death. At such times, children need acceptance of such behavior as a means to achieve comfort or recreate past times, yet they also need support for their attempts to regain their more mature level of functioning. Searching behavior also needs to be supported and allowed to continue until children feel they have made a thorough search and have had ample opportunities to discuss the repeated disappointments encountered.

Anger and guilt often interfere with the experience of pain and deflect attention from the grieving process. Children often direct their anger toward their parents and other caretakers, or toward siblings and peers. It is important to empathize with these feelings, to respect their source, and to reassure the child that such hurting is part of grieving and will eventually subside. It is helpful to emphasize the value of conversation about guilty and angry feelings and encourage their expression through drawing, writing, and playing them out as well. Expressions of anger and guilt often surface at school. They can be manifested in a social context in both acting out and withdrawn behaviors, in peer conflicts, and in relation to school tasks, by an inability to concentrate or obsessive work habits. Again, this aspect of the grieving process can be facilitated by consistent monitoring on the part of school personnel in order to respond effectively to the child and to inform the family of difficulties and progress. In addition to individual counseling, school-based group work focused on bereavement is often a highly effective forum for expressing, sharing, and "normalizing" emotions.

The third task, adjusting to a new environment that no longer includes the deceased, can be facilitated by discussions that explore the feelings around such an adjustment. The negative feelings, the guilt and anger, that might impede the process need expression; the success of adjustment can also be anxiety provoking. Many children feel uncomfortable and guilty at being able to feel happy again; they may feel disloyal and a sense of betrayal that may constrain them and prevent their moving through this task. Rather than adapt to the new situation, they may withdraw, become immobilized, or feel helpless. Such manifestations of grief are frequently seen in the school setting. They can operate in both the social and academic world of the child and need to be addressed so that the grieving child does not suffer further losses by falling behind academically or socially with peers.

The school setting can help foster a child's ability to reinvest in new relationships. It is a natural environment for children to learn about relationships, to experience the process of losing and making friends, to acknowledge and share group feelings and memories, and to recognize and foster transitions and growth.

The school also offers a structured and formalized curriculum that validates experiences and processes related to life and death, growth and change. Such support comes from the life science studies, from social studies, and from literature. By its very nature as both a socializing and educational institution, the school system supports the grieving process. The mental health professionals within the system, whether teachers, administrators, counselors, or psychologists, can further support grieving children by monitoring their progress and communicating with family about it, by continuous support and responsiveness in their needs individually and as part of a class, by offering group counseling and by referring the child and family for therapy when it is indicated. In addition to private therapists or public agencies, local communities offer a number of specialized referral agencies (see Wass & Carr, 1984, and Wass, 1980, for extensive listings of resources).

PREVENTION

Just as the school's social environment and curricula can be healing to a grieving child, so can these factors serve preventative functions for all children. Both elements of the school setting can provide lessons in bereavement. Certainly, children will learn from directly observing the grieving process of a friend or classmate. They also learn from discussions in science classes, from the elementary curriculum's lessons on living things and their requirements to the more complex biology and physics classes of adolescents. Social studies classes provide information on living in society and functioning as an individual, on the family and personal development. Growth and change are fundamental to both these physical and social aspects of life. They are also frequent topics in children's reading and literature classes. There is a wide range of books available to children of all ages that address concerns of dying and grieving. (Wass, 1980, and Thomas, 1984, provide extensive bibliographies.)

All these elements serve the prevention of mental health problems by providing a base of information and of predictability of thoughts, feelings, and behaviors associated with grieving. The greater the child's cognitive awareness of death and its effects on the survivors, the better prepared he or she will be for losses throughout life. Specialized curricula in "Death Education" have been organized and are available for a wide range of elementary school aged children (Thomas, 1984). Their major purpose is to counterbalance a perceived avoidance of the subject of death in the classroom through a focused program. Whether such a formalized program is more effective than on-going acknowledgment and discussion of issues related to death and bereavement is not clear. Nevertheless, the support that can be provided to children, families, and staff by knowledgeable, responsive mental health professionals in the school setting has been demonstrated.

CONCLUSION

A child's experience with death can have profound effects on future intrapsychic development and interpersonal relationships. The school setting provides unique opportunities to mental health professionals to serve bereaved children, their families, peers, and teachers. An ever-increasing understanding of children's intellectual and psychological conceptions of death allows for effective prevention programs for all children and for significant observations and interventions for grieving children. The curriculum offers ongoing opportunities for prevention by addressing death issues in a variety of content areas and with methods appropriate to the full range of age and developmental levels. The structure of the academic and social school routines are both a support for grieving children and a gauge by which to measure their course through the grieving process. Awareness of bereaved children's needs and perceptions, understanding of their reactions, and communication with families and teachers about their progress are a sure form of prevention of mental health problems in the future.

REFERENCES

Bank, S. P., & Kahn, M. D. (1982). *The sibling bond.* New York: Basic Books.

Bowen, M. (1978). *Family therapy in clinical practice.* New York: Aaronson.

Bowlby, J. (1960). Grief and mourning in infancy and early childhood. *Psychoanalytic Study of the Child, 15,* 9–52.

Brenner, A. (1984). *Helping children cope with stress.* Lexington, MA: D. C. Heath.

Bugen, L. A. (1977). Human grief: A model for prediction and intervention. *American Journal of Orthopsychiatry, 47,* 196–206.

Cain, A. C., Fast, I., & Erickson, M. E. (1964). Children's disturbed reactions to the death of a sibling. *American Journal of Orthopsychiatry, 34,* 741–752.

Engel, G. L. (1961). Is grief a disease? A challenge for medical research. *Psychosomatic Medicine, 23,* 18–22.

Erikson, E. H. (1950). *Childhood and society.* New York: Norton.

Flavell, J. H. (1977). *Cognitive development.* Englewood Cliffs, NJ: Prentice-Hall.

Furman, R. (1974). Death and the young child: Some preliminary considerations. *Psychoanalytic Study of the Child, 19,* 321–333.

Gorer, G. (1965). *Death, grief and mourning in contemporary Britain.* London: Cresset.

Grollman, E. A. (1976). *Talking about death.* Boston: Beacon.

Jewett, C. L. (1982). *Helping children cope with separation and loss.* Harvard, MA: Harvard Common Press.

Krell, R., & Rabkin, L. (1979). The effects of sibling death on the surviving child: A family perspective. *Family Process, 18,* 471–477.

Kubler-Ross, E. (1969). *On death and dying.* New York: Macmillan.

Lindemann, E. (1944). Symptomatology and management of acute grief. *American Journal of Psychiatry, 101,* 141–149.

Lonetto, R. (1980). *Children's conceptions of death.* New York: Springer.

Matz, M. (1979). Helping families cope with grief. In S. Eisenberg & L. E. Patterson (Eds.), *Helping clients with special concerns* (pp. 218–238). Chicago: Rand McNally.

Natterson, J. M., & Knudson, A. G. (1960). Observations concerning fear of death in fatally ill children and their mothers. *Psychosomatic Medicine, 22,* 456–465.

Parkes, C. M. (1972). *Bereavement: Studies of grief in adult life.* New York: International Universities Press.

Piaget, J., & Inhelder, B. (1969). *The psychology of the child.* New York: Basic Books.

Rosen, H., & Cohen, H. (1981). Children's reactions to sibling loss. *Clinical Social Work Journal, 9,* 211–219.

Schumacher, J. D. (1984). Helping children cope with a sibling's death. In J. C. Hansen & T. T. Frantz (Eds.), *Death and grief in the family* (pp. 82–94). Rockville, MD: Aspen Systems Corp.

Spitz, R. (1945). Hospitalism: An inquiry into the genesis of psychiatric conditions in early childhood. *Psychoanalytic Study of the Child, 1,* 53–72.

Thomas, J. L., (Ed.). (1984). *Death and dying in the classroom: Reading for life.* Phoenix, AZ: Ornyx Press.

Wass, H. (1980). *Death education: An annotated resource guide.* Washington: Hemisphere.

Wass, H., & Carr, C. A. (1984). *Helping children cope with death.* Washington: Hemisphere.

Wolfenstein, M. (1966). How is mourning possible? *Psychoanalytic Study of the Child, 21,* 93–123.

Worden, J. (1982). *Grief counseling and grief therapy.* New York: Springer.

Zeligs, R. (1974). *Children's experiences with death.* Springfield, IL: Charles C. Thomas.

9

Children and Moving

Jonathan Sandoval
University of California, Davis

Who among us enjoys moving? The process of giving up an established home and friends and relocating to another neighborhood, city, or geographical region is often accompanied by fatigue, feelings of loss and alienation, and fear of the unknown. Moving for adults may be made more pleasant by the anticipation of a more challenging or rewarding occupation, or by the intellectual stimulation of relocating to a new environment. Unfortunately, most moves are not made to improve one's life. Many moves are dictated by other life events such as deaths and divorces, and come as an added burden to those experiencing life's catastrophes. For many individuals, moving is a normal part of adult life, as with the civilian and military employees of the Department of Defense who routinely relocate every 2 to 5 years. Although there is a connection between adult attitudes and children's reactions, we cannot assume children will experience a move the same way parents do.

"I don't want to move, Dad, all my friends are here!" "What will it be like in my new neighborhood?" "I'm going to get my own room in our new house when we move, aren't I, Mom?" "Boy, I'll be glad to get out of this school!" These are some of the reactions of children to the announcement of a family move. On balance, children do not like to move any more than do adults. Under the right circumstances, however, moving can lead to growth in intellectual, social, and emotional development.

For children, moving means separation. In many cases children will be giving up friends, a neighborhood, and a school environment with which they have become familiar. According to Bowlby (1960, 1961), separation and the emotions attached to it are the most difficult events with which children must deal.

151

Relations with significant others form the core of emotional development, and disruptions in the separation and individuation process can lead to life long personality problems. Children who have already experienced separation difficulties will find moving much more traumatic than others. Moving may even be a problem for the friends of a child who is relocating. Rubin (1980) found that friends of moving children suffered increases in loneliness, irritability, and anger following their companion's departure.

There are studies of stress in humans that attempt to quantify various life events as to their stress value. On Holmes and Rahe's (1967) scale, for example, changes in residence and a change in school each receive a value of 20 on a scale of 100. (The death of a spouse received a full 100 points.) On this scale, life-event scores may be added together to yield a total life crisis value. Almost always a move will add to a person's stress when it accompanies events such as family disintegration, loss of job, or death. All things being equal, a move in the absence of other negative situations would appear to have less of a negative impact on individuals than moves accompanied by events such as illness or divorce.

IS MOVING ALWAYS DETRIMENTAL?

There is some evidence that children are not uniformly opposed to moving (Bekins, 1976; Bush, 1977; Lehr & Hendrickson, 1968). More than half of the children in a survey sponsored by Bekins, for example, did wish to move. This upper middle class sample perceived making new friends, going to a new school, traveling and learning about new localities to be exciting prospects. The minority, however, did not look forward to moving, citing the loss of friends as the major problem.

A number of studies have been done attempting to discover whether moving has a negative affect on children's academic, social, or emotional development. A sizable amount of this research has focused on children of military dependents. Research has particularly focused on whether or not the stereotype of the "Military Brat" has any validity. Very little research has contradicted the findings of Sackett (1935) who discovered that the children of military officers in Panama were performing better or equal to their stateside civilian counterparts. When the proper control base rates are considered, military children seem to have fewer intellectual and social emotional problems than other children (Gordon & Gordon, 1958; Greene & Daughtry, 1961; Kenny, 1967; Pederson & Sullivan, 1964; Seagoe, 1932). One problem in the research of military children, besides the lack of suitable control groups, is in distinguishing between the children of officers and enlisted men. For officers, a move may be perceived as a positive part of a career and leading to advancement whereas for enlisted personnel a move may simply be an annoyance. In a study of primarily officer's children, Pederson and Sullivan (1964) found that normal children had mothers who were more accepting of frequent relocation and parents who were strongly identified with the military than did children who were diagnosed emotionally disturbed.

It may be unfair to generalize from military to civilian children because military moves are scheduled and supported economically and with various planned interventions for those who have moved. Personnel who move are given time and careful orientations to their new assignments. In addition, it is sometimes the case that military children move with a cohort and do not necessarily lose all of their friends in a move. They simply find themselves in a different part of the world with some of the same classmates.

Research on nonmilitary children has more often shown that children suffer from moving, although the findings are not unanimous in detailing negative outcomes. Again, researchers have not always distinguished between those whose moves are supported and planned (presumably leading to positive outcomes for the family) and for those for whom the move is a result of negative economic or social conditions. The effect of moving on children of a high level executive is obviously going to be different than the effect of moving on the children of a seasonal worker or unskilled laborer who must travel from job to job. In this latter group, particularly, moving may be a result of life problems rather than a cause of them. In general, researchers have had difficulty in distinguishing cause and effect in the study of moving. Attention to interactions may facilitate the understanding of moving research findings. For example, Blane and Spicer (1978) found that mobility had little or no effect on children from high socioeconomic status (SES) homes but was detrimental for children from most low socioeconomic homes. Whalen and Fried (1973) found that mobility improved test scores of intelligent children but depressed scores of children with lower IQs. Perhaps the exposure to new environments, the pride that comes from mastering the challenges of moving to a new place, and the introduction to different values and ways of living that travel brings may have positive effects on children. This beneficial effect is no doubt magnified for bright children in families who perceive the move to be in their best interests and are optimistic and enthusiastic about the changes (Fassler, 1978).

Extent of the Problem

Moving has become a fact of life for modern Americans. The U.S. Bureau of Census estimated that in 1978, 41.4% of the 5- to 9-year-old population had moved between March 1975 and March 1978 (U.S. Government, 1978). A reasonable estimate would be that almost 50% of the population in an elementary school had moved at least once during their lifetime. We do not know for what percentage of these children moving turns into a crisis. Certainly it does not negatively impact all of them as indicated by the research previously cited. Nevertheless, depending on the reason for the move and the individual child's makeup, moves may be quite traumatic and require intervention from school mental health personnel such as a school psychologist. Children who move will be at some risk for developing severe learning and behavior problems in the schools.

Children at High Risk

One might hypothesize that those children with a sense of separation anxiety would have the most difficult time with a move and be more prone to exhibit the features of a crisis. Psychiatric researchers estimate that a large number of the childhood population has some vestiges of separation and related anxiety. Who else is at risk for developing a crisis? As already mentioned, children for whom a move is not a planned or economically favorable situation are probably at risk of having negative outcomes from moving. Children for whom moving is a result of another life crisis are probably at greater risk for developing a crisis around the event. In addition, however, moving may have different consequences depending on the age or developmental level of the child.

Developmental Considerations

Generally speaking, most researchers have observed very little ill effects occurring from moves in the preschool population (Inbar, 1976; Tooley, 1970). Because the major effect of a move on preschoolers is a change of environment and usually not a loss of significant others, moves may be easy for infants and toddlers. Because preschoolers have formed attachments mainly to family members and only secondarily to places and peers, to the extent that important family members stay with the child during the move, there are perhaps superficial impacts of a move on young children. Placing the child out of the home with relatives and babysitter while settling in is probably not a good idea (Stubblefield, 1955). Nevertheless, one might speculate that because a major life crisis centers around separation at the preschool age, the extent to which the move causes parents to become preoccupied with the details of the move and to ignore the child's needs for comfort and emotional support, a move will create additional problems for the very young child. A move coupled with the loss of a parent through divorce or death will be especially difficult. There is no doubt that moves can cause great stress for one or another parent, although one might speculate that mothers bear the brunt of the problems of packing, finding new housing and so on. Depending on the child's closeness to the mother and the stress-induced changes in her reactions to the child, problems might be anticipated for preschoolers because this is the age when children are most attuned to their parents' mental state.

Others have argued that middle childhood represents a time of great vulnerability (Inbar, 1976; Tooley, 1970). Inbar (1976) suggests that because children in elementary school are transferring their close relations from the family to friends, moving may be a severe handicap for the socialization process. In addition, according to Erikson (1962), young elementary school children are involved in establishing a sense of industry that occurs primarily in mastering the tasks in schools such as learning to read and write. Consequently, the disruption in school progress brought about by a move may cause considerable emotional difficulties as well as learning problems. It may be argued that the curriculum across the

United States is more uniform than it is different, and that children can easily make the transition to related curriculum materials or even find the same reading series, for example, that they left behind them.

The problem may be much easier for higher achievers, in this regard, than for learning disabled or other children who have difficulty learning and who depend on the interpersonal relationship with the teacher to facilitate learning. Although individual educational plans (IEPs) may have been developed for exceptional children these may not be as easy to transfer from one locale to another as IEP proponents hope. Also, the problem of requalifying for special education may crop up to the extent that different standards for special education exist in different regions of the country. As a result, a child with learning handicaps may not encounter a sympathetic environment when he or she moves.

Other researchers believe that adolescents experience the most trauma during moves (Tooley, 1970). The task of adolescents, according to Erikson (1962), is to establish an identity through the use of interpersonal relations with peer groups. To have the continuity of such relations with peers disrupted by a move will obviously lead to difficulties. Adolescents most fear the loss of a social group as an ego support system. Because the group facilitates role playing and experimentation that leads to identity, the loss of close friends brought about by a move is particularly destructive. In addition, adolescents often are in conflict with parents as they seek to reject family values and parental authority in the process of creating their own values as individuals. The move may provide a focal point for conflict and rebellion leading the adolescent to attempt to use the move as a way of achieving independence (by, for example, asking to remain behind, or by simply refusing to cooperate in any way with the moving plans).

Other adolescents may welcome a move as an opportunity to start over again in a secondary school with a new group of peers. They see the move as facilitating role experimentation by providing a new audience and setting for them to try different ways of acting. Moves may be viewed positively by these adolescents who wish to start over.

PREVENTION ACTIVITES

When one knows that a move is in the offing it is possible to prepare the child for the move in a way that will facilitate adjustment. There are a number of anticipatory guidance activities that can be planned for a child that will help him or her think through in advance changes that will occur and prepare for the accompanying strong feelings. To remove the fear of the unknown, children should preview the new house, actively participate in its selection, and tour the new neighborhood, school, and community. The American Movers Conference, a moving trade organization, sponsored a conference on moving and children and produced an excellent pamphlet (American Movers Conference, no date) which is designed for parents to help them prepare their child for moving. Many of their suggestions are very relevant.

First, they encourage parents to talk about the move with their children. Children should not learn about the move from another source (Switzer et al., 1961). They advise the parent to explain to each child at his or her own level of understanding the reason for the move and to anticipate what the new home and community will be like. They also suggest that parents inform their children about how they can make the move a successful one and assign them a role in the move. Additionally, they recommend that parents be accepting of children's feelings, even their particularly negative ones about the move. They believe that parents should be truthful and share their misgivings as well as hopes for the new move. Obviously, the further in advance of the move the conversations take place, up to a point, the more successful they will be (Stubblefield, 1955). A child who has moved before may have some residue of feelings about the previous move and past experiences that should also be explored openly.

1. If you are moving to a distant place help your children learn about the new area. Moving companies, the local Chamber of Commerce, tourists bureaus and state agencies are possible sources of information.
2. By using dolls, boxes and a wagon children can get a feeling for concept of moving through play acting.
3. Let the children help decide how their rooms are to be arranged an decorated.
4. Take the time to make a last visit to places your family is particularly fond of.
5. Encourage the children to exchange addresses with their friends. If practical, give thought to allowing them to have their old friends visit at the new home. A telephone call to an old friend is a low cost way to relieve post move depression.
6. Prepare a package for each child containing favorite toys, clothing and snacks. Label with the child's name.
7. Survey your new home for loose steps, low overhang and other possible accident procedures. Keep your eye on the children until they become familiar with the new home's peculiarities.
8. Take your break with the family as soon as the major unpacking is done. Don't try to do everything as soon as you arrive.
9. Both parents should spend time with all their children after the move listening to what they've learned to new school, new friends.
10. The first week in a new school may be difficult for your child. Follow his progress closely and if any problems increase or don't go away in time don't hesitate to visit with his teacher. Accompanying him to school the first few days may ease both his and your minds.
11. Younger children may react to the move by reverting to babyish actions. Be reassuring, not scolding. They will soon relax and return to normal behavior.
12. Any abnormalities that linger, particularly physical ones such as loss of appetite and constipation, menstrual disorder—should be referred to a doctor. Point out to him that your family recently relocated.

FIG. 9.1.   Suggestions for parents from the American Movers Conference Pamphlet *Moving and Children*. (Courtesy of American Movers Conference.)

The American Movers Conference pamphlet also suggests some age-appropriate suggestions. For infants, they emphasize the importance disrupting the infant and toddler's normal routine as little as possible. Preschoolers, they suggest, may be helped by directly addressing any fears that the child may be left behind and reassuring the child that favorite toys and special objects such as teddy bears or beds and chairs, although they will be packed and out of sight, will be restored to an appropriate place in the new house. The movers warn against leaving preschoolers with babysitters for a long period of time during the moving period. To do so might cause them to experience more separation than usual. They also suggest the preschooler be allowed to pack and carry along some of their own special possessions during the move. They suggest that a move is not a good opportunity to discard a number of battered and broken toys that a child has become attached to. As inconvenient as this may seem, it is probably better to wait until the child is settled to throw things away.

Children of elementary school age can be reasoned with more effectively. The pamphlet urges parents to allow them to express their concerns and to talk about the challenges of fitting in with a new group of friends and schoolmates.

The pamphlet suggests that frank discussions with teenagers may allow them to express their potential anger at the move but also to consider the advantages, such as the opportunity of meeting new people and new activities. It suggests that parents help the teenager find organizations and groups in the new area that are involved in interesting activities and encourage the teenager to bring friends into the new home, even though the new house may not be as settled and presentable as the parents may like.

Additional specific ideas for making the transition as smoothly as possible for children are to be found in Fig 9.1. These ideas embody a number of good preventive principles such as anticipatory guidance and emotional inoculation.

Prevention in the School Setting

One of the prevailing notions that parents have is that it will be easier on their child if they move their school-aged children during the summer rather than interrupting their school career. This notion is based on the idea that children will not be easily able to maintain continuity in learning if they shift from one set of curriculum materials to another in the middle of the year.

Although there is a certain amount of truth that missing school and changing teacher's curriculum materials will interrupt learning, a move during the summer may bring about a number of more serious problems. Children moving during the summer will find themselves in a new neighborhood without friends and without activities to occupy their time. They are isolated and bored until school opens in September, allowing time for anger and frustration to build. Because, when school does open, most teachers are faced with a new classroom and will not be able to identify children who have moved, the teacher will not be able to give the newly arrived children the special attention they may require.

If the child moves during the school year, he or she will move from one social setting to another. The teacher and the classmates will recognize that the child is new to the school and make some allowances for the fact. Sensitive teachers will be able to engage the new child in a number of activities to assist in the establishment of a peer group and in an appropriate curriculum that is challenging but not overwhelming or repetitive.

Helping the Child Who is Leaving. When it is known that a child will be leaving the school there are a number of activities teachers or others can engage in that will assist in the transition. Ceremonies are very important in marking passages. Making sure that children have an opportunity to say goodbye is very important. Allowing the child time to say goodbye to former teachers and others in the school besides immediate classmates may allow the child to make the separation easier.

Encouraging the child to write to former classmates may be a useful activity, not only for the creative writing involved, but in helping the child realize that friendships can endure time and distance. Departing children can also be encouraged to take with them a folder of previous work and work in progress. Taking a record of past and present accomplishments helps the child maintain a sense of continuity with the old classroom but also has the advantage of providing the new teacher with an idea of the child's level of academic functioning. A note to the new teacher along with an evening telephone number and encouragement to call can also help the moving child find appropriate placement in the new school.

As always, giving a child an opportunity to express both positive and negative feelings about the move in the classroom can be a useful exercise for the entire class. Such classroom meeting discussions should be planned for a period when there is time for a complete discussion because other children in the group, and not just the departing child, may have feelings they wish to explore about moving. No doubt there will be a number of moves each year in a classroom and these occasions present excellent opportunities for social studies lessons ranging from geography to anthropology.

Bibliotherapy is another activity that may be very helpful for the child leaving a school (Smardo, 1981a). With the help of the librarian, teachers and school psychologists can identify reading materials that focus on the experience of moving and the adjustments to a new environment. A number of children's books have been written on this topic (Bernstein, 1977; Fassler, 1978; Smardo, 1981b). When doing bibliotherapy it is important to identify materials that are relevant, are at an interest level that will engage the child, and are at an appropriate level of reading difficulty so that the child may read the materials on his or her own. Once the child has had an opportunity to read the materials, some discussion should follow. The point of bibliotherapy is to provide the child with models for effective coping and problem solving. Besides books on moving per se, stories concerning making friends and adapting to new customs and circumstances may be particularly relevant.

Helping the New Child in the Classroom. The first necessity for helping a new child become integrated in the classroom both socially and academically is to find out as much information about him or her as possible. A phone call to a previous teacher coupled within a close inspection of academic records will offer an excellent opportunity to prepare for educational planning for a new child. Often, educational records take months to arrive if they ever do. Therefore, a phone call may prove a particularly good investment. Previous teachers may be asked about interests and preferred activities, information that can be used to help the child establish friendships with similarly inclined peers in the classroom, as well as to motivate academic performance. Of course, academic strengths and weaknesses as well as successful pedagogic technique should be enquired about.

Research on friendships suggests that those of like ability are inclined to associate together and form lasting friendships (Rubin, 1980). If possible, the teacher might seat the new child with like-minded peers or include them in the same work or play groups. In secondary schools, various interest groups such as music, art, hobbies, and the like can form the basis for forming friendships. Because the curriculum in the secondary school often includes elective courses, it is in these subjects that adolescents are likely to meet potential friends.

Teachers receiving new pupils in the new classroom must be educated (by school psychologists) about possible signs of maladaption to the move. They should look for symptoms of depression, withdrawal, fatigue, even loss of appetite and bring students who are suffering some form of depression to the attention of school psychologists and counselors. Teachers seem to appreciate that moving is a crisis for children so they will be open to assistance in this regard. In the next section, I discuss crisis counseling interventions on the part of guidance personnel should teachers identify children in need of extra assistance.

Switzer and his colleagues (Switzer et al., 1961) note that often school personnel harbor hostility for new children in general. New children are perceived to be threats to the accomplishment of important goals such as building cohesive classroom groups, keeping student–teacher ratios low, and high levels of classroom achievement. To the extent that this hostility interferes with working with an individual, consultation with the teacher directed at eliminating this theme will be necessary.

It is an open question as to whether new children should be singled out and introduced to classmates. Verbal and extroverted children probably can handle this situation well and will be comfortable in groups and able to tell new classmates about their previous location and the circumstances of their move. Other children will be far too shy to engage open classroom discussions in spite of the positive outcomes that might occur in making themselves known to potential friends and integrating themselves in the classroom. Orientation programs in which new children may simply watch the classroom and familiarize themselves with procedures and practices may be best for some (Levine, 1966). Levine reports a program in which upper grade children are recruited and trained to serve as guides to children entering school. The guides show the new pupils the building, inform them of school rules, and discuss age-appropriate resources in the school and community.

CRISIS COUNSELING CHILDREN WHO HAVE MOVED OR ARE ABOUT TO MOVE

At some point, the school psychologist will encounter a child who is in a state of crisis as a result of a move. A first step, of course, is to determine what has brought about the move and whether it represents a radical change in child's home environment or parental relations. If the move was occasioned by another hazardous life event, perhaps the counseling should be directed primarily at this circumstance and secondarily at the issues associated with the move. On the other hand, the impact of the move should not be ignored in helping, for example, the child adjust to a parental divorce.

Assuming the major issue is the move and the change from one school and neighborhood to another, the focus of counseling for younger children should be on the expression of feelings of loss and the experience of apprehension at establishing new routines and friendships. The child can be lead to examine the old situation and encouraged to enumerate both positive and negative aspects of his or her relationships. If the child attempts to idealize the old, it will be important to question the child carefully to create a more balanced view.

Next, the child may explore the new situation. If the child is in crisis before the move, the counselor may ask about what ideas the child has of the new environment. By being on the lookout for mistaken ideas and by inquiring about new opportunities and advantages of the move, the helper may assist the child to establish a more favorable outlook.

Many times, the crisis will arise after the move when the child finds him or herself alone and isolated. Because the loss of friendship is so devastating at middle childhood, it may prove effective in counseling to help the child maintain or reestablish the old friendships through telephone calls, letter writing, and visits. If the child is having trouble making new friends, it may be important to determine if the child has the social skills necessary for establishing friendships or if he or she is failing to use them. If the problem is lack of skill, a number of social skills programs have been developed that may prove useful (Gresham, 1981). If the child has the skills but fails to use them, a different tactic is called for. Pointing out to the counselee how he or she has not used opportunities when they have presented themselves may facilitate action. By being an interested adult and by reinforcing prosocial behaviors, the child may soon establish an important social network.

Counseling adolescents will call for many of the same approaches modified to fit their higher level of cognitive fuctioning and their unique type of egocentrism (Elkind, 1974). As mentioned previously, adolescents, with help, can come to see a move as a new chance to try out different styles of behaving and to play new roles. A counselor can point out this relevant notion, and help the student consider what the pre-move social status has been and what it might be in a new setting.

The adolescent's egocentrism creates a condition of extreme self-consciousness and sense that they are constantly being observed and judged by others (Elkind's 1974, imaginary audience). Another aspect of counseling will be to help the adolescent test how realistic it is to be afraid and inhibited in the new social situations they are encountering at the new school. The client must learn to distinguish between his or her preoccupations and sensitive points and what is of interest and of concern to others. Role playing may be a useful technique to get the adolescent aware of another's frame of reference.

CONCLUSION

In summary, moving is a hazardous time for children. Moving presents a number of opportunities to build new skill and competencies, however. With the right preparation on the part of parents, and with sensitive school personnel, a child may experience a move as a natural part of growing up. If the move is a part of another crisis, careful attention to helping the child resolve the issues of moving can leave the child with more resources to cope with other life events.

REFERENCES

American Movers Conference. (no date). *Moving and children.* Arlington, VA: Author.

Bekins Co. (1976). *Youth consumer survey.* Glendale, CA: Author.

Bernstein, J. E. (1977). *Books to help children cope with separation and loss.* New York: Bowker.

Blane D., & Spicer, B. (1978). Geographic mobility, educational attainment and adjustment—which children are at risk? *Education Australia, 3,* 51–64.

Bowlby, J. (1960). Separation anxiety. *The International Journal of Psychoanalysis, 41,* 89–113.

Bowlby, J. (1961). Separation anxiety: A critical review of the literature. *Journal of Child Psychology and Psychiatry, 1,* 251–269.

Bush, S. (1977). Newsline: Moving can be fun. *Psychology Today, 11*(2), 28.

Elkind, D. (1974). *Children and adolescents* (2nd ed.). New York: Oxford University Press.

Erikson, E. (1962). *Childhood and society* (2nd ed.). New York: W. W. Norton.

Fassler, J. (1978). *Helping children cope: Mastering stress through books and stories.* New York: Macmillan.

Gordon, R. E. & Gordon, K. K. (1958). Emotional disorders of children in a rapidly growing suburb. *International Journal of Social Psychiatry, 4,* 85–97.

Greene, J. E. & Daughtry, S. L. (1961). Factors associated with school mobility. *The Journal of Educational Sociology, 35,* 36–40.

Greshman, F. M. (1981). Social skills training with handicapped children: A review. *Review of Educational Research, 51,* 139–176.

Holmes, T. H., & Rahe, R. H. (1967). The social readjustment rating scale. *Journal of Psychosomatic Research, 11,* 213–218.

Inbar, M. (1976). *Social science frontiers: The vulnerable age phenomenon.* New York: Russell Sage.

Kenny J. A. (1967). The child in the military community. *Journal of the American Academy of Child Psychiatry, 6,* 51–63.

Lehr, C. J., & Hendrickson, N. (1968). Children's attitudes toward a family move. *Mental Hygiene, 52,* 381–384.

Levine, M. (1966). Residential change and school adjustment. *Community Mental Health Journal, 2,* 61–69.

Pedersen, F. A., & Sullivan, E. J. (1964). Relationships among geographical mobility, parental attitudes and emotional disturbances in children. *American Journal of Orthopsychiatry, 34,* 575–580.

Rubin, Z. (1980). *Children's friendships.* Cambridge, MA: Harvard University Press.

Sackett, E. B. (1935). The effect of moving on educational status of children. *The Elementary School Journal, 35,* 517–526.

Seagoe, M. V. (1932). The transient child. *Journal of Juvenile Research, 16,* 251–257.

Smardo, F. A. (1981a). Books about moving. *Childhood Education, 58,* 37–39.

Smardo, F. A. (1981b). Geographic mobility: How do we help children cope? *Childhood Education, 58,* 40–45.

Stubblefield, R. L. (1955). Children's emotional problems aggravated by family moves. *American Journal of Orthopsychiatry, 25,* 120–126.

Switzer, R. E., Hirschberg, J. C., Myers, L., Gray E., Evers, N. H., & Forman, R. (1961). The effect of family moves on children. *Mental Hygiene, 45,* 528–536.

Tooley, K. (1970). The role of geographic mobility in some adjustment problems of children and families. *Journal of the American Academy of Child Psychiatry, 9,* 366–378.

U.S. Government, U.S. Department of Commerce, Bureau of the Census. (1978). *Geographic mobility: March 1975 to March 1978. Current population reports: Population characteristics* (Series P-20, No. 331). Washington, DC: U.S. Government Printing Office.

Whalen, T. E., & Fried, M. A. (1973). Geographic mobility and its effect on student achievement. *Journal of Educational Research, 67,* 163–165.

III

CRISES IN ADOLESCENCE

The Anthropologist Mary Douglass (1966) has described the occurrence of marginality resulting from a person's being outside the social system. Such is the case during transition from one status to another. In many societies, including ours, pubescent youngsters are marginal. They are leaving the status of childhood for that of a new life stage. We put them in a transitional institution—the junior high that has little identity of its own. The term *middle school* is revealing in itself with its meaning of "inbetweenness."

Transitions are crises in that they present the individual with a situation for which old techniques of adjustment and coping may not work. According to Douglass, the individual in transition can be dangerous and vulnerable, a threat to self and to society. In many rites of passage, the marginal person is isolated or avoided. There is also a kind of lawlessness about such persons because the roles and ascriptions of one's past status no longer apply, and the new ones have not yet been acquired.

Psychology, too, described the marginal person drawing on the topological life space theory of Kurt Lewin (1939). There is no defined phenomenological space or life role for the pubescent. Behavioral requirements are ambiguous, perhaps in recognition that the period of transition will be characterized by both forward-looking and regressive attitudes and actions. Redl (1969) has spoken of the pubescent's task of emigrating to the society of the teenager.

Unlike other transitions such as graduation or marriage, the status change from child to adolescent takes longer. There is no ceremony. It is more akin to the midlife crisis in that regard, but by middle age, one has more experience in dealing with crises and, with luck, possesses greater self-knowledge. Conflicts resulting from marginality will be muted by years of socialization, and while in a transitional phase, the middle-aged person is probably not as marginal as is the case in early adolescence.

Adolescence in itself, then, is a hazardous event resulting in numerous crises. The chapters in this section deal with crises related to peer conflict, pregnancy, the discovery of homosexuality, suicide, and parent conflict. These events (except pregnancy) may occur earlier than adolescence, but are particular problems for school personnel in secondary schools. It is important to consider how the phenomenon of adolescence interacts with these events and how interventions with adolescents are unique.

The world of the adolescent becomes a more separate one from that of adults because of decreasing supervision and increasing independence. The degree of distinctiveness of the teen world from the adult world varies by family, community, and culture. Single mothers in the inner city may have little knowledge about the activities of their teenage sons. In tightly knit families or religious groups, the teen world and the adult world may show considerable overlap.

Sherif and Sherif (1964) described the findings of participant observers in groups of adolescent boys. Substantial segments of the boys' time were devoted to activities about which parents and teachers had little knowledge. Recently in Japan, for example, school officials responded with shock, surprise, and dismay to the development of bullying, *Ijime*, within the junior high schools. The behavior had not been noted by school personnel and did not even have a name until brought dramatically to light by a number of student suicides ("All Things," 1985).

There exists in the United States, a subculture in which adults and children do not figure. To experience this, take a trip to a surfing beach, an inner-city barrio, or a high school sports event. If you are over 25 or under 10 years of age, the "locals only" sign at the beach will not apply to you. In the barrio, you probably need not fear violating the graffiti warnings of territorial boundaries posted by neighborhood gangs. At the game, parade and display in the bleachers are not for your benefit. If you are a female outside the age range, you are virtually invisible unless you look like someone's mother. As a male, you merit only a second glance to determine your authority status.

Adolescents may not completely withdraw from the world of adults, but the following survey gives an idea of where their interests lie. For 600 students, the factors listed as most important were "me, myself," "my parents," "my school grades," "my friends in school," and "elective classes." Least important were "principal," "my school counselor,' "building and its location" and "school rules" (Litowsky-Ducasa, 1981).

For the school psychologist and other school personnel it is clear that finding ways to intervene and help adolescents in crisis presents a particular challenge.

Note in the following chapters how peers are often involved in crisis intervention and how group work might be considered.

Chapter 10 by Sommer examines crises related to peer conflicts. She stresses the need to attend to the entire school climate to create a preventative program. Davis' chapter (chapter 11) on suicide also discusses the need to sensitize peers as part of a comprehensive program. The chapter on suicide addresses the need to do a careful assessment of the child's status and emphasizes the special role of referral agent for school personnel, like child abuse, suicide calls for a programmatic approach to prevention rather than therapeutic counseling.

The special world of adolescence also has its private side. Crises related to sexuality may be deliberately shielded from peers although they may be exacerbated by the peer culture. Hardy (chapter 12) discusses the crisis of pregnancy, both for the male and the female involved. Peer culture has a heavy influence in contributing to the hazard, but is not much help in resolving it. Most hidden from peers is homosexuality. Ross-Reynolds (chapter 13) outlines an approach in counseling as well as the important informational and attitudinal base that school personnel must have in working with this significant hidden minority population.

The specifics of addressing the natural but nevertheless stressful crisis of parent–child conflict appear in the final chapter by Fine and Roberts in chapter 14. These authors bring a number of insights from family therapy to play in the school work with adolescents and their parents.

B.S. & J.S.

REFERENCES

All Things Considered: Nightly news magazine (1985). *Public Broadcasting System,* Dec. 15 & 26.

Douglass, M. (1966). *Purity and danger; an analysis of concepts of pollution and taboo.* London: Routledge & Kegan Paul.

Lewin, K. (1939). Field theory and experiment in social psychology: Concepts and methods. *American Journal of Sociology, 14,* 868–897.

Litowsky-Ducasa, D. (1981). The adolescent and school violence: A developmental perspective of adolescent perceptions of high school settings (Doctoral dissertation, Boston University School of Education, 1980). *Dissertation Abstracts International, 41,* 8–A, 3492.

Redl, F. (1969). Adolescents—just how do they react? In G. Caplan & S. Lebovici (Eds.), *Adolescence: Psychosocial perspectives* (pp. 79–99). New York: Basic Books.

Sherif, M., & Sherif, C. W. (1964). *Reference groups: Explorations into conformity and deviation of adolescents.* New York: Harper & Row.

Peer Conflicts

Barbara Sommer
University of California, Davis

Peer conflict refers to a broad spectrum of behaviors that can range from low-level nonverbal harassment (stares and glares) and verbal insults, through malicious gossip, to bullying and fighting, gang confrontations, and aggravated physical assault. The conflict may involve one-on-one harassment, the ganging up of several against one, or confrontations between cliques or groups.

The incidence of violent peer conflict is described first, followed by sections describing how conflicts vary with the social ecology of the school, and how they differ by gender and age. Biological, psychological, and school variables connected with individual aggression are addressed. A section is devoted to reference groups and group conflict. Finally, specific suggestions are offered for dealing with and reducing peer conflict.

INCIDENCE OF STUDENT–STUDENT VIOLENCE

In 1978 the National Institute of Education (NIE) published *Violent Schools— Safe Schools: The Safe School Study Report to the Congress.* That study summarized data from three sources from a representative sample of 604 secondary schools: Principal Report Sheets, Student Questionnaires (50 at each school), and Student Interviews (10 at each school), all covering events for the preceding month. Figure 10.1 shows the victimization estimates from the two student data sets.

Based on the student interviews (considered the most reliable of the three measures), 1.3% of secondary school students were physically attacked at school in a month; 42% of these involved some injury, with 4% requiring medical atten-

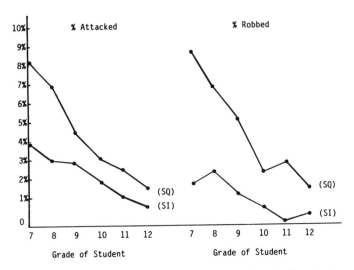

FIG. 10.1.   Percent of students victimized, by grade (SQ = Student Questionnaires, SI = Student Interviews) (NIE, 1978, Table B-3.3).

tion. The principals' estimates were a few percentage points higher. About one
half of 1% of secondary school students were robbed by force, weapons, or threats,
in a typical month.

These figures are generalizations for the entire United States. Studies in urban areas yield much higher rates of violence. In a 1978 survey of seventh graders
in a large midwestern city ($N=321$), 34% reported at least one incident of victimization in or around school between early September and late November (Blyth,
Thiel, Bush, & Simmons, 1980). Victimization referred to an actual beating or
physical injury, the threat of physical injury, or theft of more than $1 value. These
findings were based on interviews of the students. An earlier survey of youngsters,
ages 10–14, in an inner-city neighborhood showed a rate of 2.7 incidents of threat,
beating, or theft per child per year, with one third of these incidents occurring
in school (Blyth et al., 1980). Gold (1978) reported that in a national sample of
youthful offenders, 36% acknowledged that they had attacked someone inside
a school building.

Junior High versus Senior High

In the NIE study, the overall proportion of junior high students reporting attacks
was 2% versus 1% of the high school students; the percentages reporting having
been robbed in the preceding month were 1% and .4%, respectively. The differences were statistically significant.

Comparing attacks inside and outside of school, younger adolescents (ages
12–15) are more likely to be attacked in school, whereas older students (ages

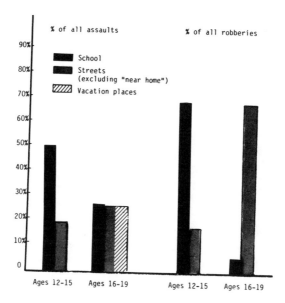

FIG. 10.2.   Percent of assaults and robberies at varying locations, by age (remaining percents in "other" locations).

16–19) are more likely to be attacked outside of school (see Fig. 10.2).

For junior high school students, school is less safe relative to other settings. For senior high school students it is more safe, relative to other settings. The difference may reflect time spent on the streets and in other public places. However, the fact that a junior high school student has a higher likelihood of attack at school than does the high school student gives pause, and suggests the need for a closer scrutiny of the institution and its pupils.

Age Effects and School Grade Structure

As noted in Fig. 10.1, the likelihood of assault or robbery declines with age. However, school structure may play a role in addition to age with respect to the higher rates for seventh graders.

Table 10.1 shows the differential in assaults and robberies between students in the 3-year junior high and those in a comprehensive high school (Grades 7 through 12). The same pattern was obtained when community type was held constant. The difference suggests that the presence of older students may have a moderating or socializing influence on the younger ones.

Three quarters of the victims and offenders were the same age. However, the age categories of ≤ 12, 12–14, 15–17, 18–20, 21 + may mask important age differences, for example, a ninth grader (age 14) attacking a seventh grader (age 12).

TABLE 10.1

Percentage (N) of Students Attacked/Robbed in Junior High Schools and Comprehensive High Schools Extending Through Twelfth Grade, for Grades 7, 8, and 9 (NIE, 1978)

Grade	Junior High		High School
7	15.4 (3,724)	*	11.0 (345)
8	11.9 (3,964)		11.1 (371)
9	9.4 (2,598)	*	7.5 (2,437)

* Differences significant at $p < .05$ level.

Although the aforementioned study minimized the likelihood of older students attacking younger ones, a different picture emerged from the Blyth and Bush (1978) study of 321 urban seventh graders. When they compared junior highs (seventh through ninth grade) with K-8 schools, they found a lower victimization rate for seventh graders in the K-8 school (Table 10.2).

They attribute the difference to older students' victimizing the younger ones, and support that assertion with the finding that sixth graders in the K-8 school had a higher rate of victimization than did sixth graders in the K-6 schools.

Offenders and Victims

For the NIE data, most offenses were committed by students against students, and the offender was usually recognized by the victim. Most offenses were one-on-one. Fifty-eight percent of attacks and 54% of robberies involved persons of the same race. Students victimized once were more likely to be victimized again. As a group, victims tended to be youngsters who were less well-adjusted in school, in academic difficulty, had fewer friends and less social support at home, were generally fearful, and lacked a sense of internal control. They also were more

TABLE 10.2

Percentage (N) of Seventh-Graders Experiencing an Incident by Nature of Victimization and School Type (Blyth et al., 1980)

	K-8 Schools (N = 115)	Junior Highs (N = 206)
Threats	9.6	17.5
Beatings	6.1	5.8
Thefts	12.2	22.8
All types (combined)	24.3	39.3

likely than nonvictims to be offenders themselves. According to teachers and administrators, there was a hard-core group of about 10–15% of the students who account for most disruption. The other 85–90% of students were seldom either victims or offenders.

Environmental Factors

Data from the interviews and principals' reports show that most violence occurs in the hallways and stairways between classes. Students also run the risk of attack in the locker room/gym, restrooms, and the cafeteria. Additional data from elementary schools indicate that for this age group, the playground is the most likely place for attack.

Other findings were that crime and violence in the immediate community were reflected in the incidence of violence in the school. The size of the school was positively related to the incidence of violence, although the relationship was not a strong one. Rates of violence were low on Monday, rose midweek, and returned to a low on Friday.

School Factors

The NIE study isolated four dimensions on which safe and violent schools differed:

1. The more firmly a school is run (i.e., greater classroom control and firmness by the principal) the less violence.
2. The absence of fairness, as perceived by students, was associated with violence. The issue of fairness was particularly significant among junior high students.
3. Student-teacher ratio—smaller class size and more continuous contact between teachers and the same students were associated with reduced violence.
4. The perceived relevance of subject matter was associated with less violence. Schools where students strive to get good grades are less violent.

Although lack of family or parental discipline was predictive of *vandalism*, this was not the case for *violence*. School discipline and control were more closely associated with less violence than was parental discipline.

In summary, junior high students are the most likely among school age youngsters to be involved in assaults at school; victims and offenders frequently are acquainted; and students involved in conflict are often those who have academic difficulty and little social support. Most violence occurs between classes in places of close contact among students and away from adult surveillance. School location (with respect to violence level in the surrounding community) and school management affected the incidence of campus violence.

SOCIAL ECOLOGY AND SCHOOL CLIMATE

There has been a considerable amount of research on school size and other factors affecting school climate—the feeling tone of a school (Barker & Gump, 1964; Epstein, 1981; Safer, 1982). The general conclusion from reviewing these studies is that size interacts with many other variables such as the interrelationships and interconnections among students, teachers, and the physical operational characteristics of the school.

One particular dimension of interest to counselors is Kelly's (1979) description of fluid versus constant environments in high school. He found that schools with high turnover rates provided fluid environments that were diverse and varied, providing more opportunity for social interaction and success. Low turnover rates led to more constant environments with stable cliques. Students were more conforming, and there was a narrower range of opportunities for success. Kelly points out that student problems will differ with the nature of the environment. In the fluid environment, a major issue will be finding a niche and establishing a personal identity. In the constant environment, problems are more likely to revolve around conformity and finding an opportunity to develop one's individuality and personal competence. We can assume that the nature of peer conflict may differ in the two settings, as well.

GENDER AND PEER CONFLICT

Males show considerably more aggression than females at all ages (Maccoby & Jacklin, 1974; White, 1983). There is a dramatic difference between males and females in the incidence of violence. The NIE (1978) study found that 88% of attacks and 85% of robberies occurring in school were committed by males, and boys were twice as likely to be victimized as were girls. A study of retarded and nonretarded students showed that males in both groups were rated significantly higher than females on the Conduct Disorder dimension—items related to aggression, disruption, and other acting out behavior (Cullinan, Matson, Epstein, & Rosemeier, 1984). Among seventh graders in a large midwestern city, boys were more likely to have experienced threats, theft, or a beating, than were girls (Blyth et al., 1980).

Principals and vice-principals reported that compared with boys, the girls tended to gang up on each other, carry grudges longer, and react negatively to gossip. Boys were described as erupting more spontaneously, were more likely to fight physically, and less likely to carry the conflict beyond its immediate expression (Reed, 1983). Although peer conflict cuts across gender, its incidence and form can be expected to differ by sex.

TABLE 10.3

Changes in Factors Contributing to Peer Conflict Across the School Years

Elementary school	Junior high/middle school	High school
1. Incidence of conflict between children declines. 2. Shift from *instrumental conflict* over possessions, objects, or privileges to *hostile conflict* directed at persons. 3. Younger children are likely to physically fight over possessions. Older children are more likely to quarrel verbally with a give-and-take of retaliatory insults.	1. Increased drive level producing activation and sexual arousal. 2. Physical growth may outstrip cognitive and emotional development. 3. Sensation seeking increases. 4. For males, interest in power symbols such as knives and guns. 5. Developing needs for autonomy and independence. 6. Reduced desire to please adults. 7. Cognitive and social skills not matching complexity of circumstances. 8. Limited capacity to articulate feelings. 9. Individual deficits in reality testing become more apparent. 10. Less direct supervision from adults. 11. Increasingly private and peer-centered world. 12. Problem youngsters still in the school system. 13. Groups and cliques not yet consolidated.	1. Improved impulse control and social skills. 2. Conflict more focused and instrumental–serving particular needs or wishes, rather than diffuse response to frustration. 3. Violence and physical aggression continues to be male-dominated. 4. Female conflict centers in the social realm—friendships, popularity, appearance, boyfriends, etc. 5. Peer conflict may take the form of peer competition, becoming more covert and socially acceptable. 6. Cliques and crowd orientations more well-defined and consolidated, e.g., cowboys, stoners, society types, etc. 7. Ratio of individual to group conflicts reflects social structure of the school and group solidarity. Strong group indentification will produce territorial disputes and intergroup rivalry. 8. In the community, locals vs. outsider conflicts likely, particularly at sporting events (and when fueled by alcohol). Gang violence may occur on or off campus.

PEER CONFLICT ACROSS THE SCHOOL YEARS

The pattern of peer conflict changes with age. These developmental differences are listed in Table 10.3 by school level.

The changes during the elementary school years stem from increases in empathy and role-taking ability, and the developing ability to recognize people's intentions. The cognitive capacities that lay the groundwork for meditating or resolving conflicts among older children and adults—the capacity to take the perspective of others—initially may produce conflict and hostility. Until children have the capacity for role-taking (around age 7), clear directions for conduct and sanctions against misbehavior are most effective, for example, stating "Do not push other children" or "We do not fight on the playground." In the later elementary years, encouraging the child's developing sense of respect for self and others becomes an effective means of reducing peer conflict (Sabatino, Sabatino, & Mann, 1983).

A number of developmental issues become particularly salient in the junior high years perhaps making it the most conflict-prone segment of a child's school career. This is also the time when most attacks on teachers occur (NIE, 1978).

Although impulse control has improved throughout the childhood years, it still may be problematic and strained by general activation and sexual drives fueled by puberty. Junior high pupils are larger and stronger than elementary school children; they can do more damage and are less easily controlled physically by adults. A rapidly maturing 15-year-old may still be thinking and acting as a child, although having the physical appearance of an adult.

Both intrinsic and extrinsic factors serving motivation are likely to be changing. The desire to please becomes less motivating. Intrinsic qualities of assignments and activities become more important (e.g., whether they are interesting or boring).

The increased complexity of the school environment and the adolescent social world may not be matched by the individual's cognitive and social skills leading to bewilderment and frustration that may be expressed in aggressive outbursts. Many pubescent-aged youngsters, especially males, are unable or unwilling to articulate feelings and such incapacity or defensiveness limits self-understanding and self-control. Affective expression may take the form of erratic or puzzling behaviors that generate conflict.

By the high school years, students possess more self-control and are less erratic in their behavior. Peer conflict is less likely to erupt in a spontaneous and overt way. Many problem students will have dropped out of the system. Conflict is more sophisticated centering on group identification, and lifestyle issues such as religious or political affiliations, and socioeconomic differences. The nature of peer conflict will reflect the surrounding community, the selection of the student body, and school administrative management policies.

AGGRESSION IN ADOLESCENCE— BIOLOGY AND EXPERIENCE

The activation of the neurophysiological mechanisms leading to aggressive behaviors in humans depends on appropriate stimulation and is subject to cognitive control (Bandura, 1983). In other words, arousal (activation of the sympathetic nervous system) increases the likelihood of an aggressive response when the circumstances, including the perception and appraisal on the part of the person, appear to warrant it (Zillmann, 1983). For adolescents, nervous system arousal is generated by the neuroendocrine changes of puberty. Another source of activation is environmental stimulation—the excitement of a hard-fought football game or stimulus-seeking activities, such as attending concerts of loud, repetitive, and discordant music. The environment may include chemical stimulation as well.

On the appraisal side, adolescence is a time of increased self-consciousness and concern with self-image. Adolescents are likely to be especially sensitive to perceived threats to body and self. They may also be actively seeking out opportunities to demonstrate strength of wit, muscle, or will, in order to dominate others or as a means of warding off potential attacks.

Even when aggression is not openly expressed, urges of sexual desire, dominance, social territory, and acceptance by peers come into conflict with learned values that are being continually reinforced by social agents. The resulting tension produces a disorder in consciousness that is expressed in bad moods, being tired (passivity), a loss of motivation, and the inability to focus or use attention (Csikszentmihalyi & Larson, 1984; Freud, 1958).

Social Learning

A further element in adolescent aggression is the individual's life history with respect to aggressive behavior. Aggression is a self-reinforcing response when it leads to the achievement of some desired outcome (Valzelli, 1981). Aggressive styles of behavior learned in childhood often continue into adulthood (Olweus, 1979). The acquisition of an aggressive style of behavior is accomplished through modeling of family behaviors and family reinforcement of aggression; through the subculture—the neighborhood or social community; and through symbolic modeling provided by the media (Bandura, 1983).

Aggressive behavior patterns acquired and established early in life are not easily altered by the usual means of socialization and often require more focused interventions. Various techniques and programs have been developed for dealing with aggressive children and adolescents at both the familial and individual levels (Eron, 1980; Feshbach & Feshbach, 1982; Mueller & Donnerstein, 1977; Parke & Slaby, 1983; Patterson, 1981; Seidman, Rappaport, & Davidson, 1980).

Aggression in School

Family factors other than learned patterns of aggressive behavior may contribute to peer conflict. Teachers report an increase in fighting among pupils whose parents are getting divorced (Goldman & King, 1985). Although not as clearly documented, other family crises may also contribute to aggressive outbursts at school—

problems with siblings, economic stresses in the home, family loss, and so on. When school personnel detect unusual behavior on the part of a child, one of the first possibilities that comes to mind is that of problems at home.

The school setting itself may provide the stimulus for aggressive behavior, for example, when an individual responds aggressively to save face, or as a defense against the humiliation of failure. The association of academic failure (measured by test scores, grades, rank within a class or grade level) with disruptive behavior in school and with later delinquency has been well-documented (Farrington, 1980; Hindelang, Hirschi, & Weis, 1981; Kelly, 1980; Pink, 1982; Robins & Ratcliff, 1980; Sanders, 1981; Wright & Jesness, 1981).

In their work on therapeutic classrooms, Holmes, Holmes, and Field (1974) found that disruptive students had poor impulse control, little tolerance for frustration, and operated in terms of anger and getting even. They also showed deficits in reality testing, and used disruption as a means of gaining attention and concealing academic deficiences—in the authors' terms, "better bad than dumb."

There is considerable controversy as to the relative contributions of school and family variables to academic achievement (or failure), and the degree to which academic outcome is a cause or effect in a longer sequence of failures and misbehavior (Harootunian & Apter, 1983). Although family variables are highly predictive of aggressive behavior, experience in school is likely to enhance or reduce the likelihood of aggressive tactics by the individual. Examples are the reinforcement or extinction of aggressive responses, behaviors modeled by teachers and peers, and the ratio of success and failure experiences of the student in academic (including the arts), athletic, or social realms.

REFERENCE GROUPS: CLIQUES, CROWDS, AND GANGS

Reference groups refer to the sets of people to which one feels one belongs, or wants to belong. It is a psychological relationship between self and other—these are the people who *count* (Sherif & Sherif, 1964). The relationship may have elements of "settling for" in that the member may not be entirely up to group standards, or the individual may have had higher aspirations for status. Such nuances may become sources of conflict.

Cliques are small, tightly knit friendship groups; crowds represent larger, more loosely connected affiliations, and gangs fall somewhere in between. Gangs are generally male, usually with a leadership hierarchy and a clear identity, demonstrated by a name, appearance, or apparel.

Group Conflict

Cliques and crowds may operate quite independently of one another on campus.

They may inhabit different places on the school grounds, attend different classes, and sit in particular areas in the cafeteria so as to avoid out-group contact entirely. Tightly knit cliques or gangs are more likely to come into conflict when they are adjacent in status or territory, than would groups with overlapping membership or little clique or gang identity. On the other hand, clearly defined and well-established territory and status may reduce open displays of conflict, particularly when there is little competition.

Conflicts over territory or status may be generated in the service of maintaining group solidarity, as will forays into the territory of others. Vandalism, racial harassment, and other forms of aggression also serve a similar purpose.

Community gang structures may be replicated on the school grounds, and off-campus conflicts and weaponry may be imported as well. Gang membership serves adolescent needs for identity and intimacy or belonging. Environmental pressures, seeing no alternative, and the possibility of rewards outweighing the costs, are other forces contributing to the development of gangs. In the words of Sherif and Sherif (1964) "Whenever the goals, interests, or activities of one group imply the defeat of those of another group, the relations between these groups in so many specific situations will be characterized by conflict" (p. 229). In other words gangs do not fight only because they are gangs (although fighting may occur in the service of group solidarity), but also because they see themselves as having something to win or lose.

Racial Conflict

Racial conflict may show up in gang violence, or may occur between cliques or individuals. In their study of desegregation in southern schools, Crain, Mahard, and Narot (1982) pointed out that elementary schools have better race relations than high schools. Low contact between races in adolescence is not simply a matter of recent desegregation. There is a well-documented pattern of picking friends from similar backgrounds in childhood. In addition, desires for status and the need for sexual expression in adolescence foster self-segregation with regard to race. Because conflict between rival groups is fairly common in secondary schools, it is not unusual for it to occur along racial lines. In the 200 high school studied, Crain et al. found that most interracial conflict was verbal rather than physical.

TRANSITORY STATES AND CONDITIONS

Children and adolescents who are absorbed in some activity are less likely to engage in conflict than those who are bored. Fatigue plus irritability may increase conflict, while fatigue plus relaxation is likely to decrease it.

The following circumstances also may affect the incidence of peer conflict (Linneweber, Mummemdey, Bornewasser, & Loschper, 1984):

- social density—number of persons in the room.
- spatial density—amount of space per person.
- spatial mobility—degree to which students are moving about.
- audience—presence of bystanders, depending on who they are, will increase or decrease the likelihood of open conflict.

REDUCING PEER CONFLICT

Intervention and Primary Prevention— Improving School Climate

Detection of emerging conflicts is more likely in a situation where there is a strong element of trust, and that generally involves prior acquaintance and interaction. School staff members who know the students, spend time with them, and who are familiar to them, are more likely to engender trust and confidence than is a stranger, no matter how well qualified. Often, students will select their own intimates from among the adults in the school. It may be a favorite teacher, the attendance clerk, a custodian, the bus driver, or a cafeteria worker—even on occasion, the vice-principal. Preliminary findings from an intervention program in Charleston, South Carolina, indicate that promoting a sense of belonging, along with improved disciplinary practices, reduces school disruption (Gottfredson, 1984).

The importance of access to a variety of people with whom to form relationships may be overlooked in the provision of specialists for pieces and parts of the individuals. Although a professional may target the reading problem or adjust the visual difficulty, there may be no provision made for the whole person. The transition from elementary school to junior high with its multiple classes, specialized teachers, and ancillary professionals is another example of the tendency to reduce the student to a set of component parts and skills.

Ironically, the professionalization of education may have contributed to there being no person who feels singularly responsible for a student. Perhaps even more serious is the likelihood that there is no one to whom the student feels any responsibility. Thus, one suggestion for reducing alienation, that may be expressed in conflict, is to encourage every adult in the school to assume a sense of responsibility for knowing and caring about particular students.

Fostering Cooperation and Interdependence.   There is a well-documented body of research from social psychology that clearly demonstrates the value of interdependent group activity in forging bonds and reducing individual and intergroup conflict (Cook, 1984). The classic Robbers Cave study of the early 1950s demonstrated how intergroup rivalry in boys could be reduced by their having to work together in the achievement of a common goal (Sherif & Sherif, 1956). With desegregation in the armed forces and the schools, many naturalistic and experimental studies have been made of interracial contact and its role in reducing conflict (Miller & Brewer, 1984).

Results of these studies show quite clearly that active interracial contact which involves cooperative interaction on tasks of mutual benefit reduces interracial conflict and increases friendship and respect. A variety of techniques have been used ranging from Aronson's jigsaw technique in which each person in a group learns part of the material and is responsible for teaching it to someone else, to studies in which teamwork is encouraged and rewarded (Johnson, Johnson, & Maruyama, 1984; Slavin, 1979). Fostering cooperative and interdependent activities, particularly when each member of the group is able to make a contribution to the group's success, is a tried and tested means of improving intergroup relations and reducing peer conflict.

Interventions with Individual Students

Behavioral Interventions. Peer conflict in the classroom may be only one of several disruptions. A number of books and articles provide guidelines for behavioral management of disruptive students in the school setting (Bybee, Gee, & Gordon, 1982; Dinkmeyer & Dinkmeyer, 1976; Duke, 1977; Gordon, 1974; Sabatino, Sabatino, & Mann, 1983; Schloss, 1983). Safer (1982) describes exemplary programs for disruptive students, with a special emphasis on junior high. These programs include the use of behavioral management techniques by classroom teachers, individualized programs, special classes, and separate day schools.

Training in psychological problem-solving skills has shown promise in modifying the behavior of aggressive adolescents (Goldstein & Pentz, 1984). In his extensive review, Durlak (1983) concluded that the approach is most effective when accomplishment of a specific task is targeted, (e.g., prevention of drug use or unwanted pregnancy). Reducing peer conflict could be addressed in a similar manner. Training in social problem-solving skills has been used in conflict mediation programs with reported success (Davis & Porter, 1985).

Counseling Victims. In many cases peer conflict will not require particular interventions with victims, for example, when the conflict is minor and when the victim's coping responses are adequate. In some cases, the stress of the conflict may lead to a crisis, as shown in Fig. 10.3.

Restoring equilibrium involves three general factors: realistic perception, situational support, and coping mechanisms. Making the same point in a slightly dif-

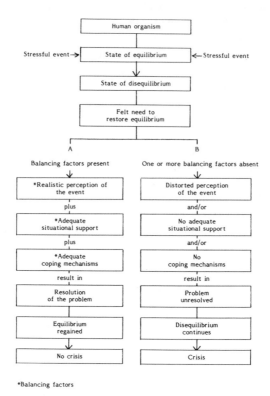

FIG. 10.3.   General responses to stressful events (Aguilera & Messick, 1982, p. 65).

ferent way, Whitlock (1978) referred to the anxiety-provoking and anxiety-suppressive aspects of crisis counseling. The anxiety-provoking aspect requires confronting the facts of the crisis—Aguilera and Messick'a realistic perception (Fig. 10.3). Facing the crisis may be the appropriate counseling response to denial and the shifting of the problem to the counselor. Maladaptive responses on the part of the student are challenged—hence the anxiety-provoking qualities of the intervention. The anxiety-suppressive components are analogous to situational support and coping—providing emotional support and allowing for the mobilization of the student's resources. Specific steps are:

- letting students tell their story
- reducing anxiety by reassurance
- identifying precipitating events and attempting to eliminate them
- decreasing pressure felt by student
- providing assistance in decision making

- using "anticipatory guidance" where necessary (helping the student to anticipate possible sequelae, such as the recurrence of anxiety, somatic symptoms, etc. associated with traumatic experiences).

More detail is provided for the anxiety-suppressive intervention than the anxiety-provoking one, perhaps a reflection of an emphasis on support which underlies much of the crisis intervention literature. However, the opportunity for increased self-knowledge should not be missed, particularly where the student's own behavior has been maladaptive. These approaches are not mutually exclusive, and can be combined in counseling sessions, particularly those extending beyond a single meeting.

In summary, when counseling victims, a fundamental requirement is careful, active listening with quiet and relaxed attention. This demonstration of interest and concern reassures youngsters and allows them to mobilize their own resources in confronting the crisis. It may be appropriate to physically remove the individual from a hazardous situation. Such a move, although not directly solving the issue, provides time for personal development. Behavioral training in social skills may be appropriate for victims as well as for perpetrators. In the NIE study, described earlier, youngsters who were victims in some instances were offenders in others.

Counseling Strategies for Mediating Differences

Chapters in this text by Sandoval and others specify the counseling principles applicable in crises in the school setting. These general principles will apply when dealing with peer conflict as well. The additional aspect is that in cases of peer conflict, the counselor may be cast in the role of third party or mediator, having to attend to both sides of a dispute instead of being in the more accustomed role of listener to one party. The following recommendations provide some guidelines (Bybee et al., 1982):

1. Try to proceed after the parties are calm, rational, and organized.
2. Use new approaches to regulate interaction if old ones have failed.
3. Recognize and acknowledge the conflict. (If recognizing it is inappropriate, i.e., creating a problem where none previously existed, proceed differently.)
4. Demonstrate the legitimacy of all parties to the conflict.
5. Develop a sense of community for parties to the conflict.
6. Make sure rules are known, clear, unbiased, and adhered to by all parties.
7. Use cooperative rather than competitive procedures.
8. Consider personality differences, but focus on the problems not the persons.
9. Reduce large conflicts to smaller components and resolve these in an orderly fashion.

10. Emphasize the similarities between parties.
11. Identify the possibilities for solutions successful to both parties.
12. Reach a consensus on the problem by having the parties
    a. describe the conflict situation.
    b. express feelings and meanings.
    c. describe the desired situation.
    d. suggest necessary changes.
    e. establish an agenda for resolving the conflict and avoiding future ones.

Conflict Mediation and Resolution

Edelson (1981) has outlined a small-group training program to teach children in the upper elementary school grades a specific set of skills for successful conflict resolution. A group format is used and the training involves (a) playing roles, (b) observing others, (c) making suggestions and giving feedback, and (d) completing assignments between group sessions.

Operating on a larger scale is a school-based conflict mediation program. The principle of mediation is to resolve conflicts through negotiation rather than to end them through authoritarian means or leaving the scene. Mediation involves three general steps: defining the conflict by listening to all parties, taking a problem-solving approach, and engaging the involved parties in generating possible solutions. A logical strategy avoiding a win–loss competition strategy is best. If the mediation process proceeds satisfactorily, consensus is reached. Working within a school-based and rule-based system, the parties negotiate, evaluate, and decide on a solution.

There are three major projects underway: The School Initiatives Program, San Francisco; Project S.M.A.R.T., New York; and the Hawaii School Mediation Alliance. The American Bar Association has published a description of these.[1] These programs evolved from community-based mediation systems developed over the past decade. In general the programs involve teaching mediation skills to volunteers, including students, and then having them serve as mediators when conflicts arise. The skills are problem solving, assertiveness, listening, leadership, and developing the ability for impartiality. The general training techniques are role playing and simulation. Some schools have mediation teams comprised of youngsters who wear identifying apparel such as T-shirts with the label, Conflict Manager, or some similar message. In some cases the conflict management program is essentially an extra-curricular one. In others it becomes part of the curriculum in social studies or language skills courses.

---

[1] Materials on conflict mediation projects in the schools are available for $8.50 from the National Resource Center, Special Committee on Dispute Resolution, American Bar Association, 1800 M Street, N.W., Washington, DC 20036, telephone (202) 331-2258.

TABLE 10.4
Outline Summarizing Steps to Reduce Peer Conflict

I. Administrative level

    A. Work to make the school a place where students, teachers, and staff want to be.
    B. Establish clear, easily-understood rules and code of conduct.
    C. Provide fair and consistent enforcement of above.
    D. Maintain clear lines of communication between all staff members.
    E. Monitor indicators of conflict (Vestermark & Blauvelt, 1978)
       1. Records of assaults and problem behaviors
       2. Unusual absentee rate
       3. Class-cutting
       4. Rumors
       5. Presence of hate literature on campus
       6. Racial unrest
       7. Student demonstrations
    F. Identify students at risk, those who are
       1. disruptive
       2. having academic difficulty
       3. having difficulty with interpersonal relationships with peers
       4. experiencing problems at home
    G. Implement programs for the above:
       1. Individualized programs remediating academic deficiencies
       2. Behavioral management and social skills training
    H. Consider the establishment of a conflict mediation program.

II. Classroom teachers, counseling staff and school psychologists

    A. Establish clear, easily understood rules and code of conduct.
    B. Provide fair and consistent discipline.
    C. Use interdependent learning tasks
    D. Implement group activities where all participants are able to contribute something of value
    E. Apply behavioral management strategies
       1. Do not ignore conflict (unless it is clearly trivial).
       2. Consider alternatives and outcomes before taking action.
       3. Alter patterns which might be reinforcing conflict behavior.
       4. Listen, explain, and encourage communication.
       5. Reinforce cooperative behaviors among students.
    F. Identify motives for conflict, e.g., attention, power, revenge, or cover for inadequacy, in order to address underlying problems and needs.

III. Physical environment

    A. Design or modify the physical setting to reduce contact leading to conflict.
    B. Maximize visibility of all areas on campus.
    C. Design or modify stairways and corridors to ease traffic flow.
    D. Provide multiple routes to and from campus areas.
    E. In high-conflict situations, consider moving teachers between classes rather than students, particularly if one teacher or staff person can await the arrival of the next.
    F. Identify places-at-risk. Find out from the students the areas that they avoid.
    G. Patrol high risk areas.

IV. Student involvement

    A. Encourage and establish active student participation in governance matters
    B. Assure representation from all segments of the school population.
    C. Establish a student-produced newsletter or newspaper committed to clear factual information and analysis, as well as the expression of opinion.

Many issues must be worked out in establishing such a program, for example, the voluntary aspects—who is eligible, parental permission, types of cases appropriate for mediation, and the degree to which it becomes a component of an on-going school program. In any case, in order to be successful a mediation program must have the support of the school principal and will need a time commitment from some staff member to serve as director or project coordinator.

Mediation procedures offer one alternative in dealing with conflict. Such programs are not panaceas. Setting up a mediation team does not mean an end to conflict. The mediators themselves may become a problem, for example, in their zeal to uncover conflicts. Mediation should serve as an educational step taken toward the development of problem-solving and social skills. At best, mediation is a fill-in measure. It cannot fully substitute for the maturity of individuals being able to settle their disputes among themselves.

SUMMARY

Peer conflicts can be reduced and managed. To do so, however, requires the combined efforts of concerned administrators, classroom teachers, school counselors, school psychologists, and students. Attention must be given to the physical environment as well as to ways to improve communication and to clarify rules and expectations. Table 10.4 (see p. 183) provides an outline summarizing the steps necessary to reduce peer conflict. Schools should be safe places for individuals, and the conflict that does occur should be in the service of individual learning and development.

ACKNOWLEDGMENTS

Preparation of this chapter was supported in part by the Center on Administration of Criminal Justice, University of California Davis. The author gratefully acknowledges the assistance of Lucy Knowles, Donna Myszak, Stacy Nagel, Jim Nieters, and Susan Slager. Dr. William Watkins of the Davis Unified School District made many helpful comments on the manuscript.

REFERENCES

Aguilera, D. C., & Messick, J. M. (1982). *Crisis intervention: Theory and methodology* (4th ed.). St. Louis: C. V. Mosby.

Bandura, A. (1983). Psychological mechanisms of aggression. In R. G. Geen & E. I. Donnerstein (Eds.), *Aggression: Theoretical and empirical reviews* (pp. 1–40). New York: Academic Press.

Barker, R. G., & Gump, P. (1964). *Big school, small school.* Stanford, CA: Stanford University Press.

Blyth, D; & Bush, D. (1978). The transition into early adolescence: a longitudinal comparison of youth in two educational contexts. *Sociology of Education, 51,* 149–162.

Blyth, D. A., Thiel, K. S., Bush, D. M., & Simmons, R. G. (1980). Another look at school crime: Student as victim. *Youth and Society*, *11*, 369–388.

Bybee, R. W., Gee, E. G., & Gordon, E. (1982). *Violence, values, and justice in the schools*. Boston: Allyn & Bacon.

Cook, S. W. (1984). Cooperative interaction in multiethnic contexts. In N. Miller & M. B. Brewer (Eds.), *Groups in contact: The psychology of desegregation* (pp. 155–185). New York: Academic Press.

Crain, R. L., Mahard, R. E., & Narot, R. E. (1982). *Making desegregation work: How schools create social climates*. Cambridge, MA: Ballinger Publishing.

Csikszentmihalyi, M., & Larson, R. (1984). *Being adolescent: Conflict and growth in the teenage years*. New York: Basic Books.

Cullinan, E., Matson, J. L., Epstein, M. H., & Rosemeier, R. A. (1984). Behavior problems of mentally retarded and nonretarded adolescent pupils. *School Psychology Review*, *13*, 381–384.

Davis, A., & Porter, K. (1985). *Mediation in American schools*. (Available from Mediation Project, Administrative Office of the District Court, Holyoke Square, Salem, MA 01970, 617-745-9010).

Dinkmeyer, D., & Dinkmeyer, D., Jr. (1976). Logical consequences: A key to the reduction of disciplinary problems. *Phi Delta Kappan*, *57*, 664–666.

Duke, D. K. (1977). A systematic management plan for school discipline. *National Association of Secondary School Principals Bulletin*, *61*, 1–10.

Durlak, J. A. (1983). Social problem-solving as a primary prevention strategy. In R. D. Felner, L. A. Jason, J. N. Mortisugu, & S. S. Farber (Eds.), *Preventive psychology: Theory, research and practice* (pp. 31–48). New York: Pergamon Press.

Edelson, J. L. (1981). Teaching children to resolve conflict: A group approach. *Social Work*, *26*, 488–493.

Epstein, J. L. (Ed.). (1981). *The quality of school life*. Lexington, MA: Lexington Books.

Eron, L. D. (1980). Prescription for reduction of aggression. *American Psychologist*, *35*, 244–252.

Farrington, D. (1980). Truancy, delinquency, the home, and the school. In L. Hersov & I. Berg (Eds.), *Out of school* (pp. 49–63). New York & Chichester, England: Wiley.

Feshbach, N. D., & Feshbach, S. (1982). Empathy training and the regulation of aggression: Potentialities and limitations. *Academic Psychology Bulletin*, *4*, 399–413.

Freud, A. (1958). Adolescence. In R. S. Eissler, A. Freud, H. Hartmann, & M. Kris (Eds.), *The psychoanalytic study of the child* (Vol. 13, pp. 255–278). New York: International Universities Press.

Gold, M. (1978). Special analysis of offender data. In NIE (National Institute of Education), *Violent schools—safe schools. The safe school study report to the Congress* (Vol. 1) (pg. 32, Footnote 3) Washington, DC: U.S. Government Printing Office.

Goldman, R. K., & King, M. J. (1985). Counseling children of divorce. *School Psychology Review*, *14*, 280–290.

Goldstein, A. P. & Pentz, M. A. (1984). Psychological skill training and the aggressive adolescent. *School Psychology Review*, *13*, 311–323.

Gordon, T. (1974). *Teacher effectiveness training*. New York: David McKay.

Gottfredson, D. C. (1984). *An assessment of a delinquency prevention demonstration with both individual and environmental interventions*. Paper presented at the annual meeting of the American Psychological Association, Toronto, Canada.

Harootunian, B. & Apter, S. J. (1983). Violence in school. In Center for Research on Aggression, *Prevention and control of aggression* (pp. 66–83). New York: Pergamon Press.

Hindelang, M. J., Hirschi, T., & Weis, J. G. (1981). *Measuring delinquency*. Beverly Hills, CA: Sage.

Holmes, M., Holmes, D., & Field, J. (1974). *The therapeutic classroom*. New York: Aronson.

Johnson, D. W., Johnson, R., & Maruyama, G. (1984). Goal interdependence and interpersonal attraction in heterogeneous classrooms: A metanalysis. In N. Miller & M. B. Brewer (Eds.), *Groups in contact: The psychology of desegregation* (pp. 187–212). Orlando, FL: Academic Press.

Kelly, D. H. (1980). The educational experience and evolving delinquent careers: A neglected institutional link. In D. Shichor & D. H. Kelly (Eds.), *Critical issues in juvenile delinquency* (pp. 99–114). Lexington, MA: Lexington Books.

Kelly, J. G. (Ed.). (1979). *Adolescent boys in high school: A psychological study of coping and adaptation*. Hillsdale, NJ: Lawrence Erlbaum Associates.

Linneweber, B., Mummemdey, A., Bornewasser, M., & Loschper, G. (1984). Classification of situations specific to field and behaviour: The context of aggressive interactions in schools. *European Journal of Social Psychology, 14*, 281-295.

Maccoby, E. E., & Jacklin, C. N. (1974). *The psychology of sex differences*. Stanford, CA: Stanford University Press.

Miller, N., & Brewer, M. B. (Eds.). (1984). *Groups in contact: The psychology of desegregation*. Orlando, FL: Academic Press.

Mueller, C., & Donnerstein, E. (1977). The effects of humor-induced arousal upon aggressive behavior. *Journal of Research in Personality, 11*, 73-82.

National Institute of Education. (1978). *Violent schools—safe schools. The safe school study report to the Congress* (Vol. 1; Stock No. 017-080-01830-6). Washington, DC: U.S. Government Printing Office.

Olweus, D. (1979). Stability of aggressive reaction patterns in males: A review. *Psychological Bulletin, 86*, 852-875.

Parke, R. D., & Slaby, R. G. (1983). In P. H. Mussen (Ed.), *Handbook of child psychology* (4th ed., Vol. 4, pp. 547-641). New York: Wiley.

Patterson, G. R. (1981). *Coercive family processes*. Eugene, OR: Catilia Press.

Pink, W. T. (1982). Academic failure, student social conflict, and delinquent behavior. *Urban Review, 14*, 141-180.

Reed, R. J. (1983). Administrators' advice: Causes and remedies of school conflict and violence. *National Association of Secondary School Principals Bulletin, 67*, 75-79.

Robins, L. N. & Ratcliff, K. S. (1980). The long-term outcome of truancy. In L. Hersov & I. Berg (Eds.), *Out of school: Modern perspectives on truancy and school refusal* (pp. 65-83). Chichester, England and New York: Wiley.

Sabatino, D. A., Sabatino, A. C., & Mann, L. (1983). *Discipline and behavioral management: A handbook of teachers, strategies, and programs*. Rockville, MD: Aspen Systems.

Safer, D. J. (1982). Some factors influence school conduct. In D. J. Safer (Ed.), *School programs for disruptive adolescents* (pp. 5-20). Baltimore: University Park Press.

Safer, D. J. (Ed.). (1982). *School programs for disruptive adolescents*. Baltimore: University Park Press.

Sanders, W. B. (1981). *Juvenile delinquency: Causes, patterns, and reactions*. New York: Holt, Rinehart & Winston.

Schloss, P. J. (1983). An integrated social learning approach to the treatment of aggressive reactions. *Education, 104*, 104-112.

Seidman, E., Rappaport, J., & Davidson, W. S. (1980). Adolescents in legal jeopardy: Initial success and replication of an alternative to the criminal justice system. In R. Ross & P. Gendreau (Eds.), *Effective correctional treatment*. Toronto: Butterworths.

Sherif, M., & Sherif, C. W. (1956). *An outline of social psychology* (rev. ed., pp. 301-328). New York: Harper & Row.

Sherif, M. & Sherif, C. W. (1964). *Reference groups: Explorations into conformity and deviation of adolescents*. New York: Harper & Row.

Slavin, R. (1979). Effects of biracial learning teams on cross-racial friendships. *Journal of Educational Psychology, 71*, 381-387.

Valzelli, L. (1981). *Psychobiology of aggression and violence*. New York: Raven Press.

Vestermark, S. D., & Blauvelt, P. D. (1978). *Controlling crime in school*. West Nyack, NY: Parker.

White, J. W. (1983). Sex and gender issues in aggression research. In R. G. Geen & E. I. Donnerstein (Eds.), *Aggression: Theoretical and empirical reviews* (Vol. 2, pp. 1-26). New York: Academic Press.

Whitlock, G. E. (1978). *Understanding and coping with real-life crises*. Monterey, CA: Brooks/Cole.

Wright, W. E., & Jesness, C. E. (1981). Quality of school life, school problem behavior, and juvenile delinquency. In J. L. Epstein (Ed.), *The quality of school life*. (pp.) Lexington, MA: Lexington Books.

Zillmann, D. (1983). Arousal and aggression. In R. G. Geen & E. I. Donnerstein (Eds.), *Aggression: Theoretical and empirical reviews* (Vol. 1, pp. 75-101). New York: Academic Press.

Suicide and the Schools: Intervention and Prevention

John M. Davis
University of California, Davis

Guess this is our last goodbye
And you don't care so I won't cry
And you'll be sorry when I'm dead
And all this guilt will be on your head
I guess you'd call it suicide.
　　　　　　　　　—The Police

Whether it is "Can't Stand Losing You" by the Police, Elton John/Bernie Taupin's "Think I'm Gonna Kill Myself," or the theme song fom M.A.S.H., "Suicide is Painless," the "deadly alternative" permeates our young adult, adolescent, and pre-adolescent music, TV, and motion picture cultures, not to mention our daily newspapers. Because of this awareness and the accumulated statistics on suicide, our state and federal governments search to find ways of understanding and preventing suicide.

The purpose of this chapter is to address four aspects of suicide: the incidence, underlying theory, and strategies for intervention and prevention. The incidence section presents the magnitude of the problem. The theory section contains typologies of suicide, the development of the concept of death in children, and the dynamics of suicide. The intervention and prevention sections address indicators of children and adolescents at risk for suicidal behavior, assessment, intervention options, and prevention. Depression as one of the indicators of suicide potential is discussed, but a review of childhood depression and treatment is beyond the scope of this chapter. Therefore, the focus of intervention is only on suicide evaluation and referral, not on the treatment of the underlying anger and depression.

TABLE 11.1
Suicides by Sex and Race (Ages 15-24)

Sex/Race	All Races	White	Black	All Others
Both sexes	12.4	13.1	7.0	7.5
Male	18.9	20.0	11.6	12.2
Female	6.1	6.6	2.8	3.2

Note: From Bureau of Vital Statistics, 1980.
Per 100,000 population

INCIDENCE OF SUICIDE IN CHILDREN AND ADOLESCENTS

Although estimates differ, it is agreed upon that completed suicides among youths are relatively rare, whereas suicidal ideation and behavior is not. In 1978, only 2 of the more than 32 million children under 10 years of age in the United States committed suicide (Schaffer & Fisher, 1981). Kosky (1983) reported that only one or two children under age 12 per million inhabitants in the United States complete suicide.

In the 15- to 24-year-old category, the number of suicides jumps to 12.4 per 100,000 (Vital Statistics of the United States, 1980). This 1980 figure represents an increase of over 300% since 1950. The rate of 12.4 per 100,000 places suicides third to accidents and homicides as causes of death in this age. Table 11.1 displays the incidences of suicides in the 15- to 24-year-old age group according to sex and race.

Suicide attempts are even more common. Ross (1985), in a survey of a nonclinical population of California high school seniors, found that 12% of the seniors admitted to one or more suicide attempts during their lives, some attempts as early as 6 years old. Suicidal ideation is almost the norm. Hackel (personal communication, March 8, 1985) reported that over 50% of the freshmen class at a small urban college in California admitted to contemplating suicide at least once in their young lives.

Among clinical populations, the incidence of suicide can be greater and these attempts can be made by children as young as 2½ (Rosenthal & Rosenthal, 1984). Pfeffer, Conte, Plutchik, and Jerrett (1979) reported that 72% of an inpatient latency-aged clinic population and 33% of a latency-aged outpatient clinic population (Pfeffer, Conte, Plutchik, & Jerrett, 1980) revealed suicidal ideation, threats, or attempts.

There seem to be reliable sex differences in suicidal behavior, suggesting it is largely a male phenomenon. Schaffer and Fisher (1981) report that the ratio of males to females in the completed 10- to 14-year-old category is approximately 5:1 and in the 15- to 19-year-old category the ratio is approximately 4.2:1. Also boys, like their older male counterparts, tended to use more violent and lethal methods, although as Table 11.2 shows, the gap is narrowing.

TABLE 11.2
Suicide Methods by Sex (Ages 25–24)

Method	Male	Female
Firearm/explosives	63.7	51.0
Drugs/poisons	5.3	23.2
Hanging/suffocation	16.8	9.3
Gas	6.5	6.2
All others (jumping, cutting, drowning, etc.)	7.7	10.3
	100.0	100.0

Note: From Bureau of Vital Statistics, 1980.
      Per 100,000 population

But what about the accuracy of these statistics? Statistics can be inaccurate owing to over- or underreporting. It is safe to assume that suicides are not over-reported because of the denial and social stigma associated with suicide, particularly with children (Toolan, 1975). It is unanimously agreed upon that underreporting is a problem. Ross (1985) stated that she felt suicides were underreported by about 4:1. Perhaps the most careful investigation of the phenomenon is Schaffer's (1974) research. In his study reviewing coroner's records for children, he found that underreporting or misreporting suicidal deaths as accidents probably occurred but the effect on the suicide statistics was relatively slight, the rate increasing from .98 to 1.44 in the 10- to 14-year-old category and from 8.87 to 10.7 in the 15- to 19-year-old category. Thus, a range of estimates exists.

In spite of a generally low rate of completions, given a high school population of 2,000 children, a school psychologist could expect suicidal ideation in perhaps as high as 25-30% of the student body, suicide attempts by as many as 50 students each year, and about one successfully completed suicide every 4 years.

SUICIDE THEORY

Typologies of Suicide

Gould (1965), Beebe (1975), and Everstine and Everstine (1983) have all developed typologies of suicide. Much congruence and overlap exists among these authors' descriptions, so the following is a consolidation of their works. The "types" are indicative of the underlying rationale or processes occurring within the child at the time of the suicide attempt. It serves as an informal diagnostic guide that can help to conceptualize the level of psychopathology, the type of treatment, and the first issues that would need to be addressed in treatment. Seven "types" are discussed.

Psychosis or Personality Disintegration. This type is best represented by a child experiencing auditory hallucinations ordering him or her to kill him or herself or to die. Other children die functioning under an active delusional system. For example, the child or adolescent, under the delusion of being Superman, might leap off a tall building, killing him or herself.

Self-Homicide. The primary causative factor in this type of suicide is intense rage at another. However, for some reason, the rage cannot be outwardly expressed so is turned inwards. Self-murder symbolically represents the murder of someone else.

Retaliation for Real or Imagined Abandonment. In this type, the child hopes that the suicide will accomplish two things when the child is threatened by rejection or abandonment. First, the child beats the adult to the punch (i.e., you can't kick me out, I'm leaving). Second, the child uses suicide as a demonstration of power to compensate for feelings of helplessness and lack of control.

Blackmail and/or Manipulation. In this type, suicide is the ultimate threat. "If you don't treat me better you'll be sorry." This and the previous type are most often seen in families where suicidal threats or gestures are used as power ploys.

Rejoining a Powerful Lost Love Object. In this type, death is thought of as a way to become reunited with a dead significant other, most often a parent or grandparent, but any significant other whose loss is experienced as insurmountable. This type of suicide occurs when the child is unable to move through the grieving process concerning the loss of a loved one.

Atonement for Unpardonable Sins. In this type, death is perceived to be the only way to be relieved of the guilt and "badness" a child feels he or she has engendered. Although very infrequent in occurrence as a suicide type, injury-prone children often fit into a less extreme version of this dynamic.

A Cry for Help. This is probably the type that is the most familiar and most successfully treated. Although they are overwhelmed, regardless of the kind of underlying problem, children in this type are at least aware they have a problem and that they would like to have some other means of coping with it. They either know no other way to cope or to call for help, or other channels have been blocked to them by their guardians, so they turn to suicidal behavior.

A Cognitive-Developmental Perspective

Unfortunately, there appear to be no studies on the evolution of children's ideas about suicide. A small body of literature on the development of children's ideas about death, however, exists. Although helpful, the warning of Orbach and Glaubman (1979) should be remembered:

> Many children show a split in the death concept; they may have a mature concept of impersonal death, but a rather childish concept of their own personal death. Only the exploration of the emotional and personal aspects of the death concept is of value diagnostically and therapeutically. (p. 677)

Nagy (1959) and Anthony (1971) were the first to address the issue of the child's conceptions of death. Although not specifically Piagetian, their findings fit Piaget's theoretical framework. Koocher (1973, 1974) and Wass (1982) use the Piagetian framework to conceptualize their data. All agree that children proceed through at least three distinct phases that are roughly equivalent to Piaget's preoperational, concrete, and formal operational stages (see chapter 8 for an extended discussion).

Safier (1964) says that the youngest children (those here considered preoperational) saw life and death in terms of flux or interchange. At this age, death is "sleeping" or "resting," and is temporary and reversible; therefore, the child cannot conceptualize death as nonexistence so could not be motivated to take his or her own life to achieve it.

In the concrete operational mode, based on logical and naturalistic thinking, death is now understood as an irreversible event. However, children in this phase see death as something that is unlikely to happen to them until they are very old. That is, they see death as concrete and externalized, something that happens to them. It could be that these children are so strongly involved in rule learning, and following, that the rules seem immutable. The strength of the prohibitions on taking one's life, then, would have more force in middle childhood than at other stages. No data on this possibility has yet been published.

In the formal operational period of development (approximately post 12-year-olds), death is seen as not only irreversible but also personal, part of an internal principle which encompasses the self and others. And, as such, suicide would be understandable as a means to an end. Elkind's (1978) idea of "adolescent egocentrism" and the "imaginary audience" would also help explain the rise in suicide in adolescence. He stated:

> The imaginary audience has other negative consequences as well. Suicide, which is rare in childhood, becomes more frequent in adolescence. Although such self-destructive behavior has many determinants, one of these is the imaginary audience. A common fantasy among suicidal persons is the imagined reactions of an audience. Many suicidal persons see their action as a way of punishing those they feel have rejected them. Such persons take pleasure in imagining the grief and remorse of those they leave behind. These imagined reactions are a powerful motive for carrying out the suicidal idea. (p.124)

Thus, as in all other areas, the more developed cognition becomes, the more options become available; that includes negative options such as suicide.

The Dynamics of Suicide

Focus on the Individual. The traditional intrapsychic view began with Steckel (cited in Friedman, 1967), who theorized in 1910 that suicidal ideation and impulse stem from guilt feelings generated by the super-ego. Shortly thereafter, in 1917, Freud (1957) adopted Steckel's formulation and introduced his concept of melancholia, which he postulated was a state between the guilt and the actual suicidal impulse. In other words, Freud implied that melancholia, or the depressive state, is the cornerstone of suicidal behavior.

Within this Freudian view, depression is discussed as both a descriptive syndrome (Carlson & Cantwell, 1982; Toolan, 1975) and as a symptom (Pfeffer et al., 1979), one or both being seen as common prerequisites to suicidal behavior. Carlson and Cantwell (1982) report that "there is a direct association between feeling depressed and feeling suicidal" (p. 365). The inference is that the more depressed the child the more hopeless and helpless he feels until not living, or suicide, is viewed as the only alternative. As can be seen from the typologies, not all suicides can be understood from this perspective.

The interactional view of suicide is well formulated by Everstine and Everstine (1983). Their position is based on a combination of Menninger's (1938) "wish to kill" concept, Bateson, Jackson, Haley, and Weakland's (1956) views as creators of the interactional context, and Schneidman's (1969) notion of a "dyadic suicide." From these writings they distil the following premises:

1. Suicide is an event that is intended to send a message from one person to another;
2. There is one specific person who is expected to receive the message of suicide; for that person, above all, the suicidal act is performed; and
3. The primary content of the message being conveyed is anger. (Everstine & Everstine, 1983, p. 207)

Symbolically, the suicide "victim" is not a victim. Rather, what the suicide attemptor is trying to create is a set of circumstances whereby he or she places the survivor, according to the Everstines, in the "mythic role of murderer" (p. 211) for which the survivor has to bear the burden.

In a study by Cohen-Sandler, Berman, and King (1982), which utilized a variety of life stress and symptomatology measures, they found that "Although 65% of our suicidal children also were diagnosed as depressed, only 38% of depressed children engaged in suicidal behavior. . . . Depressed children are not necessarily suicidal; conversely, not all suicidal children met the criteria for depression" (p. 183).

Cohen-Sandler et al. also stated that the "results of this study suggest further that children's suicidal behavior may be best understood from an interpersonal perspective. . . . Their investments in these relationships [to their families] was often expressed as rage; nearly two thirds of suicidal children also made homicidal threats, gestures, or attempts'' (p.184)

Focus on the Family.   There have also been reports on the families of children who attempt suicide. Investigators taking this interactional position look at the family's hostility and death wishes toward the suicide attemptor (Rosenbaum & Richman, 1970). Pfeffer (1981) lists five features of fixed and long duration that tend to occur in these families:

1. Lack of generational boundaries, authority is not well defined, there are shifting alliances in power that make it unclear as to who is in charge of whom;
2. Severely conflicted marital relationship;
3. The projection of parental feelings onto the child (for example, instead of a father saying ''I hate your mother,'' he will deny this and say that the child hates his/her mother);
4. Symbiotic-like parent–child relationship with one of the parents; and
5. Rigid and inflexible family system within which the child feels no power.

Sabbath (1982) went so far as to offer the concept of the ''expendible child,'' and Rosenbaum and Richman (1970), in their study if the family's role in suicide, found that the majority of the families of suicidal children expressed the feeling that all would be better off if he or she was dead or gone, whereas very few families of the nonsuicidal children expressed such a belief.

A more benign view of the family process in these situations is offered by Cohen-Sandler, Berman, and King (1982), who thought that these families fostered the use of suicide as a coping strategy. Regardless of how benign or malignant the family may be, and there is most probably a continuum rather than an either/or dichotomy, it is clear that the family is in some way actively involved in the suicide process.

INTERVENTIONS

Suicidal Indicators

The American Association of Suicidology (1977) lists five general ''danger signs'': (a) a suicide threat or other statement indicating a desire or intention to die, (b) a previous suicide attempt, (c) mental depression, (d) marked changes in behaviors and/or personality, and (e) making final arrangements. Let us look at these more closely and consider if or how they would become manifest at different developmental stages.

A Suicide Threat.   People who are thinking about suicide often tell others. It may be direct or, unfortunately, indirect. An indirect form at adolescence could be through joking or through references in school assignments, particularly creative writing or art pieces. In concrete and preoperational children it comes indirectly with acting-out, violent behavior often accompanied by suicidal and/or homicidal threats. In discussing latency-aged children, Pfeffer et al. (1980) found that the "specific high-risk factors of childhood suicidal behavior are the wish to die (often verbalized), intense preoccupations with death, and suicidal behavior in the parents" (p. 708).

A Previous Attempt.   It is important not to dismiss previous attempts even if they seemed superficial or attention-getting. This check is a critical part of a suicide evaluation. As previously noted, suicidal attempts and/or ideation in the parents needs to be explored, as well as whether any family abuse (Cohen-Sandler, Berman, & King, 1982) or "death wishes" (Rosenbaum & Richman, 1970) on the part of parents exist.

Specific methods to achieve suicide do not seem to be tied to age. Pills, guns, hanging, and leaping to one's death span all ages. However, there are some obvious differences (e.g., suicide by automobile in adolescents). Something somewhat comparable in middle and early childhood is jumping out of moving vehicles and dashing into traffic. These kinds of attempts are often not viewed as suicidal behavior, but they are often intended as such.

Depression and Marked Changes in Behavior.   Prolonged sadness or apathy, hopelessness, and a move toward social isolation are key and dangerous indicators. Common thoughts are that things are awful, will never get better, and no one can help; there is little interest or pleasure in formerly enjoyable endeavors. Other symptoms that often emerge are changes in eating and sleeping habits, sudden and quite noticeable changes in behavior and/or personality, acting-out behavior, hyperactivity (an agitated depression), school problems, substance abuse, psychosomatic ailments, high risk-taking behavior, and constant accidents or other forms of self-destructive behavior.

Final Arrangement.   This behavior may take many forms. In adolescents it might be giving away prized possessions (e.g., jewelry, skis, records, books, etc.). Although no mention of this behavior appears in the research literature, it seems likely that preoperational children lack the cognitive skills necessary to plan for this kind of behavior. Concrete operational children are more capable of planning, but whether they do so as often as their formal operational counterparts is open to research and speculation.

Suicide Evaluation

The following nine areas need to be addressed so that decisions regarding the child or adolescent can be made. Examples of the kinds of questions found useful for interviewing children and parents are provided in Table 11.3. It is assumed that a positive rapport has been established before questioning. If rapport has not been established, it is then safest to hospitalize, given that the hospital staff will have more time to develop a rapport and to insure closer monitoring until needed information is obtained.

TABLE 11.3
Examples of Evaluation Questions for Children and Parents

Child Questions	Parent Questions
• It seems things haven't been going so well for you lately. Your parents and/or teachers have said _____. Most children your age would feel upset about that.	• Has any serious change occurred in your child's or your family's life recently (within the last year)?
• Have you felt upset, maybe some sad or angry feelings you've had trouble talking about? Maybe I could help you talk about these feelings and thoughts.	• How did your child respond?
	• Has your child had any accidents or illnesses without a recognizable physical basis?
• Do you feel like things can get better or are you worried (afraid, concerned) things will just stay the same or get worse?	• Has your child experienced a loss recently?
• Other children I've talked to have said that when they feel that sad and/or angry they thought for awhile that things would be better if they were dead. Have you ever thought that? What were your thoughts?	• Has your child experienced difficulty in any areas of his/her life?
	• Has your child been very self-critical or have you or his/her teachers been very critical lately?
• What do you think it would feel like to be dead?	• Has your child made any unusual statements to you or others about death or dying? Any unusual questions or jokes about death or dying?
• How do you think your father and mother would feel? What do you think would happen with them if you were dead?	• Have there been any changes you've noticed in your child's mood or behavior over the last few months?
• Has anyone that you know of attempted to kill themselves? Do you know why?	• Has your child ever threatened or attempted suicide before?
• Have you thought about how you might make yourself die? Do you have a plan?	• Have any of his friends or family, including yourselves, ever threatened or attempted suicide?
• Do you have (the means) at home (available)?	• How have these last few months been for you? How have you reacted to your child (anger, despair, empathy, etc.)?
• Have you ever tried to kill yourself before?	
• What has made you feel so awful?	

Note: Words and phrasings should be changed to better fit the child and/or interviewer.
Two things need to be accomplished during this questioning: (a) to gather more information about the child and (b) to try to evaluate the parents in terms of their understanding, cooperation, quality of connection with their child, energy to be available to a child in crisis.

Suicidal Potential.   Pfeffer et al. (1979) proposed a 5-point spectrum of suicidal potential ranging from "nonsuicidal" to "serious attempt." The 5-point spectrum of potential is as follows: (a) nonsuicidal; (b) suicidal ideation (including controlled thoughts and uncontrolled thoughts such as hallucinations or delusions); (c) suicidal threat (e.g., "I'm going to jump off the roof, out of the car, hang myself," etc.); (d) mild attempt (a self-destructive act that the child *believes* would not have killed him or her); (e) serious attempt (any attempt which obviously would have killed the child or the child *genuinely believed* would have been fatal).

Suicidal Plan.   As Beebe (1975) cautioned, suicidal thoughts must be distinguished from actual planning. In evaluating the suicidal potential of a person the lethal potential of his or her plan, the availability of the means, and the sophistication (including developmental level) must be taken into account. There are developmental differences here in that planning is relatively nonexistent in a preoperational child but increases with developmental level. However, there is no guarantee that formal operational adolescents are going to formulate a plan rather than act impulsively, and if they do, there is no guarantee that they will directly communicate it.

Past Suicide Attempts.   This includes both the child's past attempts or any significant others' past attempts. The latter is often overlooked but is of necessity, as stated in the dynamics section of this chapter, because of the profound influence of the child's family and the possibility of covert messages.

Affects and Behaviors.   Pfeffer et al. (1979) found the following feelings and behaviors associated with suicidal children: anxiety, anger, sadness, hopeless resignation, temper tantrums, psychomotor retardation or increase in activity level, defiance, trouble sleeping, social withdrawal, weight loss, alcoholism, drug addiction, running away, firesetting, or other evidence of transformed rage or masked depression.

Family Background.   Is there any drug, alcohol, or child abuse? Are there recent separations or deaths? What is the level of parental depression and/or other psychopathology? What discipline is used, and do the parents have any plan or course of action to deal with the crisis?

Precipitating Events.   Perhaps the most common antecedent is some loss or threat of loss. Other possibilities are health or medication problems, social disgrace, school problems, or loss of the reason to live. Seldom is suicide attempted due to only one event, rather the precipitating event is more akin to the straw that broke the camel's back.

Response from the Support Network.   Under this heading comes Beebe's (1975) notion of a lifeline. "A lifeline is one or more interested persons who want the patient to stay alive. An immobilized other, no matter how significant, is not a lifeline. In fact, if he is immoblized enough, he may unconsciously drive the patient to suicide" (p. 38). It may be that a temporary hospitalization or out-of-home placement may be necessary until an "immobilized other" (an exhausted single parent would be a good candidate) can regain adequate functioning.

Concept of Death. The evaluation of the child's understanding of death is important both to suggest how to reason with the child during counseling as well as to predict how potentially lethal the situation is.

Ego Functioning. Ego functions (e.g., reality testing, intelligence, impulse control, and regulation of affect) and defenses need to be assessed. The more disturbed the ego functions and more primitive the defenses, the less hopeful the prognosis and the more cautious and conservative the interventions.

Post-Evaluation Options

The two primary questions that need to be answered by the suicide evaluation are: (a) In your professional opinion, is the child or adolescent at risk for attempting suicide?; and (b) What interventions are necessary given the answer to the first question?

Hospitalization. If the child or adolescent is assessed to be in imminent danger and needs constant monitoring, hospitalization is required. If the danger is not imminent, a halfway house, crisis intervention, or outpatient psychotherapy are alternatives. The choice depends on a combination of three factors: (a) suicidal risk, (b) family strengths and dynamics, and (c) community resources.

If danger is imminent and legal guardians agree and are cooperative, hospitalization can move smothly as long as the evaluator is aware of the local resources. If the legal guardians disagree or are uncooperative, the evaluator can proceed to initiate the state "involuntary hold"[1] code that usually entails calling the police or sheriff's department and having the child or adolescent taken to the emergency/crisis clinic or a psychiatric clinic or hospital.

When dealing with minors, especially adolescent minors, there is sometimes a gray area when the legal guardians agree to the hospitalization but the child or adolescent does not. If the guardians cannot control the child or adolescent and facilitate the hospitalization, the law enforcement authorities should be sum-

---

[1] In California this is referred to by State Law number 5150. This enables authorized personnel, usually the police or an emergency or crisis center, to hospitalize patients without consent for 72 hours if they are suicidal, homicidal, or gravely disturbed, for further evaluation. In California, if at the end of 72 hours more evaluation is needed, a 5151 or 14-day hold can be invoked.

moned. Should this occur it is very important that the guardians are informed about what will happen (e.g., their child may well be handcuffed and taken away in a police vehicle).

After hospitalization, when it is deemed safe for the child or adolescent to leave the protection of the hospital, the decision as to whether the child returns home, to a halfway house, or to a foster home needs to be made. This decision is most often made by the hospital staff after an extended evaluation.

Outpatient Treatment.   Once the crisis has resolved to this point it is unlikely that the school psychologist will be involved. Most experts (e.g., Pfeffer, 1984; Toolen, 1975) agree that long-term (usually more than a year) psychotherapy is necessary and few school psychologists have the time or training to do this. But, the issues that first need to be addressed in therapy are frequency of sessions, medication, and modality of treatment.

The actual treatment, as summarized by Pfeffer (1984), "should focus on helping the child (1) alter his expectation of abandonment and punishment, (2) decrease emphasis on an ideal self, (3) develop healthier identifications, and (4) modify aggressive responses to frustrations and disappointments and reduce depression and hopelessness while increasing self-esteem" (p. 367). Modifications within the family structure and communications system need to be addressed, as might parental psychopathology.

PREVENTION

This section examines a range of intervention and prevention activities. Caplan's (1964) schema for "preventive psychiatry" is used to organize the material. Caplan defines preventive psychiatry as:

> the body of professional knowledge, both theoretical and practical, which may be utilized to plan and carry out programs for reducing (1) the incidence of mental disorders of all types in a community ("primary prevention"), (2) the duration of a significant number of those disorders which do occur ("secondary prevention"), and (3) the impairment which may result from those disorders ("tertiary prevention"). (p. 1617)

Within this context, I consider primary prevention efforts to be those aimed at the total school population prior to any suicidal threats or attempts with the goal of reducing the incidence of suicide; secondary preventive efforts are those interventions aimed at a subpopulation of the total school population who have had contact with the youth who has attempted or completed suicide with the goal of counteracting any "contagion effect" and being available for any crisis precipitated by the event; and tertiary prevention has the goal of intervening with family and friends close to the person who has completed a suicide to help them work through the issues (i.e., guilt, anger, etc.) of the mourning process to reduce impairment.

Primary Prevention

This would consist of any programs or curricula focusing on suicide among youths for the education of students, school personnel, or parents.

One example of a comprehensive curriculum-based preventive approach for students, teachers, and parents is evolving in California. As a result of Senate Bill 947, 1983 and the California Education Code Section 10200, California has established a goal to develop a youth suicide prevention program consisting of classroom instruction, nonclassroom school or community-based alternative programs, and teacher training.

The classroom instruction is to be designed to achieve any of the following:

1. to encourage sound decision making and to promote ethical/moral development;
2. to increase pupils' awareness of the relationship between drug and alcohol use and youth suicide;
3. to teach pupils to recognize signs of suicidal tendencies in self and others and other facts about youth suicide;
4. to inform pupils of available community youth suicide prevention services;
5. to enhance school climate and relationships among teachers, counselors, and pupils; and
6. to further cooperative efforts of school personnel and community youth suicide prevention program personnel.

The nonclassroom programs may include, but are not limited to:

1. positive peer groups or peer-counseling programs;
2. 24-hour "hotline" telephone services staffed by trained professional counselors;
3. procedures for collecting data on youth suicide attempts;
4. intervention and postvention services; and
5. parent education and training.

The content of the teacher training is not specified in the legislation.

During 1984-1985 the project developed drafts of three major curriculum documents: a *Teacher's Guide*, a *Parent Meeting Discussion Guide*, and a brochure, *Teenage Suicide: What A Parent Needs to Know*. These materials were pilot-tested in eight high schools during the 1985-1986 school year.

The 86-page *Teacher's Guide* contains sections on special concerns in teaching about suicide, background information about suicide, an overview of the curriculum, and teaching resources. The classroom curriculum consists of five lessons, each with specific objectives, an introduction and approach, a summary, and a detailed lesson plan. The five lessons are tentatively titled, "What We Know About Suicide," "Pain and Depression Don't Have to Lead to Suicide," "Recognizing the Cry for Help," "How to Help a Friend: Intervention Skills," and "Resources for Helping."

The *Parent Meeting Discussion Guide* includes suggestions on preparing for the meeting, an agenda, a leader's outline, and lecture material. The lecture content summarizes the five lessons, and focuses on five topics: "Teenage Suicide: A Problem Which Must Be Confronted," "The Pressures on Adolescents Today," "The Dynamics of Depression," "Recognizing Danger Signs," and "How to Help a Teen Who is Feeling Suicidal."

The brochure on *Teenage Suicide: What A Parent Needs to Know* summarizes information for parents on the rise in teenage suicide, teenage depression, high-risk adolescents, the danger signs, and what they can do to help.

If materials like the aforementioned are not available, local Suicide Prevention and community mental health centers are willing to provide or collaborate on suicide prevention programs. What may be more difficult than deciding how to begin a preventive program is getting permission from the district to do so. In this section and the following two sections, it is assumed that the political groundwork and education necessary to support these types of interventions have been accomplished. There are many myths and religious and ethical considerations that must be worked through before such a program can begin (see Sandoval, Davis, & Wilson, in press, for a more thorough discussion of these issues).

Secondary Prevention

Let us assume that suicide has been attempted, or worse, completed. The suicidal ideation has been transformed into a well-planned or impulsive action that has resulted in serious consequences and a whole new range of thoughts, feelings, and behaviors may be observed in the suicidal adolescent and peers. Three sets of behaviors should be set in motion by the school psychologist: direct interventions, referral, and consultation.

Direct Interventions.   Interventions may include an assessment as previously outlined, but usually does not because medical and psychiatric personnel are typically involved by this point. Singer (1980) discusses another form of direct intervention. She provides an example of a New Jersey high school where four suicides occurred within an 18-month period. Overcoming resistance, the school's counseling staff and mental health workers from outside the school set up a situation offering counseling to any interested student. About half of the 1,600-member student body participated. The focus of most of the counseling seemed to be the offering of assurance that the student would not kill him or herself, in fact helping the students talk about their primary fear that suicide is contagious. A secondary gain reported was that the students became more sensitive to each other's needs and became more willing to help other students get assistance.

Referral. Most often it is as a result of the direct interventions that referrals get made. The most obvious is the child who survives an attempt along with the child's family if they have not yet come to the attention of the medical and psychiatric personnel.

The other common referral would be those students (and very rarely staff) who were so close to the suicide attemptor or completor that their feelings of guilt, responsibility, and so on, cannot be alleviated by brief counseling in the students' cases or consultation in the staff's cases. Another possibility is a member of the staff or student body who did not know the person but who had been having suicidal ideation or feelings themselves and this event has brought them too close to the edge. Contagion exists. Suicides do serve as powerful models and grant permission to behave in a similar way. However, as Singer's example stresses, it is silence that supports the acting-out while talking about it defuses the situation and reassures the people in difficulty.

Consultation. Consulting to school personnel can be important in three unique ways. First, it can be helpful to the person to air and alleviate some of the feelings and fears and be therapeutic for him or her. Second, if the personnel can be more aware of their feelings with less need to deny these feelings they can become more helpful to students who are feeling the depression, helplessness, and hopelessness that can lead to suicide. And third, as they become knowledgeable, school personnel can become more willing and able to assess suicidal crises and make earlier and more appropriate referrals.

Tertiary Prevention

This area is not generally in the domain of the school psychologist. One form of intervention can be the therapy of the family who survive a completed suicide so they do not decompensate or become symptomatic. Another form is working with the family and the victim of a suicide attempt who has survived but has incurred some permanent disability (e.g., a paralysis) from the attempt.

In the latter situation, the psychologist in the school can help in the evaluation and planning of a continuing educational plan for the now handicapped student. The psychologist may also be called upon to collaborate and/or consult with staff and family around issues that arise during the planning.

CONCLUSION

This chapter addressed what is known about suicide among youths, how it can be understood, and some of the things school psychologists functioning within a school district can do to be helpful. Perhaps, if as professionals we are not feeling as helpless and hopeless as those who attempt suicide, we can intervene in ways that save lives.

What this chapter does not address are the fears, anxieties, and counter-transferential reactions that we experience when forced into life and death decision-making situations. With training, experience, and our own consultations and therapies, we will, ideally, be able to deal with these issues.

REFERENCES

American Association of Suicidology. (1977). *Suicide and how to prevent it.* West Point, PA: Merck, Sharp, & Dome.

Anthony, S. (1971). *The discovery of death in childhood and after.* New York: Basic Books.

Bateson, G., Jackson, D. D., Haley, J., & Weakland, J. (1956). Toward a theory of schizophrenia. *Behavioral Science, 1,* 251–264.

Beebe, John E., III. (1975). Evaluation of the suicidal patient. In C. P. Rosenbaum & J. E. Beebe, III (Eds.), *Psychiatric treatment: Crisis, clinic, and consultation.* New York: McGraw-Hill.

Caplan, G. (1964). *Principles of preventive psychiatry.* New York: Basic Books.

Carlson, G. A., & Cantwell, D. P. (1982). Suicidal behavior and depression in children and adolescents. *Journal of the American Academy of Child Psychiatry, 21*(4), 361–368.

Cohen-Sandler, R., Berman, A. L., & King, R. A. (1982). Life stress and symptomatology: Determinants of suicidal behavior in children. *Journal of the American Academy of Child Psychiatry. 21*(2), 178–176.

Elkind, D. (1978). *The child's reality: Three developmental themes.* New York: Wiley.

Everstine, D. S., & Everstine, L. E. (1983). *People in crisis: Strategic therapeutic interventions.* New York: Brunner/Mazel.

Freud, S. (1957). Mourning and melancholia. In J. Strachey (Ed. and Trans.), *The standard edition of the complete psychological works of Sigmund Freud.* (Vol. 14, pp. 237–259). London: Hogarth Press. (Originally published 1917)

Friedman, P. (Ed.). *On suicide.* New York: International University Press.

Gould, R. E. (1965). Suicide problems in children and adolescents. *American Journal of Psychotherapy, 19,* 228–246.

Koocher, G. P. (1973). Childhood, death and cognitive development. *Developmental Psychology, 9,* 369–375.

Koocher, G. P. (1974). Talking with children about death. *American Journal of Orthopsychiatry, 44*(3), 404–411.

Kosky, R. (1983). Childhood suicidal behavior. *Child Psychology and Psychiatry, 24,* 457–468.

Menninger, K. A. (1938). *Man against himself.* New York: Harcourt, Brace.

Nagy, M. (1959). The child's view of death. In H. Feifel (Ed.), *The meaning of death* (pp. 79–98). New York: McGraw-Hill.

Orbach, I., & Glaubman, H. (1979). The concept of death and suicidal behavior in young children. *Journal of the American Academy of Child Psychiatry, 18,* 668–678.

Pfeffer, C. R. (1981). The family system of suicidal children. *American Journal of Psychotherapy, 35*(3), 330–341.

Pfeffer, C. R. (1984) Modalities of treatment for suicidal children: An overview of the literature on current practice. *American Journal of Psychotherapy, 38*(3), 364–372.

Pfeffer, C. R., Conte, H., Plutchik, R., & Jerrett, I. (1979). Suicidal behavior in latency age children: An empirical study. *Journal of the American Academy of Child Psychiatry, 18*, 679–692.

Pfeffer, C. R., Conte, H., Plutchik, R., & Jerrett, I. (1980). Suicidal behavior in latency age children: An outpatient population. *Journal of the American Academy of Child Psychiatry, 19*, 703–710.

Rosenbaum, M., & Richman, J. (1970). Suicide: The role of hostility and death wishes from the family and significant others. *American Journal of Psychiatry, 126*(11), 1652–1655.

Rosenthal, P. A., & Rosenthal, S. (1984). Suicidal behavior by preschool children. *American Journal of Psychiatry, 141*, 520–525.

Ross, C. (1985). *A survey of high-school seniors.* Reported at presentation on The Youthful Suicide Epidemic, Berkeley, CA.

Sabbath, J. C. (1982). The suicidal adolescent—the expendable child. *Journal of the American Academy of Child Psychiatry, 8*, 272–289.

Safier, G. (1964). A study in relationships between the life and death concepts in children. *Journal of Genetic Psychology, 105*, 283–294.

Sandoval, J., Davis, J. M., & Wilson, M. P. (in press). The prevention of adolescent suicide in the schools. *Special Services in the Schools.*

Schaffer, D. (1974). Suicide in childhood and early adolescence. *Journal of Child Psychology and Psychiatry, 15*, 275–291.

Schaffer, D., & Fisher, P. (1981). Suicide in childhood and early adolescence. In C. F. Wells & I. B. Stuart (Eds.), *Self-destructive behavior in children and adolescence.* New York: Van Nostrand Reinhold.

Schneidman, E. S. (1969). Prologue: Fifty-eight years. In E. S. Schneidman (Ed.), *On the nature of suicide.* San Francisco: Jossey-Bass.

Singer, M. T. (1980). Teenage Suicide: A growing problem. *Forcast for Home Economics, 25*, 34–36.

Steckel, W. (1967). Presentation (1910). In P. Friedman (Ed.), *On suicide* (pp. 1–24). New York: International University Press.

Steckel, W. (1910). Reported by Friedman (1967), In P. Friedman (Ed.), *On suicide* (pp. 1–24). New York: International University Press.

Toolan, J. M. (1975). Suicide in children and adolescents. *American Journal of Psychotherapy, 29*, 339–344.

Vital Statistics of the United States. (1980). *State and metropolitan data book—1979.* Washington DC: U.S. Department of Commerce, Bureau of the Census.

Wass, H. (1982). Parents, teachers and health professionals as helpers. In H. Wass & C. A. Corr (Eds.), *Helping children cope with death: Guidelines and resources.* Washington, DC: Hemisphere.

12

Adolescent Parenthood:
Crisis for Males and Females

Barbara S. Hardy
St. John Parish, Louisiana

Adolescence is a period marked by rapid physical growth, the challenge of numerous complicated developmental tasks, and the need to adjust to physical, intellectual, social, and emotional changes. Today's adolescents mature physically at a younger age than those of past generations (Foster & Miller, 1980). In achieving an appropriate sense of identity, the adolescent must confront issues of anticipated future achievement, self-concept, relations with authority, and peer acceptance. Personal relationships become important and meaningful during this period, not only because of peer acceptance but also because of the need for intimacy with others. This intimacy may extend to sexual involvement with the opposite gender (Levering, 1983).

Since the earliest studies concerning sexual behavior between unmarried young people (Bromley & Britten, 1938; Davis, 1929; Hamilton, 1929), societal attitudes concerning sexual behavior have been gradually changing toward more tolerance of sexual expression of feelings (Dreyer, 1982). The implications of society's increasingly tolerant attitudes and the adolescents' management of their sexual behavior should be areas of concern to the adolescent, parent, and educator. Knowing the needs of today's adolescents and the resulting behavior may help to provide proper guidance and direction for adolescents.

SCOPE OF THE PROBLEM

Adolescent Sexuality

Adolescent sexual behavior has increased markedly since the 1930s. Although it is difficult to determine the reason for the rise in sexual activity among teenagers and college-age youth, it is possibly a result of the need to achieve personal identity through intimacy rather than the result of promiscuity (Dreyer, 1982). The increase in sexual activity among adolescents can largely be attributed to the sexual revolution of the late 1960s, which was characterized by a sharp increase in premarital intercourse among adolescents. Trends that began in the late 1960s and 1970s that contributed to adolescent pregnancy include a rise in divorce rates, a more accepting attitude by society toward sexual behavior and "alternative" lifestyles, the rise of the feminist movement, and the availability of reliable birth control in the form of the pill (Lewis, 1982). Today, approximately 7 million teenage men and 5 million teenage women are sexually active (Guttmacher, 1981).

A survey of adolescents ages 13 to 17 reported 44% of males and 30% of females in the United States have had sexual intercourse by age 16 (Sorenson, 1972). Sorenson reported that by 19 years of age, 51% of females and 72% of males have engaged in sexual intercourse.

Although the number of sexually active teenagers has increased, the number of teenage marriages continues to decline. In 1978, 6.9% of adolescent women and 1.6% of adolescent men between 14 and 19 years of age were married (Guttmacher, 1981). This decline in marriage may be attributed in part to the decreasing concern of teenagers to marry in order to legitimize a premaritally conceived child (Lewis, 1982).

Prevalence of Pregnancy Among Adolescents

Although the birth rate for females 16 years and over decreased during the late 1970s and 1980s, the birth rate for females under 16 years of age increased during this same period (Chilman, 1979). The rate of illegitimate births for females under 17 years of age has increased 60% since 1965 and 300% since 1942 (Bolton, 1981). Bolton estimated that approximately 13 million American adolescent females are currently sexually active, and of these, over 10% become pregnant annually. Although two-thirds of these pregnancies are unintended, over half of these females choose to bear their children (Foster & Miller, 1980). There are approximately 1.1 million births to teenagers in the United States annually with over 90% of these teenage mothers opting to raise their children. As a consequence, approximately one of every six babies born are raised by teenage mothers (Guttmacher, 1981).

Gender and Ethnic Differences in Sexuality and Attitudes Toward Pregnancy

Traditionally, permissiveness has been associated with higher educational levels, lower socioeconomic status (SES), greater sexual experience, greater age, being male, and being black. Studies in the 1970s (Cvetkovich & Grote, 1976; Jessor

& Jessor, 1975; Jurich & Jurich, 1974) indicate these associations to not be as strong as in the past. Although men in the past have had more permissive sexual attitudes than have women, men today are only slightly more permissive than females. This change in the way sexual behavior is viewed may be attributed to the general increase in the acceptance of sexual activity among the unmarried (Dreyer, 1982).

Blacks have had and continue to have more permissive sexual attitudes than do whites (Dreyer, 1982). Although the proportion of sexually active black teenagers tends to be higher than that of whites, the increase in sexual activity among whites has narrowed the gap (Lewis, 1982). The average age of first coitus for an adolescent white female is 16.4 and for an adolescent black female 15.5 (Guttmacher, 1981).

Research indicates ethnic differences in birth rate among adolescents with the rate for blacks being higher. Just as there are ethnic differences in birth rate, there are also ethnic differences in pregnancy management, with black teens more likely to oppose abortion and choose to raise their child. White teenagers are more likely to marry before the birth of their child, to have an abortion, or to choose adoption (Burden & Klerman, 1984).

CONTRIBUTIONS TO ADOLESCENT PREGNANCY

The explanations for adolescent pregnancy have varied since the 1920s. During the 1920s, bad peer associations and mental deficiency were considered to lead to adolescent pregnancy, whereas in the 1930s broken homes and poverty were associated with unwed motherhood. Psychological factors such as low educational goals and poor parent relationships were associated with pregnancy of the 1940s, but there was a shift back to the sociological perspective of delinquent behavior in the 1950s (Foster & Miller, 1980). Since the 1960s, however, it has become apparent that there is no single cause of adolescent pregnancy, but many factors that interact (Burnside, Ebersole, & Monea, 1979).

Factors Associated with Adolescent Sexual Attitudes

Sociological. Studies of factors associated with adolescent sexual attitudes have primarily focused upon the sociological variables of race, educational level, nationality, and region of the United States (Dreyer, 1982). Although these factors remain important, there exist other sociological factors, as well as psychological and biological factors, that also contribute to adolescent sexual attitudes. In today's society our teenagers have greater exposure via mass media such as television, movies, and magazines, to permissive sexual norms and explicit sexual activity.

There is probably no period in life when peer pressure is more influential than in adolescence. This pressure often leads to adolescents engaging in coitus with little or no knowledge of the risks involved. If today's youth associate with peers who either have sexually permissive attitudes or are sexually active, they themselves tend to feel pressure to also become sexually active. In addition, many of today's teenagers are subjected to peer pressure to be both attractive to and to please the opposite sex (Dreyer, 1982; Foster & Miller, 1980).

The most important sociological factor contributing to adolescent pregnancy concerns societal standards regarding sex education. Teenagers risk pregnancy by being misinformed, not being informed early enough, or being ill-informed on sexuality, sexual relationships, and contraception because sex education is not taught well or at all in the schools. As a result, the burden rests on the parents to educate their adolescents about these topics. Unfortunately, parents have not accepted this challenge, with the result that today's youth are never properly exposed to this information (Foster & Miller, 1980).

Psychological.   Psychological factors are also contributors to adolescent coitus (Dreyer, 1982). Low educational aspirations, an unhappy home life, beliefs in commitment to a partner, and lack of self-control all are attitudes that have been associated with early sexual activity, particularly in teenagers from low socio-economic backgrounds. These attitudes lead to a sense of hopelessness and help-lessness where sexuality is the only arena for achievement and the only source of gratification.

Limited communication between parents and youth and poor relationships with one's parents are additional factors contributing to adolescent coitus. Because of a poor relationship with one's parents, teenagers tend to reject parental stan-dards, thus leading them to engage in sexual relationships to escape the home environment. The need for the affection that youth have not been and are not receiving from their parents often encourages the teenager to engage in a rela-tionship to meet this need (Chilman, 1979). Some adolescent females believe that a baby and/or a commitment from a partner will address the emptiness in their life. They believe that a baby will fill the void of love and affection not received during childhood from their parents. Additionally, as a consequence of possess-ing strong feelings for a male, some adolescent females engage in coitus, which may result in pregnancy and possibly a commitment by the child's father (Nahashima, 1978).

In younger adolescents, self-control is not as well developed as it is in older adolescents, thus increasing the desire for affection, dependency, and self-esteem. This lack of self-control may make the adolescent more vulnerable psychologically and lead to early participation in coitus (Teitze, 1978).

Biological.   The biological factors associated with adolescent coitus are limited. As a result of the baby boom following World War II there are more adolescents today. In 1979 there were 33 million more women between the ages of 15 and 19 than there were in 1950. Today's youth also reach puberty at an earlier age than those in the past, with the average age of menarche for girls today being 12.5, and the average age for females to conceive being 14. The age of fertility in males today is 15 (Nahashima, 1978).

Factors Associated with Use of Contraception

Knowledge about contraception and the use of contraceptives has not kept up with the increase of sexual activity among adolescents. Numerous studies (Brown, Lieberman, & Miller, 1975; Finkel & Finkel, 1975; Fox, 1975; Kantner & Zelnick, 1972; Miller, 1976; Presser, 1974; Settlage, Baroff, & Cooper, 1973; Sorenson, 1973) report inadequate birth control knowledge and failure to use contraceptives as major problems that have great impact on adolescents and their families.

Data from studies (Fox, 1975; Presser, 1974; Sorenson, 1973) show that only approximately 50% of sexually active female high school and college-age youth used contraceptives at the time of their first intercourse. Studies (Cvetkovich & Grote, 1976; Finkel & Finkel, 1975) reported that approximately 90% of the blacks and 70% of the whites who were sexually active in high school had unprotected intercourse at least once.

Teenagers risk pregnancy by not being informed properly on contraception (Roosa, 1983). Even following instruction on contraceptive methods, they continue to believe that contraception limits the naturalness of sexual relations, that contraceptives may be physically harmful, or that contraceptives are not necessary because pregnancy could never happen to them (Foster & Miller, 1980). The longer an adolescent female is involved in a relationship, however, the more likely she is to use contraceptives and to use them effectively.

A lack of contraceptive use may be attributed to several factors. In some instances, there is a reliance of adolescent women upon men for contraceptive use (Bauman & Udry, 1972; Bauman & Wilson, 1974). A contributing factor to an adolescent's poor use of contraceptives may be associated with the fact that many teenage females are ambivalent about getting pregnant and do not fear pregnancy (Goldsmith, Gabrielson, & Gabrielson, 1972; Luker, 1975; Sorenson, 1973). For many female youth, pregnancy offers a number of advantages including confirmation of the young girl's status as a woman, elevation to the status of motherhood, feeling equal to her own parents, establishment of independence from parents, providing a child to love, testing the father's commitment, proving one's fertility, and gaining the attention of her parents and other adults (Burnside et al., 1979; Chilman, 1979).

According to current research (Cvetkovich & Grote, 1976; Kantner & Zelnick, 1972; Lindemann, 1974; Luker, 1975; Presser, 1974; Rosen, Martindale, & Griselda, 1976; Shah, Zelnick, & Kantner, 1975) there are certain characteristics of women less likely to use contraceptives or to use them effectively (see Table

TABLE 12.1
Characteristics of Contraceptive Misuse

Demographic Variables	Situational Variables	Psychological Variables
Age less than 18	Not in a steady relationship	Desire for pregnancy
Single status	Never pregnant	Ignorance of risk of pregnancy
Low socioeconomic status	Infrequent intercourse	Ignorance of family planning services
Minority group member	Lack of access to a family planning service	Feelings of inferiority
No plans for college	Lack of parental guidance on sexuality	Passivity in relationships
Religious beliefs	Lack of friends using contraceptives	High level of anxiety
	Recent initiation into coitus	Low ego-strength
		Unrealistic view of sexual behavior
		Risk-taking attitude
		Pleasure-seeking attitude
		Fear of side effects and infertility
		Poor communication skills

12.1). These characteristics indicate that a multifactor approach is necessary in response to the various situational and psychological factors contributing to poor contraceptive practice if pregnancies among adolescents are to be prevented.

Because many adolescent females have difficulty accepting their sexual activity, they ignore the use of contraceptives. However, this concept does not appear to be true of females over 18 years of age. These older adolescents are more likely to accept their sexual activity, choose to use contraceptives, and use contraceptives effectively. Characteristics of females using contraceptives includes involvement with one man over an extended period of time and/or engagement in intercourse regularly, which leads to planning for sexual activity. Adolescent females from middle and upper socioeconomic classes are more likely to use contraceptive methods than are females from low socioeconomic backgrounds. Previous experience of having an abortion or a baby as well as the fear of pregnancy are other factors influencing the use of contraceptive methods (Kantner & Zelnick, 1972; Lindemann, 1974; Presser, 1974).

Thus, there is a need for sex education in the schools. Rather than wait until adolescence, this education should begin before youth reach adolescence. Emphasis upon reproduction, methods of contraception by males and females, and instruction on sexuality should be stressed.

PRIMARY PREVENTION OF PREGNANCY

Although it is important that schools incorporate sex education into their curricula, as of 1976 only six states mandated sex education, and 60% of all schools banned discussion of birth control (Cattanach, 1976). The reluctance to provide education in birth control is consistent with the approach of federal agencies that currently promote sexual abstinence as the most effective, if unrealistic, method of contraception (Everett, 1984). School psychologists advocating education on contraception should, therefore, be aware of the possible controversy such a position may provoke. With schools reluctant to educate youth regarding family planning, community-based services designed to meet the special needs of adolescents are a necessity, and practitioners might consider coordinating services with agencies such as Planned Parenthood.

For the majority of teenagers, the classroom teacher is the first source of birth control instruction (DeAnda, 1983). Although schools may provide sex education for the adolescent, more informative instruction on sexuality and contraception is imperative at an earlier age. Programs for upper elementary school children, designed to help them understand the physical changes they are to encounter, should be incorporated into the curriculum. Junior high and high school programs should de-emphasize instruction of human physiology and examine such issues as dating, premarital relationships, details of contraception, and various aspects of married and/or family life (Cattanach,1976). Programs that discuss an individual's rights, needs, and desires in a relationship may help adolescents decide whether to involve themselves in a sexual commitment (DeAnda, 1983). Training of school personnel by professionals who, themselves, have been trained to deal with adolescent sexual dilemmas may foster more effective school programs (Chilman, 1979). With the increasing rate of adolescent pregnancy it is important that schools incorporate sex education into their curricula.

Besides improving awareness of contraceptives, counseling goals should be designed to develop responsibility, socialization skills, personal efficacy, and a positive orientation of future goals. The school psychologist or other guidance personnel should encourage the adolescent to accept his or her sexuality and the adult responsibility that sexual activity connotes. These individuals must learn to accept the conventions of society, take responsibility for their actions, develop a feeling of competency, and establish an internal locus of control of reinforcement. The school psychologist should help each teenager to develop coping and problem-solving skills relating to sexuality, which include knowledge of birth control and reproduction. The school psychologist should help teenagers to plan their future by emphasizing the importance of future goals.

Programs designed to further the education and counseling of adolescents' parents regarding sexuality and birth control may also be warranted. Increasing parent knowledge of adolescent concerns can help them to better guide their teenagers through difficult decisions regarding intimate relationships during adolescence (Chilman, 1979).

School psychologists can play a variety of roles in these primary prevention activities thereby increasing school personnel and adolescents' awareness of the psychologist as someone both interested in and capable of providing services to adolescent parents. As experts in psychosexual development, they may effectively provide teacher training in skills needed to counsel adolescents concerning sexuality issues. They might also serve as guest instructors for sex education classes focusing on personal values and relationship–responsibilities. As a liaison between the school, adolescents, and their parents, psychologists may actively coordinate parent groups, the goal of which is to capacitate parents to open communication regarding sexual matters. Primary prevention programs should begin in elementary school and extend through high school.

SECONDARY PREVENTION

Teenage pregnancy results in risks to both the adolescent parents and the child. Although hazards to the adolescent parents are predominately social and emotional, the child is at multiple risk physically, socially, and cognitively (Landerholm, 1982). The child may suffer medical complications resulting from prematurity, inadequate prenatal care by the mother, and a marginal nutritional status of the mother during pregnancy (McKenry, Walters, & Johnson, 1979). Thus, the role of the psychologist in counseling the adolescent parents should be twofold. First, the practitioner must increase the adolescent female's awareness of the importance of good health and regular visits to the physician during the pregnancy. Second, the psychologist must provide to the adolescent parents information regarding the risks involved to both of them as well as the child. The physical risks to young mothers may be great.

The emphasis of secondary prevention programs should be on identifying and serving those adolescent females who have a possibility of becoming pregnant and who would be excellent candidates for special counseling programs. Although some aspects of these programs may be similar to primary prevention programs, the population served and the counseling goals slightly differ.

Table 12.1 describes characteristics of the most likely adolescent females to avoid using contraceptive measures. These females, along with academically low-achieving females, lonely sexually active females, and females who have been pregnant before are excellent candidates for special preventive programs. Because today's youth are given little consistent guidance for their sexual attitudes and behaviors, adolescents usually are ambivalent about their own sexual attitudes and behaviors (Dreyer, 1982) and are thus good candidates for counseling.

There are several aspects that such a program should address with sexually active females. First might be a focus on relationships and why the teenage female wants to or feels the need to engage in a sexual relationship. Various contraceptive measures and consequences for engaging in coitus without the use of contraceptives should be emphasized. During the program, the female should receive assistance in seriously examining her future goals and how she might obtain them. The guidance counselor or psychologist should try to help the adolescent imagine how achievement of these goals may be more difficult should she have a child to raise.

It is imperative that the psychologist or guidance counselor promote an open-door policy that encourages teenagers to come and discuss personal situations without feeling embarrassed or threatened. In a school setting, the psychologist or guidance counselor may hear of females who may benefit from this program. When this occurs the counselor should seek out these females and encourage them to share problems. The counselor should provide information about adolescence and sexuality. Literature should be made available on contraceptives to enhance female awareness. Literature on outside agencies may also prove useful. To insure the continuation of these teenagers returning for advice or support, confidentiality must be established early.

CRISIS INTERVENTION

The adolescent involved in teen pregnancy confronts two maturational crises in addition to those arising from adolescence—the challenges of adulthood, and the acceptance of parenthood. At a time when support systems are needed, the adolescent discovers there are few resources available for either help or support. Crisis counseling by school psychologists can be beneficial in filling this void. The psychologist can serve both the male and female adolescent involved in pregnancy by offering support and a nonjudgmental attitude, serving as confidant, informing the adolescent of alternatives and resources, and assisting with decision making. Crisis counseling should be directed toward helping individuals accept responsibility for their situation and developing strategies for coping with the pregnancy (Foster & Miller, 1980).

The Adolescent Female

During counseling the practitioner must not only provide information, but must also carefully listen to and assess the individual's reasoning and logic to ensure that alternatives have been thoroughly examined before decisions are reached (Resnick, 1984). In counseling the female adolescent, the school psychologist should prepare her for emotional crises that may be precipitated by : (a) discovering and confirming a pregnancy; (b) disclosing the pregnancy to others; (c) having to make decisions regarding pregnancy alternatives; (d) experiencing labor and delivery; (e) confronting alternatives for raising the child; and (f) having to reassess educational goals.

During the discovery and confirmation period, the psychologist should explore the teenager's feelings and fears about the possible pregnancy. During this time the teenager expresses guilt, hostility, and anger. Should the adolescent find she is not pregnant, family planning, as well as referring the individual to information on sexuality may be recommended. Should the diagnosis of pregnancy by the physician be positive, the psychologist must establish a support system and a trusting relationship with the adolescent. Disclosing the pregnancy to others is one of the most difficult tasks for the adolescent. The psychologist can ameliorate anxiety through positive approaches such as role plays to help prepare the person for others' reactions, or being present to offer support and guidance when the female informs others (Foster & Miller, 1980).

One of the greatest problems for the pregnant adolescent is maintaining a relationship with her own parents. Depending on the age of the minor, in some states, the parents will have some say about the decisions that will be made. In any case, they will need to be informed about the pregnancy at some point. The issue of communication with parents must be dealt with squarely and techniques to help the pregnant teenager prepare for the reactions of her parents must be included in counseling. Chapter 14 in this volume contains more information on parent–child crises.

The practitioner must be prepared to assist teenagers in deciding whether or not to maintain the pregnancy, and if deciding to bear the child, whether to release the child for adoption. Regardless of whether the adolescent chooses to abort, adopt, or keep the child, counseling should continue beyond the point of decision. Depending on the adolescent's choice, the practitioner should assist in contracting appropriate agencies or in enrolling the young parent in classes that offer support and skills necessary for child rearing (Foster & Miller, 1980). Anticipating guidance will prove useful as well as an examination of post-choice emotions such as guilt and depression.

The psychologist should reinforce the importance of education and encourage its continuation during and after the pregnancy. The greatest difficulty the adolescent will face will be the ability to cope with the reactions of peers and teachers. The adolescent will probably feel singled out, alienated, and different from her peers. Thus, it is incumbent upon the psychologist to prepare the individual for these reactions and to explore alternative educational experiences such as homebound programs and adult education (Foster & Miller, 1980).

During the pregnancy, the teenager will have fears about labor and delivery. The psychologist must help the adolescent develop adaptive strategies for coping with labor and delivery. Attendance at childbirth classes should be recommended. The psychologist may assume the role of explaining and discussing labor and delivery to the adolescent (Foster & Miller, 1980).

The Adolescent Male

Little attention or support has been given to the adolescent male in programs or literature involving teenage parenthood; yet adolescent fathers are also in need of counseling and guidance. Research indicates that they are willing to participate in counseling particularly when there is a lack of friends with whom to share their feelings, fears, and concerns (Barret & Robinson, 1981). The participation of the adolescent father, however, rests on his awareness of the programs and the individuals that can assist him. The psychologist might seek out adolescent fathers in neighborhoods or in schools rather than wait for them to come for help, but how and if this is done depends on rights of privacy and confidentiality. In order to make services less threatening and woman-oriented, male psychologists should be available. Expectant father support groups can be formed to provide youths the opportunity to share feelings, fears, concerns, and solutions, and reduce the social isolation common to adolescent fatherhood. Finally, the psychologist can assist in locating teen–parent programs that teach parenting and coping skills.

Adolescent fathers have a variety of needs and concerns. In crisis counseling, the school psychologist should prepare the male for emotional upheaval that may be initiated by (a) a lack of involvement or control in the pregnancy decision and later child care; (b) communication problems with the mother; (c) a lack of communication with members of the mother's family; (d) a reexamination of educational goals; (e) financial obligations to the child and mother; (f) the restriction of freedom concomitant with fatherhood; and (g) the minimal visitation rights with the child after birth. Because of his young age, the adolescent father is typically ill-prepared psychologically for the demands posed by these issues (Barret & Robinson, 1981).

Because the adolescent father may be ambivalent regarding the pregnancy, the school psychologist should inform him of alternatives and encourage him to discuss these with the mother. The practitioner may assist in the couple's decision-making process by facilitating communication during the couple's discussion of alternatives. The adolescent father is usually not cognizant of his role as caretaker and provider (Rothstein, 1978). Because this role may interfere with attainment of educational goals, the psychologist should reiterate the importance of education, assist in the adolescent's re-examination of these goals, and provide alternatives to the male for achieving these goals when faced with financial obligations.

Paternal involvement with the mother and child following pregnancy can be problematic. Cattanach (1976) reported only 29% of unmarried mothers continued seeing the father one or more times per week following pregnancy. Although the majority of adolescent fathers maintain contact with their children for up to 5 years after birth, visitation frequency declines. Given that paternal involvement contributes to the cognitive and social development of the child (Parke, Power, & Fisher, 1980), the psychologist should encourage the adolescent to maintain the contact important for the child's development.

Accepting responsibility in the pregnancy, overcoming feelings of guilt, depression, and adjusting to the social isolation often accompanying fatherhood are issues to be confronted during counseling (Barret & Robinson, 1981). As for the adolescent mother, services for the father should be provided not only during the pregnancy, but should continue into the postpartum period as the father copes with his paternal role and responsibilities.

The Adolescent Couple

Options for the Adolescent Parents—Role of the Psychologist.   Within the first 12 weeks, the adolescent parents must make a decision about the pregnancy. The adolescents are faced with two alternatives: to terminate or to continue the pregnancy. If the second alternative is chosen, the parents must decide between keeping the baby or giving it up for adoption. The psychologist's responsibility is to present both alternatives and to provide the adolescent parents with the opportunity to explore each. The psychologist should aid in the discussion of each alternative. If the parents choose to terminate the pregnancy, they will need support and counseling before and following the abortion to resolve any feelings of guilt.

Should the parents opt to keep the baby, the psychologist should provide a support system. The psychologist will need to assist the adolescent parents in coping with the frustrations of pregnancy and the attitudes significant others may have of them during the pregnancy. During the postpartum period the psychologist should continue to offer support and serve as a resource to assist in teaching parenting skills and in identifying vulnerable areas in the bond that exists between the mother and child.

Should the adolescent parents choose adoption, they must first accept the reality of the baby's existence. Although in the past mothers were not allowed to see their baby before giving it up, today professionals believe differently. Today it is felt that the mother should be allowed to see her child and accept it as reality before giving it up for adoption. The psychologist's role proves to be invaluable to the adolescent mother and father during this period. Because the adolescent parents may feel grief over their decision, it is imperative that the psychologist serve as a support and a source of reinforcement in helping the parents accept their decision of adoption (Foster & Miller, 1980).

SUMMARY

Although there is a role for the school psychologist in adolescent pregnancy, it is still difficult for the practitioner alone to provide the range of services essential in a program to help the adolescent parents. Not only should the school psychologist provide the adolescent parents with information about community services and resources, the practitioner should also help the teenage parents to feel better about themselves, accept their sexuality, and develop coping strategies to adjust psychologically to their new role as parents. The key to developing a better self-concept during this difficult period is through an active and continuous counseling program.

The role of the school psychologist should be to provide services to both parents. Although it is more difficult to engage the teenage father in a counseling program, the psychologist should seek out these males, provide male practitioners to them for counseling, and encourage them to actively participate in the pregnancy as well as the decision-making process. Just as with female youth, counseling with males should continue beyond the postpartum period.

During the provision of services, the school psychologist must be accepting of the adolescents confronting this crisis by maintaining a nonjudgmental attitude. The practitioner must also provide an environment in which the adolescents feel safe to discuss their feelings and concerns. In addition, the school psychologist plays a vital role in offering pregnancy alternatives and facilitating problem-solving strategies. The psychologist should continue to reinforce the importance of education by offering educational alternatives and assist in developing ways to maintain the adolescent parents' interest in the continuation of their education.

REFERENCES

Barret, R. L., & Robinson, B. E. (1981). Teenage fathers: A profile. *Personnel and Guidance Journal, 60,* 226–228.

Bauman, K. E., & Udry, J. R. (1972). Powerlessness and regularity of contraception in an urban Negro male sample. *Journal of Marriage and the Family, 34,* 112–114.

Bauman, K. E., & Wilson, R. (1974). Contraceptive practices of white unmarried university students: The significance of four years at one university. *American Journal of Obstetrics and Gynecology, 118,* 190–194.

Bolton, F. G. (1981). *The pregnant adolescent.* Beverly Hills, CA: Sage.

Bromley, D., & Britten, F. (1938). *Youth and sex.* New York: Harper & Row.

Brown, S., Lieberman, J., & Miller, W. (1975). *Young adults as partners and planners: A preliminary report on the antecedents of responsible family formation.* Paper presented at the 103rd Annual Meeting of the American Public Health Association, Chicago.

Burden, D. S., & Klerman, L. V. (1984). Teenage parenthood: Factors that lesson economic dependence. *Social Work, 29,* 11–16.

Burnside, I. M., Ebersole, P., & Monea, H. E. (1979). *Psychological camry throughout the life span.* New York: McGraw Hill.

Cattanach, T. J. (1976). Coping with intentional pregnancies among unmarried teenagers. *The School Counselor, 23,* 211–215.

Chilman, C. S. (1979). Teenage pregnancy: A research review. *Social Work, 24,* 492–498.

Cvetkovich, G., & Grote, B. (1976, May). *Psychological factors associated with adolescent premarital coitus.* Paper presented at the National Institute of Child Health and Human Development, Bethesda, MD.

Davis, K. (1929). *Factors in the sex life of twenty-two hundred women.* New York: Harper & Row.

DeAnda, D. (1983). Pregnancy in early and late adolescence. *Journal of Youth and Adolescence, 12,* 33–42.

Dreyer, P. H. (1982). Sexuality during adolescence. In B. B. Wolman (Ed.), *Handbook of developmental psychology* (pp. 559–601). Englewood Cliffs, NJ: Prentice-Hall.

Everett, B. A. (1984, October). Adolescent pregnancy. *Washington report, 1.* Washington DC: Society for Research in Child Development.

Finkel, M., & Finkel, D. (1975). Sexual and contraceptive knowledge, attitudes and behaviors of male adolescents. *Family Planning Perspectives, 7,* 256–260.

Foster, C. D., & Miller, G. M. (1980). Adolescent pregnancy: A challenge for counselors. *Personnel and Guidance Journal, 58,* 236–240.

Fox, G. (1975, August). *Sex role attitudes as predictors of contracepive use*. Paper presented at the Annual Meeting of the National Council on Family Relations, Salt Lake City.

Goldsmith, S., Gabrielson, M., & Gabrielson, I. (1972). Teenagers, sex and contraception. *Family Planning Perspectives, 4*, 32–38.

Guttmacher, A. (1981). *Teenage pregnancy: The problem that hasn't gone away*. New York: The Alan Guttmacher Institute.

Hamilton, G. (1929). *A research in marriage*. New York: A. & C. Boni.

Jessor, S., & Jessor, R. (1975). Transition from virginity to nonvirginity among youth: A social-psychological study over time. *Developmental psychology, 11*, 473–484.

Jurich, A., & Jurich, J. (1974). The effects of cognitive moral development upon the selection of premarital sexual standards. *Journal of Marriage and the Family, 32*, 390–399.

Kantner, J., & Zelnick, M. (1972). Sexual experiences of young unmarried women in the U.S. *Family Planning Perspectives, 4*, 9–17.

Landerholm, E. (1982). High-risk infants of teenage mothers: Later candidates for special education placements? *Journal of the Division for Early Childhood, 6*, 3–13.

Levering, C. S. (1983). Teenage pregnancy and parenthood. *Childhood Education, 59*, 182–185.

Lewis, G. M. (1982). Adolescent pregnancy: An interdisciplinary challenge for school psychologists. In J. Grimes (Ed.), *Behavioral strategies for psychological intervention* (pp. 387–422). Des Moines, IA: Department of Public Instruction.

Lindemann, C. (1974). *Birth control and unmarried young women*. New York: Springer.

Luker, K. C. (1975). *Taking chances: Abortion and the decision not to contracept*. Berkley: University of California Press.

McKenry, P. C., Walters, L. H., & Johnson, C. (1979). Adolescent pregnancy: A review of the literature. *The Family Coordinator, 28*, 17–28.

Miller, W. B. (1976, September). *Some psychological factors predictive of undergraduate sexual and contraceptive behavior*. Paper presented at the American Psychological Association meeting, Washington, DC.

Nahashima, I. I. (1978). Teenage pregnancy: Its causes, costs, and consequences. *Nurse Practitioner, 3*(4), 10–13.

Parke, R. D., Power, T. G., & Fisher, T. (1980). The adolescent father's impact on the mother and child. *Journal of Social Issues, 36*, 88–106.

Presser, H. (1974). Early motherhood: Ignorance or bliss? *Family Planning Perspectives, 6*, 2.

Resnick, M. D. (1984). Studying adolescent mothers' decision making about adoption and parenting. *Social Work, 29*, 5–10.

Roosa, M. W. (1983). A comparative study of pregnant teenagers' parenting attitudes and knowledge of sexuality and child development. *Journal of Youth and Adolescence, 12*, 213–223.

Rosen, R., Martindale, L., & Griselda, M. (1976, March). *Pregnancy study report*. Detroit, MI: Wayne State University.

Rothstein A. A. (1978). Adolescent males, fatherhood, and abortion. *Journal of Youth and Adolescence, 7*, 203–214.

Settlage, D., Baroff, S., & Cooper, D. (1973). Sexual experience of younger teen-age girls seeking contraceptive assistance for the first time. *Family Planning Perspectives, 5*, 223.

Shah, F., Zelnick, M., & Kantner, J. (1975). Unprotected intercourse among unwed teen-agers. *Family Planning Perspectives, 7*, 39.

Sorenson, R. (1972). *Adolescent sexuality in contemporary America*. New York: World Publishing.

Sorenson, R. (1973). *Adolescent sexuality in contemporary America: Personal values and sexual behavior ages 13–19*. New York: World Publishing.

Teitze, C. (1978). Teenage pregnancies: Looking ahead to 1984. *Family Planning Perspectives, 10*, 209–216.

Intervention with the Homosexual Adolescent

Gary Ross-Reynolds
Nicholls State University

THE PHENOMENOLOGICAL WORLD OF THE HOMOSEXUAL ADOLESCENT

I've been having these feelings for other guys for at least 12 years and sometimes I'm OK with them and I feel good about myself. And then other times, well, . . . I hope they'll go away and I deceive myself for awhile but they don't go away. I think about what mom and dad would say if they knew. They'd be so hurt and I've already hurt them a lot.

I've never done anything with any other guys except maybe once, but I'm not sure. I was drinking and doing some dope with this other guy and we were feeling good, like hippies in the 60s, you know, out looking at the leaves on the trees and going "wow!" And I put my arm around him and softly stroked his arm, and he said to cut the shit that it was just the drugs, but I knew it wasn't. And then I had a blackout, and I don't know what happened, but I wonder.

If anybody knew about me they would freak. I look straight and nobody would suspect. And you really can't talk to anybody about it or I'd be an outcast. I told a couple of counselors once. One said it was just a phase I was going through and everybody has those feelings, and the other one said it was because I masturbated. So I really didn't deal with it, and they gave me an excuse to keep on deceiving myself. I also told some friends once and they flipped out. One guy had been seduced when he was little and he was afraid I was going to do something to him. The other wouldn't have any more to do with me. And then this guy at work that was married with kids, he looked rough with a scraggly beard and I thought he was a red neck, and he found out and it was no big deal to him. So you can never tell how somebody is going to react. . . .

219

I'm not here to find out if I'm gay. I want to feel better about myself, to stop pretending to myself. Like I have these sexual dreams about other guys and I feel real good in the dream and after I wake up I feel bad. I'm embarrassed about telling you about the dreams, ashamed. There's not a day that goes by that I don't have these feelings for other guys, sometimes several times a day, not always, but yet it's always there. So I'm always aware of being different, of not fitting, of having to hide, of being unacceptable. You can't possibly know what that feels like. It's real lonely sometimes but mostly I've handled it. But I don't know what I'll do in the future. I know that there's certain things I can't do that I want to do like have a family. I'm interested in education but if anyone found out about me I could never have a career in that field. . . . It's scary talking about this stuff, but it feels good, too, to finally be straight with somebody about it, to really be heard and not judged or excused.

—Bill, age 18

Bill's story, intact with minor details changed, spilled forth in his initial counseling session. Although its theme and variations could be repeated by thousands of Bill's or Linda's anywhere, the pain and conflict are uniquely, solely his. As a member of possibly the largest and certainly the most invisible minority group in the United States, Bill and others like him are left to grapple with powerful, undeniable feelings that the homophobic society of which they are a part has condemned as pathologic, sinful, and unlawful. Their collective struggle typically occurs in lonely isolation, outside the institutions of the school, church, family, or hostile peer culture. As adolescents, they are left with the daunting task of developing a positive self-identity as they struggle with shame, guilt, and self-contempt inculcated by the rejecting majority culture.

In the following pages, issues of definition, prevalence, and origin are presented. Problems confronting adolescents grappling with homosexual feelings are examined within the context of the social milieu in which they are raised. Finally, the role of the school psychologist in facilitating positive identity formation is discussed.

WHO IS HOMOSEXUAL?

Definition

On the face of it, arriving at a definition of *homosexuality* may seem to be simple; in fact, the issue of definition is quite complex. Compare, for example, Eric, who has frequently engaged in sex with males since his early teens yet vehemently denies he is homosexual, with Paul, who identifies himself as homosexual in the absence of any same-sex sexual experience. Although these examples may represent extreme positions in the interest of making a point, they are by no means contrived.

The popular misconception that one can readily distinguish homosexuals by mannerisms, dress, or lifestyle aside, there are few enduring criteria by which to discriminate homosexuals from heterosexuals. Although Kinsey, Pomeroy, and Martin (1948) long ago recognized that homosexuality and heterosexuality were not dichotomous, or as they put it, "the world is not to be divided into sheep and goats" (p. 639), there has been a propensity in both professional and popular circles to do just that. Some writers have attempted to avoid the complexities inherent in a definition of homosexuality by opting for a strictly behavioral definition. For example, Kremer, Zimpfer, and Wiggers (1975) view such behavior as that which "occurs when people of the same sex seek sexual stimulation or satisfaction with each other" (p. 96). Such a definition ignores the intrapsychic dimensions (evident in Paul's arriving at a self-definition as homosexual in the absence of overt behavior), the context in which the behavior occurs, and the quantitative dimensions. Homosexual behavior in the context of a same-sex environment such as a prison or boarding school may carry a different meaning than when it occurs in mixed society. Similarly, such behavior during latency or early adolescence may simply "be used for such developmental purposes as information-gathering, comparison, reassurance, and experimentation" (Glasser, 1977, p. 218) and not carry any prognostic significance. Finally, a behavioral definition ignores the issue of relative frequency of same-sex versus opposite-sex contact. For these reasons, a strict behavioral definition is, therefore, at once too limiting and too inclusive in its scope to be of practical value.

Kinsey et al. (1948) recognized both the behavioral and psychological dimensions of sexuality by classifying individuals on separate unidimensional, bipolar continua of 0 (exclusively heterosexual) to 6 (exclusively homosexual) based on both psychosexual reactions and overt behavior. Money and Ehrhardt (1972), too, discussed the need to discriminate between homosexuality defined as a sexual act as opposed to a "permanent state of erotic disposition and preference" (p. 228). More recently, just as masculinity and femininity have been conceptualized as independent from each other rather than as a unidimensional, bipolar continuum, Storms (1980) promulgated a two-dimensional model of sexual orientation yielding four possible sexual orientation categories: asexual, heterosexual, homosexual, and bisexual.

In the context of this chapter, homosexuality is defined as a phenomenon arising in early childhood characterized by emotional attachments and erotic fantasies directed toward persons of the same sex. Such responsiveness usually, but not necessarily finds its expression in overt sexual experiences, and does not preclude heterosexual arousal (Marmor, 1980a; Saghir & Robins, 1973). This definition, gives primacy to the psychosexual rather than the behavioral component of sexuality, or as T. S. Weinberg (1983) expressed it, to the concept of "being" homosexual with the implication that individuals identify themselves as such as opposed to "doing" homosexual wherein self-identity as homosexual cannot be assumed. The importance of this distinction is discussed in the context of adolescent self-disclosure and identity formation later in the chapter.

Many individuals who identify with the definition of homosexuality as articulated in the preceding paragraph would, nevertheless, take issue with the label *homosexual* due to its negative connotations. The term unduly emphasizes sexual acts and carries society's implications of shame and guilt as well as the still-recent stigma of a psychiatric diagnosis (Norton, 1976; G. Weinberg, 1973; Woodman & Lenna, 1980). The term *gay*, on the other hand, connotes emotional, spiritual, intellectual, and affectional involvement with members of the same sex rather than just sexual involvement. "Gay is proud, angry, open, visible, political, healthy, and all the positive things that homosexual is not" (Morin & Schultz, 1978, p. 139). For G. Weinberg (1973) the gay-identified person has developed a positive self-identity, eschewing non-gay society's negative attributes with which the homosexually identified person is still burdened. The power of labels and the importance they have for an individual's self-perception cannot be dismissed (T. S. Weinberg, 1983). Although "homosexual," not to mention "faggot," "fairy," "dyke," and "queer" are epithets, "gay"—a relatively new word in the lexicon—is an affirmation of a positive self-identity.

Prevalence

Besides definitional difficulties, given the opprobrium associated with homosexuality in American society it is impossible to determine what percent of the population is homosexual because unknown numbers of individuals remain closeted all their lives. Homosexual individuals can be found in all strata of society. They are represented in every profession, at every socioeconomic level, in every racial and ethnic group, and in every political, religious, and social organization. Although dated, the Kinsey findings are still considered reliable, although possibly low estimates of the prevalence of homosexuality in American society. Kinsey et al. (1948) estimated that 25% of men have had more than incidental homosexual experience for at least 3 years between ages 16 and 55; 10% are predominantly homosexual for at least 3 years, and 4% remain so throughout their lives. At least 37% of adolescent males and 60% of preadolescent males engage in some homosexual behavior. For females, the prevalence is much lower than for males, ranging from 2% to 6% of the population among both adolescents and adults (Diepold & Young, 1979; Kinsey, Pomeroy, Martin, & Gebhard, 1953). The greater visibility of homosexuals in society today notwithstanding, it is generally agreed that the incidence of homosexuality has remained fairly constant over the decades.

Origins of Homosexuality

As Marmor (1980a) noted, in the face of powerful cultural taboos against homosexuality, it is intriguing why millions of men and women, nevertheless, are homosexual. Although writers vigorously promulgate various causes, there is no single underlying causative factor for homosexuality. Like heterosexuality, its roots are multiple, diverse, and complex; in spite of voluminous literature addressing the issue, its origins are still shrouded in mystery.

Although there is considerable disagreement among professionals about the origin and nature of homosexuality, there are also some areas of consensus. For example, in spite of the widely publicized concern of Anita Bryant that openly gay individuals may influence children's sexual orientation (Raspberry, 1977), there is agreement among philosophically diverse professionals that modeling is irrelevant in acquiring a homosexual identity (Bieber, 1976; Marmor, 1980a; Stoller et al., 1973; Warren, 1980). In fact, children of openly gay or lesbian parents are apparently no more frequently homosexual than their peers growing up in non-gay households (Green, 1978; Hotvedt & Mandel, 1982; Kirkpatrick, Smith, & Roy, 1981). Sexual orientation, whether homosexual or heterosexual, is established early in life, probably prior to age 5, and certainly before the onset of adolescence. Further, it is generally agreed that the prevalence of homosexuality in a society is little influenced by whether the greater society is accepting or rejecting of such behavior.

In searching for causes of homosexuality, many mental health professionals have regarded disturbed parental relationships as the smoking gun (Bieber et al., 1962; Socarides, 1968). However, their conclusions that a family pattern characterized by a dominant, seductive mother, and an aloof, weak, and rejecting father is the sine qua non of homosexual identity formation are without empirical support (Green, 1980). Such a reductionistic and simplistic viewpoint ignores both the homosexual for whom this family pattern does not fit and the heterosexual for whom it does. Similarly, biologic theories have failed to explain adequately the occurrence of homosexuality. No consistent biologic differences between homosexuals and heterosexuals have been discovered whether examining hormones, chromosomes, gonadal changes and morphology, genetics, or cerebral function (Hendryx, 1980; Money, 1980; Newton & Risch, 1981). Interestingly, individuals whose gender at birth is ambiguous due to problems of genital morphology almost invariably display heterosexual interest with respect to their arbitrarily assigned gender regardless of their biologic gender (Money & Dalery, 1976; Money & Ehrhardt, 1972).

Although homosexuality was declassified as a mental disorder by both the American Psychiatric Association and the American Psychological Association (Conger, 1975), many individuals still regard it as such (Bieber, 1976; Marmor, 1980b; Socarides, 1978). Although psychoanalysts remain the most vocal proponents of the homosexuality-as-disease model, Freud himself emphasized that pathology was not inherent in homosexuality and that homosexuals should not be considered sick nor treated as such (Freud, 1951; Marmor, 1980b). The data, gathered long after Freud's death, are on his side. For example, Reiss (1980) concluded from a review of 23 studies conducted between 1967 and 1977 that homosexuals could not be distinguished from heterosexuals on the basis of projective test responses. Similarly, the MMPI and other tests such as the 16PF have failed to identify any consistent differences between homosexuals and heterosexuals (Dean & Richardson, 1964, 1966; Gonsiorek, 1982). In short, there are no psychological assessment instruments that reveal greater pathology among homosexuals than heterosexuals (Green, 1980; Marmor, 1980b; Reiss, 1980), and in the light of current data, "theories contending that the existence of differences between homosexuals and heterosexuals implies maladjustment are irresponsible, uninformed, or both" (Gonsiorek, 1982, p. 80).

COUNSELOR ATTITUDE AND TRAINING

As noted earlier, to be homosexual in American society carries a profound stigma. Psychologists and other mental health professionals confronted with an adolescent in the throes of a sexual identity crisis immediately find themselves face-to-face with their own beliefs, attitudes, biases, and stereotypes about homosexuality. Having been reared themselves in a homophobic and heterosexist society, their professional status neither shields them from these values nor bestows rationality, objectivity, or competence in dealing with this highly charged issue.

For example, in the absence of any validating data, the usually rational Albert Ellis stated, "I used to think that most homosexuals were neurotic. Now I think that maybe 50% of them are borderline psychotics" (Karlen, 1971, p. 223). Garfinkle and Morin (1978) demonstrated the presence of bias among psychologists who were asked to rate an individual from a case history. The histories were identical except for the gender and sexual preference of the person depicted. Nevertheless, heterosexual clients were rated as more healthy than the homosexual clients, and male psychologists were more negative in their attributions of homosexuals than were females. A study of a variety of mental health practitioners revealed that social workers displayed the most negative attitudes toward homosexuality and psychologists least (DeCrescenzo, 1983/1984). However, it was not clear whether the groups in DeCrescenzo's study were matched on such intervening variables as personal sexual preference, marital status, or religious values, all of which were found to be related to degree of homophobia.

Mental health professionals are generally ill-prepared to effectively intervene with homosexual individuals (Graham, Rawlings, Halpern, & Hermes, 1984), and the ineptitude the practitioners demonstrated in assisting Bill at the opening of this chapter cannot be dismissed as an isolated phenomenon. Although the therapists responding to the Graham et al. study were extremely liberal in their attitudes toward homosexuals, they "demonstrated only a modicum of basic information about lesbian and gay male lifestyles that is available in the scientific literature" (p. 486); recognizing this, 83% reported that they needed special training and knowledge to counsel homosexual clients effectively. As therapists, their major concerns centered primarily on their own biases and prejudices that could interfere with therapy, followed by lack of knowledge of homosexuality and homosexual lifestyles.

Liberal bias may be expressed by the belief that sexual orientation really makes no difference. Such an attitude negates the fact that for most lesbians and gays their sexual orientation has had a profound and pervasive impact on their lives that cannot be cavalierly dismissed (Messing, Schoenberg, & Stephens, 1983/1984). At the other extreme, homophobic professionals may react with hostility, or they may exaggerate the significance of the client's sexual orientation even though it is not relevant to the presenting problem. Still others may show pity or deny the possibility of a homosexual love interest as in the therapist who was observed to repeatedly refer to a lesbian client's lover as "he." The therapist had missed the fact that the client herself had repeatedly, assiduously, and awkwardly avoided using a pronoun or name to refer to her lover. When she finally told the therapist that her lover was female he immediately tried to dismiss the relationship as a transitory reaction to a bad heterosexual marriage.

In order for professionals to serve their homosexual clients effectively they must become knowledgeable of lesbian and gay male lifestyles and informed about social support systems within the gay community. They must examine personal biases and become aware of how these prejudices affect their therapy. Becoming better informed about homosexuality by reading professional and positive gay literature is an important component of the professionals' education. However, it is also essential that psychologists and others explore their personal boundaries and broaden their experience through participation in gay consciousness-raising groups and interpersonal involvement with gay and lesbian individuals. Participation in gay and lesbian cultural, social, and political events can provide an excellent avenue for becoming aware of and mitigating one's homophobia and stereotypes.

CRISIS COUNSELING

Homosexual/Heterosexual Differentiation

Concerns about homosexuality may surface for the school psychologist in a variety of ways. Students, themselves, may broach the issue either as a presenting concern or one that may arise during the course of counseling centering on other issues. Some students may first present a smoke screen of several non-issues which serve to test the trustworthiness of the school psychologist before risking the censure that they fear may accompany a disclosure of homosexual concerns. At other times the intervention of the school psychologist may be sought by teachers who feel inadequate in dealing with an adolescent who has confided a homosexual orientation. Other school personnel, too, such as principals or guidance counselors, may seek the services of the school psychologist in managing a situation in which a student is targeted by peers for persecution for real or imagined homosexual activity. Parents, either as the result of disclosure by their child of his or her homosexuality, or their discovery of their child in a sexually compromising position with another person of the same sex, may also seek the counsel of the school psychologist.

Regardless of the avenue through which the issue of homosexuality comes to the attention of the school psychologist, both the professional and client are soon likely to confront the need to differentiate whether the adolescent is, indeed, homosexual. In some situations the psychologist may have serious concerns that the adolescent has inappropriately or prematurely labeled him or herself as gay. Possibly, the youth has attached unwarranted meaning to exploratory homosexual behavior common among adolescents, both heterosexual or homosexual. In other instances the student may inappropriately have accepted the judgment of peers who have labeled the student based on astereotypic interests or behaviors. The issue of differentiation may also arise in the absence of homosexual behavior but in the presence of a strong same-sex attraction. More rarely, the psychologist may also be confronted with a youth who denies any homosexual inclination while engaging in frequent same-sex liaisons.

Differentiating whether or not a student is homosexual may provide the illusion of clarity and the sense of security of having been properly categorized both for the psychologist and the client. At best, such differentiation may represent for some adolescents the affirmation of a positive self-identity as an individual who is gay. At worst, the closure represented by differentiation may prematurely and inappropriately result in a self-label at variance with the adolescents' emerging and changing awareness of their sexual self, thereby hindering or delaying the formation of a positive sexual identity, either as heterosexual or homosexual. Many now consider the very concept of a homosexual identity to be destructive because it places individuals in a stigmatized, dehumanizing category and does not recognize the possibility that their identity may change in the course of their development (Cass, 1983/1984).

Differentiation, although perhaps sometimes necessary and desirable in the counseling process with adolescents, is difficult enough when working with adults. For example, many individuals holding theoretical orientations as diverse as psychoanalytic and behavioral question whether homosexuality even exists as an identifiable psychological syndrome (Birk, 1980; Gundlach, 1969; Morin, 1977; National Institute of Mental Health, 1969; Stoller, 1975). Stoller (1975; Stoller et al., 1973) argued that for a syndrome to be present there must be a constellation of symptoms shared by a group of people, based on similar underlying dynamics (pathogenesis) and having a common etiology. Homosexuality does not constitute a syndrome because only a sexual preference is evident, not an identifiable cluster of symtoms, and because there is no common underlying psychodynamic or etiology among homosexuals. Indeed, the inability of psychology or medicine to differentiate reliably between homosexuals and heterosexuals, as well as the professions' failure to account for the variety and diversity of adult sexual practices lends support to this assertion.

The issue of differentiating between homosexual and heterosexual children and adolescents is even more complex. Often adults and children inappropriately and harmfully label the child who displays cross-gender behaviors (i.e., the feminine boy or the masculine girl) as homosexual. Retrospective evidence does indicate that adult homosexual men and women more frequently report that they engaged in cross-gender behavior as children (Saghir & Robins, 1973; Whitam, 1977) although there appears to be little difference between heterosexual and homosexual adults in their self-ratings of masculinity, femininity, and androgyny (Heilbrun & Thompson, 1977; Storms, 1980). Further, significant proportions of homosexuals do not report this pattern of cross-gender behavior in childhood while some heterosexuals do. It is, therefore, impossible to discriminate whether effeminate boys, for example, are preheterosexual, prehomosexual, or pretranssexual (Green, 1980).

Although the majority of males engage in same-sex sexual behavior at some time during preadolescence or adolescence, most neither continue such behavior as adults nor go on to develop a homosexual identity. Conversely, sizeable numbers of homosexuals engage in no homosexual behavior until after high school (Schofield, 1965). Further, homosexual behavior in early adolescence may be less predictive of future sexual orientation than the same behavior in late adolescence. Therefore, the presence or absence of such behavior is neither a valid nor reliable indicator of a homosexual identity.

Empathy

When adolescents declare, in whatever manner, that they are gay or that they are concerned about a possible homosexual orientation, the first concern of the school psychologist is to communicate acceptance both of the individual and of the possibility of the individual's homosexuality. Because of the extreme stigma attributed to homosexuality in American society, it is almost certain that adolescents coming to the psychologist with this concern have adopted the larger society's negative evaluation of homosexuality and will be particularly sensitive to any signs of disapproval by the psychologist. The acceptance by the school psychologist in the face of such a potentially damning and high-risk disclosure from the youth's point of view will facilitate, perhaps more than any other intervention the psychologist may make in the course of counseling, the development of a positive self-image.

Establishing Client Concerns

Having created a context of genuine acceptance, the school psychologist needs to determine exactly what the adolescent means when he or she raises the issue of homosexuality. Is he concerned because peers label him such due to astereotypic interests and/or effeminate mannerisms? Is she concerned because of a strong crush on a female teacher? Does the concern arise from a transient homosexual desire or isolated homosexual experience? Does the youth truly accept himself as homosexual but find himself unable to cope any longer with the mounting isolation and loneliness while fearing the consequences of disclosure? Are the adolescent's concerns grounded in significant ignorance and misinformation about homosexuality that can be easily and quickly allayed through education? Are negative attitudes about homosexuality the source of anxiety that brought the adolescent to the psychologist?

Clarifying Issues

If the issue concerning the adolescent is one of identity confusion, Woodman and Lenna (1980) have identified several factors that can be explored: (a) degree of sexual arousal of same versus opposite sex, sex of masturbatory fantasies and visual stimuli sought; (b) extent to which same-sex experiences are purposefully initiated and enjoyed by the individual rather than random or incidental; (c) relative frequency of same-sex versus opposite-sex sexual encounters, and gender of client's principal choice for relationships; (d) pattern of same-sex relationships characterized by duration and intensity to the exclusion of opposite-sex attractions; (e) future expectations and fantasies featuring relationships with the same sex; (f) self-identification as gay or homosexual (it is particularly important to distinguish between self-perception and the acceptance of labeling by others, especially in adolescence); (g) discomfort with pressures to date, homosexual jokes, or news of homosexual oppression.

The presence of one or more of these indicators does not mean that the person is gay, nor does the absence of overt homosexual experience indicate that the person is not gay. Although the psychologist can employ the aforementioned variables to assist clients in discovering whether or not they may be gay, the conclusion should be the clients' and not the psychologist's. Both the psychologist and client should be aware that (a) both homosexual and heterosexual experimentation is common among teenagers; (b) finding pleasure in a homosexual act does not necessarily indicate the individual is homosexual; (c) overt homosexual or heterosexual activity by itself is not indicative of sexual orientation; and (d) as a time of sexual discovery there is no need for the adolescent to adopt a self-label or accept a label imposed by others unless it fits with their self-image (Woodman & Lenna, 1980).

HOMOSEXUAL IDENTITY FORMATION— COMING OUT

There are no psychological problems inherent in developing a homosexual identity per se. Probably the event would pass with little more note than that given to heterosexual identity formation were it not for the hostile social context in which it occurs, for to be homosexual in American society today still constitutes a profound stigma. Of modern western societies, the United States remains one of the most hostile toward homosexuality (M. Weinberg & Williams, 1974). A 1970 survey on attitudes toward homosexuality by the Institute for Sex Research (Levitt & Klassen, 1974) revealed that 85% viewed sex acts between two persons of the same gender as always wrong or almost always wrong. Over 75% would deny homosexuals the right to work as judges, teachers, or ministers, and 66% would prohibit them from occupations as physicians and government officials. Approximately 70% of the 3,000 people surveyed believed erroneously that homosexuals try to become sexually involved with children and 50% viewed it as a social corruption with potential to cause the downfall of civilization. Paradoxically, 55% felt that homosexuality was in itself no problem, but what people made of it could be a serious problem, and 84% regarded homosexuality as obscene or vulgar to a moderate or high degree. Nearly 50% would deny homosexuals the right to organize for social and recreational purposes or permit gay bars and 17% would deny gays church membership; yet 68% agreed that what consenting homosexual adults do in private is no one else's business.

Such hostile attitudes are not limited to the adult population. Having had the heterosexist and homophobic values of their parents' culture inculcated since birth, peers of gay adolescents, too, hold generally negative and hostile views toward homosexuality (Price, 1982; Sobel, 1976; Young & Whertvine, 1982). Further, attitudes apparently have changed little over the past 16 years. A recent *Los Angeles Times* (1985) poll found that 73% said homosexuality was wrong, a figure essentially unchanged since 1973.

For both heterosexual and homosexual individuals, societal support for developing a heterosexual identity is strong. The vast majority of adolescents grow up in heterosexual households surrounded by heterosexual role models. Heterosexist values are both overtly and covertly inculcated, and few question the assumption that they will someday grow up, get married, and have children. Heterosexual imprinting begins in childhood before children are aware that another alternative is possible (Penelope, 1979). Concurrent with the positive promotion of a heterosexual identity, strong antihomosexual societal proscriptions serve to reinforce the desirability of heterosexuality and discourage the adoption of a homosexual identity (Lukenbill, 1978).

For homosexual adolescents, this process is obviously inimical to the development of an identity as a gay person. Positive identity formation requires not only that society refrain from attempting to actively eradicate homosexuality through intervention programs but also that it provide active support for the development of a gay identity (Morin & Schultz, 1978). In the current social climate, adolescents greet their dawning awareness of their nascent homosexual preferences with anxiety, guilt, shame, and fear of social disapproval. Isolated from disapproving peers and adults, they withdraw into themselves to cope with feelings of loneliness, inferiority, and difference at a time in their development when affiliation needs are strongest. Not only do they bear the burden of others' disapproval; having themselves adopted the negative values of the greater society, they may struggle against self-loathing as desires over which they have no choosing press for recognition and expression. Possessing a deep stigma not immediately apparent to others, homosexual adolescents constantly face the task of "managing information about (their) failing. To display or not to display; to tell or not to tell; to let on or not let on; to lie or not to lie; and in each case to whom, how, when and where" (Goffman, 1963, p. 43). Such discreditable adolescents live in constant fear of the consequences of discovery ranging from rejection and ridicule to physical danger and eviction from their home. Consequently, they live in secrecy and isolation while torn by a longing to disclose this most important aspect of themselves to those they care deeply about.

Homosexual adolescents confront their dilemma, according to Malyon (1981), either by repressing their homosexual desires, suppressing them and adopting a heterosexual or asexual orientation, or by disclosing their homosexuality. Each course of action is fraught with unique consequences for the individual. The most primitive and unsatisfactory response is made by adolescents who repress their same-sex desires that almost invariably later manifest themselves precipitously and unexpectedly resulting in panic, disruption of coping strategies, and disorganization. Adolescents suppressing their homosexual desires delay positive identity formation sometimes until their 30s or 40s. They may attempt to adopt heterosexual norms of behavior including marriage. Consistent with this view, Troiden and Goode (1980) found that individuals with more high school heterosexual experience were older when they labeled themselves as gay. As homosexual impulses are finally acknowledged and integrated during the delayed coming out process the individual may repeat many of the hallmarks of adolescence such as intense but brief intimate involvements, intense sexual experimentation, and concern with physical appearance. This "biphasic adolescence" (Malyon, 1981) facilitates the completion of adult identity formation.

Those disclosing their homosexual identity during adolescence avoid the developmental hiatus accompanying suppression. However, they risk increased alienation, persecution, and isolation from their peers and family members, difficulties that may be attenuated if there is a community of other gay individuals with whom they can affiliate. Depending on the strength of other personal resources such as degree of self-esteem, disclosure, in spite of its hazards, can lead to increased self-acceptance and freedom from shame and the incessant anxiety of being "found out" (Bales, 1985; Ross-Reynolds, 1982). That 10% of the population manage to achieve a homosexual identity in the absence of visible positive role models and in the face of strong homophobic attitudes and resulting stigma attests to the strength of the phenomenon. That this group of individuals is generally as well adjusted as their heterosexual peers is even more remarkable given the social context from which their identity emerges.

COUNSELING ISSUES

In counseling the gay adolescent, school pscyhologists must be knowledgeable of the developmental process of coming out in which the emerging sexual preference is first recognized and then incorporated into the individual's personal and social identity. Although different writers view the process slightly differently (Dank, 1971; DeMonteflores & Schultz, 1978; McDonald, 1982; Troiden, 1979), in general it is thought to begin with the individuals' awareness of their same-sex attractions and progress to same-sex experience, self-designation as homosexual, significant same-sex relationship, disclosure to significant non-gay others, and finally the achievement of a positive identity as a gay person.

The aforementioned progression notwithstanding, the practitioner should expect, nevertheless, significant individual differences in this process with regard to order, time lapses between milestone events, and age at which milestones are achieved. For example, same-sex attraction may occur after same-sex experience, or a significant same-sex relationship may precede self-designation as homosexual. Likewise, some individuals may be aware of same-sex attractions for many years before they move to the next phase of homosexual activity, whereas others may act on their attractions soon after they emerge into awareness. Finally, with regard to the age at which the process of coming out begins, some homosexuals report they were aware of their same-sex sexual preference during their early elementary years, whereas for others such an awareness did not emerge until adulthood. However, for the majority, the development of a homosexual identity is very much an adolescent phenomenon with awareness of same-sex attraction emerging around the age of 13 and the achievement of a positive gay identity occurring in the early 20s (McDonald, 1982). It appears that homosexual identity formation is occurring at an earlier age now than in the past (Troiden & Goode, 1980); Rector's (1982) study of 33 adolescent homosexuals revealed that the mean age of awareness of attraction was 10.9 with a range from 5 to 15. His sample publicly identified at the age of 16.6 compared to 23 for McDonald's sample whose mean chronological age at the time of the study was 31.

Central to the development of a positive self-identity as a gay individual is disclosure of one's sexual preference to others, particularly non-gay others. Jourard (1971) eloquently articulated the role of self-disclosure in the development of a healthy personality, noting that people can only fully know themselves as they reveal themselves fully to others. As previously noted, disclosure may have its costs, but concealment may be detrimental to psychological well-being (Minton & McDonald, 1984; M. Weinberg & Williams, 1974). The act of revealing undisclosed aspects of the self to another can, of itself, be healing as the burden of maintaining the previously shameful secret is dissolved (Ellenberger, 1966). At the point of initial disclosure of one's identity to another, the gay adolescent is extremely vulnerable because the reaction of the other can have very important consequences for the continued development of a positive identity (Coleman,

1982). Acceptance by the other of the disclosure can be a powerful factor influencing acceptance by the self. Positive responses from close friends and family will, obviously, exert a more powerful positive influence on the adolescent than would a similar response from a stranger. As Coleman notes, rejection by significant others at this vulnerable stage can have very deleterious consequences for positive identity formation, and the process may consequently be aborted, delayed, or made more difficult. For this reason, it is critical that practitioners working with adolescents assist them to carefully choose individuals to whom they will disclose. Although another's reaction cannot be assured, it can be predicted. After adolescents have received numerous positive responses to their disclosure they are less vulnerable to negative reactions. It is important to be aware that for most individuals disclosure is a life-long process with the decisions of whether or not to disclose, how, and when constantly evaluated by the individual in light of the context and probable consequences.

AIDS

AIDS, Acquired Immunodeficiency Syndrome, has recently become an ominous fact of the homosexual milieu. As of March, 1986 over 18,000 cases of AIDS had been reported to the Centers for Disease Control, and approximately 9,600 or 53% of these individuals had died (Louisiana Department of Health and Human Resources, 1986). Homosexual men account for 74% of all AIDS cases in the United States. Geographically, 31% of all victims come from New York City and 11% come from San Francisco.

The current epidemic has fanned the fires of antihomosexual sentiment. A *Los Angeles Times* (1985) poll revealed that 28% of those surveyed viewed AIDS as God's wrath for a sinful lifestyle and 23% said victims have gotten what they deserve. Persons with AIDS (PWA's) fundamental civil liberties are abrogated. At the same time they face the enormous physical and psychological challenge of coping with a debilitating and terminal illness, PWA's have also faced eviction from their residences, loss of employment, abandonment by friends, family and colleagues, and refusal of frightened and ignorant health-care workers and school officials to provide services.

Adolescent males grappling with a homosexual identity may adopt a cavalier, fatalistic, concerned, or fearful attitude toward AIDS. Regardless, school personnel counseling adolescents who may be or soon become homosexually active must realistically address the issue of AIDS, impressing upon youth the seriousness of the risk and ways it might be minimized. It is not sufficient to warn the youth to avoid sexual contact that involves the exchange of body fluids. Such a general warning is at once too delimiting, leaving the adolescent with a sense that essentially all sexual activity is proscribed, especially sexual activity that seems potentially exciting, or too vague, leaving open to misinterpretation exactly what sexual practices are safe. For example, the adolescent may erroneously believe, based on the exchange of body fluid proscription, that anal intercourse is safe if it does not result in orgasm.

Although many psychologists, counselors, and social workers (and their adolescent counselees) may be relatively comfortable discussing a homosexual orientation, candid discussion of explicit sexual practices may elicit squeamishness and embarrassment on both sides. Professionals may cope with their embarrassment through desensitization by viewing sexually explicit films of homosexual activity such as are often shown in sex education classes. Their ability to discuss sexual practices forthrightly communicates a nonjudgmental attitude to the adolescent and models the assertive skills the adolescent will need in communicating with present or future partners about safe sex practices.

In the context of AIDS, responsible sexual behavior involves both selecting the proper partner and engaging in accepted safe sexual activity. With regard to the former, adolescents should not only be informed that they should avoid sexual contact with persons known or suspected of having AIDS, with those having multiple sexual partners, or with those who abuse intervenous drugs, but also that they, themselves, should refrain from multiple sexual partners and intervenous drug use, especially the practice of sharing needles and syringes. In addition, professionals should caution adolescents against the use of amyl and butyl nitrites (poppers) which may be linked to Kaposi's Sarcoma in PWA's.

Safe sexual practices include mutual masturbation, social (dry) kissing, massage, body-to-body rubbing, and using one's own sex toys. Possibly safe practices include French kissing, anal intercourse with a condom, and fellatio interruptus. Anal intercourse without a condom (both receptive and insertive, manual-anal intercourse (fisting), fellatio, urine and oral-anal contact are all considered unsafe (New Orleans/Aids Task Force, no date).

Simple knowledge of appropriate partners and the parameters of safe sex practices will, by itself, probably not result in safe and responsible sexual activity. To apply this knowledge, the adolescent must be sufficiently comfortable to directly inquire about the previous sexual activity of a potential partner, and to openly discuss the parameters of any planned sexual activity. Assertion training focusing on such sexual content may provide the adolescent with the skills necessary to put this knowledge into action. In addition, erotic gay fiction emphasizing safe sexual practices (Preston, 1985) may make such practices more attractive to the adolescent who may otherwise find such guidelines quite restricting. In introducing such material school psychologists are cautioned to remain mindful of community standards and take steps to minimize the likelihood of any possible repercussions.

CONCLUSION

In order to effectively work with gay adolescents, school psychologists must do more than familiarize themselves with the process of gay identity formation; they must also examine their own biases and myths about homosexuality and familiarize themselves with gay and lesbian lifestyles and culture. It is important to realize that counseling is not value-free, and in the initial phase practitioners should discuss their biases with respect to homosexuality, and how these biases will influence the content and goals of intervention (Malyon, 1982). Intervention with the gay adolescent does not require different skills as much as a different sensibility to accompany the specific knowledge-base necessary to work effectively with gay adolescents. One of the main objectives of intervention ''is to provide corrective experiences to ameliorate the consequences of biased socialization'' (Malyon, 1982, p. 62). In addition to exploring the role negative socialization plays in the crisis the adolescent may be experiencing, school psychologists must be prepared to provide positive information on gay and lesbian lifestyles and facilitate supportive contact for the adolescent in the gay community.

REFERENCES

Bales, J. (1985, December). Gay adolescents' pain compounded. *APA Monitor*, p. 21.

Bieber, I. (1976). A discussion of ''Homosexuality: The ethical challenge.'' *Journal of Consulting and Clinical Psychology*, *44*, 163–166.

Bieber, I., Dain, H. J., Dince, P. R., Drellich, M. G., Grand, H. G., Gundlach, R. H., Kremer, M. W., Rifkin, A. H., Wilbur, C. B., & Bieber, T. B. (1962). *Homosexuality: A psychoanalytic study*. New York: Basic Books.

Birk, L. (1980). The myth of classical homosexuality: Views of a behavioral psychotherapist. In J. Marmor (Ed.), *Homosexual behavior* (pp. 376–390). New York: Basic Books.

Cass, V. C. (1983/1984). Homosexual identity: A concept in need of definition. *Journal of Homosexuality*, *9*, 105–126.

Coleman, E. (1982). Developmental stages of the coming-out process. In W. Paul, J. D. Weinrich, J. C. Gonsiorek, & M. E. Hotvedt (Eds.), *Homosexuality: Social, psychological and biological issues* (pp. 149–158). Beverly Hills, CA: Sage.

Conger, J. J. (1975). Proceedings of the American Psychological Association, Incorporated, for the year 1974: Minutes of the annual meeting of the Council of Representatives. *American Psychologist*, *30*, 620–651.

Dank, B. M. (1971). Coming out in the gay world. *Psychiatry*, *34*, 180–197.

Dean, R., & Richardson, H. (1964). Analysis of MMPI profiles of 40 college-educated overt male homosexuals. *Journal of Consulting Psychology*, *28*, 483–486.

Dean, R., & Richardson, H. (1966). On MMPI high-point codes of homosexual versus heterosexual males. *Journal of Consulting Psychology*, *30*, 558–560.

DeCrescenzo, T. A. (1983/1984). Homophobia: A study of the attitudes of mental health professionals toward homosexuality. *Journal of Social Work and Human Sexuality*, *2*(2/3), 115–136.

DeMonteflores, C., & Schultz, S. J. (1978). Coming out: Similarities and differences for lesbians and gay men. *Journal of Social Issues*, *34*(3), 59–72.

Diepold, J., Sr., & Young, R. D. (1979). Empirical studies of adolescent sexual behavior: A critical review. *Adolescence*, *14*, 45–64.

Ellenberger, H. G. (1966). The pathogenic secret and its therapeutics. *Journal of the History of the Behavioral Sciences*, *2*, 29–42.

Freud, S. (1951). A letter from Freud (April 9, 1935). *American Journal of Psychiatry*, *107*, 786–787.

Garfinkle, E. M., & Morin, S. F. (1978). Psychologists' attitudes toward homosexual psychotherapy clients. *Journal of Social Issues*, *34*, 101–112.

Glasser, M. (1977). Homosexuality in adolescence. *British Journal of Medical Psychology*, *50*, 217–225.

Goffman, E. (1963). *Stigma: Notes on the management of a spoiled identity*. Englewood Cliffs, NJ: Prentice-Hall.

Gonsiorek, J. C. (1982). Results of psychological testing on homosexual populations. In W. Paul, J. D. Weinrich, J. C. Gonsiorek, & M. E. Hotvedt (Eds.), *Homosexuality: Social, psychological, and biological issues* (pp. 71–80). Beverly Hills, CA: Sage.

Graham, D. L. R., Rawlings, E. I., Halpern, H. S., & Hermes, J. (1984). Therapists' needs for training in counseling lesbians and gay men. *Professional Psychology: Research and Practice*, *15*, 482–496.

Green, R. (1978). Thirty-five children raised by homosexual or transsexual parents. *American Journal of Psychiatry*, *135*, 692–697.

Green, R. (1980). Patterns of sexual identity in childhood: Relationship to subsequent sexual preference. In J. Marmor (Ed.), *Homosexual behavior* (pp. 255–266). New York: Basic Books.

Gundlach, R. H. (1969). Childhood parental relationships and the establishment of gender roles of homosexuals. *Journal of Consulting and Clinical Psychology*, *33*, 136–139.

Heilbrun, A. B., Jr., & Thompson, N. L., Jr. (1977). Sex-role identity and male and female homosexuality. *Sex Roles*, *3*, 75–79.

Hendryx, S. W. (1980). In defense of the homosexual teacher. *Viewpoints in Teaching and Learning*, *56*, 74–84.

Hotvedt, M. E., & Mandel, J. B. (1982). Children of lesbian mothers. In W. Paul, J. D. Weinrich, J. C. Gonsiorek, & M. E. Hotvedt (Eds.), *Homosexuality: Social, psychological, and biological issues* (pp. 275–286). Beverly Hills, CA: Sage.

Jourard, S. M. (1971). *The transparent self*. Van Nostrand Reinhold.

Karlen, A. (1971). *Sexuality and homosexuality*. New York: W. W. Norton.

Kinsey, A. C., Pomeroy, W. B., & Martin, C. E. (1948). *Sexual behavior in the human male*. Philadelphia: W. B. Saunders.

Kinsey, A. C., Pomeroy, W. B., Martin, C. E., & Gebhard, P. H. (1953). *Sexual behavior in the human female*. Philadelphia: W. B. Saunders.

Kirkpatrick, M., Smith, C., & Roy, R. (1981). Lesbian mothers and their children: A comparative survey. *American Journal of Orthopsychiatry*, *51*, 545–551.

Kremer, E. B., Zimpfer, D. G., & Wiggers, T. T. (1975). Homosexuality, counseling, and the adolescent male. *Personnel and Guidance Journal*, *54*, 94–101.

Levitt, E. E., & Klassen, A. D. (1974). Public attitudes toward homosexuality: Part of the 1970 national survey by the Institute for Sex Research. *Journal of Homosexuality*, *1*, 29–43.

Los Angeles Times. (1985, December 22). Gays still rejected but more sympathy is found in survey. *The Times-Picayune*, p. A-14.

Louisiana Department of Health and Human Resources. (1986). *Acquired immunodeficiency syndrome (AIDS) surveillance report*. Baton Rouge, LA: Author.

Lukenbill, W. B. (1978). *Homosexual conflicts and their resolution in five adolescent novels: A psychological inquiry*. Paper presented at the annual meeting of the Popular Cultural Association, Cincinnati. (ERIC Document Reproduction Service No. ED 169 560)

Malyon, A. K. (1981). The homosexual adolescent: Developmental issues and social bias. *Child Welfare*, *60*, 321–330.

Malyon, A. K. (1982). Psychotherapeutic implications of internalized homophobia in gay men. In J. C. Gonsiorek (Ed.), *Homosexuality and psychotherpy* (pp. 59–70). New York: Haworth.

Marmor, J. (1980a). Overview: The multiple roots of homosexual behavior. In J. Marmor (Ed.), *Homosexual behavior* (pp. 3–22). New York: Basic Books.

Marmor, J., (1980b). Epilogue: Homosexuality and the issue of mental illness. In J. Marmor (Ed.), *Homosexual behavior* (pp. 391–401). New York: Basic Books.

McDonald, G. J. (1982). Individual differences in the coming out process for gay men: Implications for theoretical models. *Journal of Homosexuality*, *8*, 47–60.

Messing, A. E., Schoenberg, R., & Stephens, R. K. (1983/1984). Confronting homophobia in health care settings: Guidelines for social work practice. *Journal of Social Work and Human Sexuality*, 2(2/3), 65–74.

Minton, H. L., & McDonald, G. J. (1984). Homosexual identity formation as a developmental process. *Journal of Homosexuality*, 9, 91–104.

Money, J. (1980). Genetic and chromosomal aspects of homosexual etiology. In J. Marmor (Ed.), *Homosexual behavior* (pp. 59–72). New York: Basic Books.

Money, J., & Dalery, J. (1976). Iatrogenic homosexuality: Gender identity in seven 46, XX chromosomal females with hyperadrenocortical hermaphroditism born with a penis, three reared as boys, four reared as girls. *Journal of Homosexuality*, 4, 357–371.

Money, J., & Ehrhardt, A. A. (1972). *Man and woman, boy and girl: Differentiation and dimorphism of gender identity from conception to maturity*. Baltimore: Johns Hopkins Press.

Morin, S. F. (1977). Heterosexual bias in psychological research on lesbianism and male homosexuality. *American Psychologist*, 32, 629–637.

Morin, S. F., & Schultz, S. J. (1978). The gay movement and the rights of children. *Journal of Social Issues*, 34(2), 137–148.

National Institute of Mental Health. (1969). *Task force on homosexuality: Final report*. Rockville, MD. (ERIC Document Reproduction Service No. ED 173 696)

New Orleans/AIDS Task Force. (no date). *Aids risk reduction*. New Orleans, LA: Author.

Newton, D. E., & Risch, S. J. (1981). Homosexuality and education: A review of the issue. *The High School Journal*, 64, 191–202.

Norton, J. L. (1976). The homosexual and counseling. *Personnel and Guidance Journal*, 54, 374–377.

Penelope, J. (1979). *The articulation of bias: Hoof in mouth disease*. Paper presented at the 69th annual meeting of the National Council of Teachers of English, San Francisco. (ERIC Document Reproduction Service No. ED 179 998)

Preston, J. (Ed.). (1985). *Hot living: Erotic stories about safer sex*. Boston: Alyson.

Price, J. H. (1982). High school students' attitudes toward homosexuality. *Journal of School Health*, 52, 469–474.

Raspberry, W. (1977, May 3). Could gay rights be wrong after all? *Los Angeles Times*, part 2, p. 7.

Rector, P. K. (1982). The acceptance of a homosexual identity in adolescence: A phenomenological study. *Dissertation Abstracts International*, 43, 883B. (University Microfilms No. 82–19, 284)

Reiss, B. F. (1980). Psychological tests in homosexuality. In J. Marmor (Ed.), *Homosexual behavior* (pp. 296–311). New York: Basic Books.

Ross-Reynolds, G. (1982). Issues in counseling the "homosexual" adolescent. In J. Grimes (Ed.), *Psychological approaches to the problems of children and adolescents* (pp. 55–88). Des Moines, IA: Iowa Department of Public Instruction. (ERIC Document Reproduction Service No. ED 232 082)

Saghir, M. T., & Robins, E. (1973). *Male and female homosexuality*. Baltimore: Williams & Wilkins.

Schofield, M. C. (1965). *Sociological aspects of homosexuality*. London: Longmans Green.

Sobel, H. J. (1976). Adolescent attitudes toward homosexuality in relation to self concept and body satisfaction. *Adolescence*, 11, 443–453.

Socarides, C. W. (1968). *The overt homosexual*. New York: Grune & Stratton.

Socarides, C. W. (1978). The sexual deviations and the diagnostic manual. *American Journal of Psychotherapy*, 32, 414–426.

Stoller, R. J. (1975). *Perversion: The erotic form of hatred*. New York: Basic Books.

Stoller, R. J., Marmor, J., Bieber, I., Gold, R., Socarides, C. W., Green, R., & Spitzer, R. L. (1973). A symposium: Should homosexuality be in the APA nomenclature? *American Journal of Psychiatry*, 130, 1207–1216.

Storms, M. D. (1980). Theories of sexual orientation. *Journal of Personality and Social Psychology*, 38, 783–792.

Troiden, R. R. (1979). Becoming homosexual: A model of gay identity acquisition. *Psychiatry*, 42, 362–373.

Troiden, R. R., & Goode, E. (1980). Variables related to the acquisition of a gay identity. *Journal of Homosexuality*, *5*, 383–392.

Warren, C. (1980). Homosexuality and stigma. In J. Marmor (Ed.), *Homosexual behavior* (pp. 123–141). New York: Basic Books.

Weinberg, G. (1973). *Society and the healthy homosexual*. Garden City, NY: Anchor Books.

Weinberg, M. & Williams, C. (1974). *Male homosexuals: Their problems and adaptations*. New York: Oxford University Press.

Weinberg, T. S. (1983). *Gay men, gay selves: The social construction of homosexual identities*. New York: Irvington.

Whitam, F. L. (1977). Childhood indicators of male homosexuality. *Archives of sexual behavior*, *6*, 89–96.

Woodman, N. J., & Lenna, H. R. (1980). *Counseling with gay men and women*. San Francisco: Jossey-Bass.

Young, M., & Whertvine, J. (1982). Attitudes of heterosexual students toward homosexual behavior. *Psychological Reports*, *51*, 673–674.

14

Parent–Adolescent Crises

Marvin J. Fine, Linda D. Roberts
University of Kansas

A number of ''experts'' writing on adolescence have emphasized the increased stress on the adolescent brought about by significant societal changes. Many of these changes relate to the home and include economic stress, divorce, the need for both parents to be employed, and ''culture shock'' changes that create an even greater gap between the growing up experiences of parents and their children (Elkind, 1984; Preto & Travis, 1985; Youniss & Smollar, 1985).

Parent–adolescent crises often occur within the context of the adolescent's striving for independence. Although the crisis may revolve around some specific concern such as choice of friends, curfew, clothing styles, grades, use of family car, drug and alcohol use, or sexual behavior, the underlying issue is frequently that of the adolescent's move toward a more equal position vis á vis the parents.

Several avenues of intervention are available to school mental health professionals within the short-term and action-oriented parameters of crisis intervention. Crisis intervention focuses initially on the present with a problem-solving orientation. The immediate goal is usually to restabalize a situation before moving into a more proactive and ameliorative stance. Although a family orientation would encourage the mental health professional to concurrently include student and parent, this may not always be feasible or even desirable. A number of options exist that could focus on the student or the parents alone. Both parent and student may need to acquire more effective communication and problem-solving skills through separate sessions before coming together.

This chapter examines parent–adolescent crises against the background of the child growing up within a family system. Characteristics of healthy families include clear generational boundaries, support within the family for changing roles and expectations of children as they mature, and constructive communication patterns. The "normal" crises of adolescence becomes exacerbated when nested within a dysfunctional family. The kinds of behavior that get defined as a crisis, who gets involved and how they respond, and traditional patterns of crisis resolution emerge in part out of the family background with its history of parent–child relationship. The new variable is the presence of a school-based mental health professional; the school psychologist, counselor, or social worker. This person can assume leadership in (a) anticipating a crisis and behaving proactively, (b) responding at the time of crisis, and (c) helping the involved parties to exploit the opportunities inherent in a crisis situation toward the modification of crisis-precipitating factors.

A VIEW OF CRISIS INTERVENTION

The discussion draws on the general crisis intervention literature, much of which has already been presented in earlier chapters, but will underscore specific aspects of crisis intervention germane to parent–adolescent crises.

In recent years there has been an increase in both quantity of literature on crisis intervention and on the quality of conceptualization and theory building around crisis intervention. Most persons would agree with Aguilera and Messick (1978) that "The goal of crisis intervention is the resolution of an immediate crisis. Its focus is on the generic present, with the restoration of the individual to his precrisis level of functioning or probably to a higher level of functioning" (p. 26).

But what is an "immediate crisis," and how is this concept useful in relation to parent–adolescent crises? Consider Slaikeu's (1984) definition of a *crisis* as "a temporary state of upset and disorganization, characterized chiefly by an individual's inability to cope with a particular situation using customary methods of problem solving, and by the potential for a radically positive or negative outcome" (p. 13).

Certainly, the sudden precipitation of an event such as the student verbally threatening or physically attacking a teacher, or the school contacting the parents to report that their teenager passed out intoxicated at a school dance, would be generally classified as a *crisis*. Both of these events are likely to energize concerned persons such as school officials and parents, into an active role.

Even though there is evidence of a precipitating event, the history of the development of the crisis and the awareness and involvement of persons may differ. For example, in one situation, a student may appear to others to be getting along well, but in another situation may act strangely enough to concern family, teachers, or friends. Although often in retrospect people can identify some indicators that sensitive observers, parents, friends, and others should have noticed, the behaviors were cloaked enough to cover up their crisis nature. In another instance, for example, that of a student deciding to quit school which provokes a strong parental reaction and throws the family in turmoil, the student may have evidenced a history of school failure with parent–adolescent conflict over grades and study time; however, it was only the decision of the student to actually drop out of school that precipitated the crisis.

Much of the literature on crisis intervention deals with life-threatening, desperate kinds of situations, with suicide being a prime example. Adolescent suicide is indeed of great concern (Grob, Klein, & Eisen, 1983; Jacobs, 1980), but the preponderance of involvements by school mental health professionals is much broader and often less dramatic in focus. Admittedly, crisis issues will vary from one situation to another but the greater frequency of professional involvements are with issues such as school failure, drop-outs, visible depression, drug and alcohol abuse, aggressive/assaultive acts, pregnancy and other sexually related problems such as gay issues, and thefts and vandalism. Additionally, one can envision home-based conflicts between parent and adolescent that are at an impasse, spilling over into the school setting and correspondingly involving school-based personnel.

The question of "who has the problem?" can present a dilemma to the school mental health professional. Although society, in the form of teachers, parents, policemen, or the courts, may perceive the adolescent as being in crisis, the young person may insist he or she can manage without outside help. Also, an adolescent may voluntarily seek out the mental health professional or may confide in a teacher that he or she is experiencing a high stress situation and is having difficulty coping. Alternately, persons familiar with the adolescent and familiar with mental health crisis indicators (e.g., moodines, irritability, reclusiveness, breaking off of old relationships, changes in sleeping or eating habits, sudden drop in grades, etc.) through the media or a school mental health program, now become concerned, cease considering the adolescent's behaviors as a normal variation that will soon pass; and view the adolescent as one who is in crisis and who needs help.

These multiple possibilities for a student coming to the attention of the school mental health professional raise the question of whether the professional should initiate contact with an "involuntary" client, thereby placing the student in the position to refuse involvement and to tell the professional that someone else (i.e., the concerned other) has the problem. Connected to the voluntarism issue is the important question of when should parents be involved? Fine (1982) spoke to that question in relation to counseling adolescents.

> A number of adolescents have conflict around gaining independence and autonomy, and the involvement of their parents may escalate the adolescent's anger . . . it may be judicious in some cases to keep the parents out, until the adolescent feels more comfortable and prepared to deal with them in a counseling situation. (pp. 396-397)

Such judicious judgments may be inappropriate in crisis situations where legal considerations and/or the nature of the crisis may prompt the mental health professional to contact and involve parents.

THE FAMILY CONTEXT OF ADOLESCENCE

Erikson's (1968) writings on the identity issues of adolescence helped professionals and indeed parents to better understand what adolescents might be experiencing. The adolescent's questioning of family values, stronger peer-group identification, and emotional reactivity were seen as the adolescent's struggle to establish a sense of personal identity. The adolescent's need to experience competence and power also become moving forces in terms of the adolescent forming new relationships, seeking new experiences, and asserting him or herself more within the family. Jones (1980) has described how adolescents who are unable to achieve a sense of personal significance, competence, and power tend to exhibit behavior problems.

Popular writers such as Ginott (1969) presented useful information to parents on how to set limits and on how to separate their concern for the child's behavior with their continuing love and support of the child. What was missing from some of the popularized books and even texts on adolescent development was a picture of the family as an organized entity, and how the child was developing within the family. The readily observable physical changes of adolescence can obfuscate the fact that important internal cognitive changes are also occurring (Elkind, 1984; Youniss & Smollar, 1985). The adolescent reasons at a higher level than the younger child and is better able to reflect on issues and indeed on thought, and can comprehend "grey areas." Simultaneously, however, there is a greater emotional investment in friends and the potential for highly moralistic stances. The parents' apparent hypocrisies are revealed and played back. "Well, you drink hard liquor while all I do is have a few beers"; "Your constant cigarette smoking is worse than my occasional pot smoking."

The literature focusing narrowly on the adolescent, his or her response to pubescence, and the personal identity issues, has not paid enough attention to the overall family development picture, parental changes and stress, and the interaction effects of parent–adolescent and family–adolescent relationships. A good example is *The Vanishing Adolescent* (Friedenberg, 1959) in which the adolescent-in-society and educational implications are considered, but in which, even in the chapter on emotional development, the family is "short-shrifted."

This point is underscored by Kidwell, Fischer, Dunham, and Baranowski's (1983) observation that "much of the stress expressed by families during the adolescent years arises out of normative life stage developmental events, experienced to varying degrees in *all* families in which there is an adolescent" (p. 75).

DYNAMICS OF PARENT–ADOLESCENT CRISES

The earlier protective and indeed controlling functions of the family for its child members needs to change as children mature into adolescence (Elkind, 1984; Preto

& Travis, 1985; Youniss & Smollar, 1985). The child is now more likely to challenge the existing family boundaries in terms of values and behaviors, sometimes as mentioned earlier with a highly moralistic logic, or with individualizing statements such as "I'm me, not you," and "I need to decide what's right for me." If the ensuing struggle is won by the parents, then the adolescent's emotional growth may be restricted. If the adolescent wins the struggle, then key family values may be rejected on a wholesale basis, leaving the adolescent even more anxious and unsure in terms of personal values. When parent–child (really family–child) conflict escalates to where indelible lines are drawn, for example, on the order of "If you do _____, you're no longer a member of our family," then, the involved persons become resistive and the issues can get polarized forcing the parties into rigid stances.

The boundaries of the family need to become more permeable to allow for a healthy in-and-out flow of new ideas as the adolescent brings back to the family his or her new ways of viewing the world and modified values. The stands the adolescent takes can challenge key aspects of the family structure such as the authority position of the parents, and in the adolescent's attempt to debate issues, (as if he or she had the right to do so) some cherished family values may be breached. From a more rigid parental stand, the adolescent is being a "smart ass," trying to be in charge, or disrespectful. Under these conditions, tension and conflict grow, and crises are predictable. A common adolescent response to perceived closedness and rigidity of the family system is active rebellion, be it in terms of rejecting school, engaging in sexual activity, drug or alcohol usage, violating family rules, increased arguments and even physical encounters between parents and adolescents.

Crises and Family Histories

One also needs to consider some historical family patterns and dynamics that might have either precipitated or exacerbated the crisis and will eventually need to be addressed in the process of crisis resolution. For example, has the family been relatively disengaged in terms of emotional relationships? Has the adolescent grown up perceiving him or herself as "alone against the world"? Has this been a family that has historically been very supportive of each other with a positive history of family relationships to fall back upon in times of crisis? Some families are so emotionally enmeshed that any move toward individual thinking or value exploration precipitates a family crisis with the adolescent being seen as rejecting the cherished family values and likely to do something "wrong." In the latter case, it is clear that the resolution of the crisis will eventually require some fairly major shifts in the family orientation toward individual behavior.

One aspect of family structure that therapists frequently look to in their attempts to understand family dynamics is the concept of generational boundaries. In some families, if one were just to read a transcript of family interaction, it would be difficult to determine who were the parents and who were the children. One finds examples of this in families of gifted children where verbal precocity sometimes moves the child into a pseudo-parenting role. There are also some families in which a child becomes the ''parental child'' and somehow, possibly through underfunctioning parents, has been allowed or encouraged over the years to assume a more parental role in relation to other family members.

Another window into family dynamics is through understanding the historic alliances and collusions that have been created. In one White family the father and daughter had maintained a supportive relationship over the years and they considered themselves to have a very special understanding. The mother correspondingly often found herself on the outside of their discussions and in instances where there were parent–child disagreements it was typically the mother trying to exercise some restriction on the daughter. The usual family pattern involved the daughter pulling the father into a rescuer role with him often softening whatever limits were placed on the daughter by her mother. It was against this background that the family found itself in conflict over the daughter's intentions to date a Black classmate. Although both parents shared in their strong feelings against the dating the mother was especially hostile toward the father. She maintained that it was his permissiveness toward the daughter that allowed the daughter to reach this point in her dating relationships. The daughter's anger at both parents over what she saw as their bigotry was particularly hurtful to the father who was experiencing the destruction of what to him had been a very special relationship with his daughter. The effects of the conflict eventually moved into the school setting. Teachers commented on the girl's moodiness and her friends became very concerned by what they saw as depression and even possible suicidal thinking.

The counselor scheduled a session with the parents and the daughter to find out what was happening and to see what kind of intervention was appropriate. The first such session produced an immediate surfacing of each family member's anger and frustration with the other. It was apparent that neither mother nor father were equipped by the history of family relationships to discuss the issue in a reasonable fashion. Their attempts at trying to make sense out of what was happening quickly deteriorated into accusations and defensive responses. This event was exceedingly painful to the teenager who, although initially caught up in anger at her parents' reactions, now saw herself as the main cause of this horrible discord. The crisis dimension of the situation expanded rapidly in the counselor's office as his initial interest in gathering some information moved the family into a reenactment of the conflict.

This example illustrates how virtually impossible it is for the crisis counselor to not be confronted with some of the historical family conflicts and therefore the need to deal to some extent with the family history at the time of crisis intervention. The crisis counselor will have to decide whether the extent of historic family discord and dysfunctionality is such that rather than attempting a school-based crisis intervention that an immediate referral to an agency able to offer comprehensive services might be appropriate.

Parental Change and Adolescent Crisis

Another way of viewing parent–adolescent tensions is to consider that not only is the adolescent going through some major personal changes, but the parents are as well (Kidwell et al., 1983). The parents, typically in their late 30's to 40's, may be going through crises related to life goals, job satisfaction, changes in marital relationship, and personal–physical changes. A number of unresovled parental issues may interfere with, or be provoked by the adolescent's behavior (Fine, 1979, 1982; Kidwell et al., 1983; Preto & Travis, 1985). As Kidwell et al. (1983) observed:

> Stress theory would suggest that when the parents' transition periods coincide with the offspring's transitions, the family system will undergo greater strain than when the parents' transition periods occur before or after the adolescence of their children. The presence in the home of an adolescent who questions parental values and customs may exacerbate the parents' own inner turmoil. (pp. 81-82)

The parents preoccupation with their own issues and their sense of vulnerability as they face life-transition decisions, may undermine the kinds of understanding, tolerance, and good humor, needed by parents to cope with changing adolescent behavior.

INTERVENTION STRATEGIES

As discussed earlier, the school mental health professional may have several entrees into a crisis situation. The adolescent may approach the professional with a problem, or the parents may contact the school expressing concern about what they are experiencing with the adolescent, or even third parties such as a friend of the student may contact the professional. The initial considerations of the mental health professional have to do with the urgency and life-threatening nature of the situation and concomitantly the rights of the parent and adolescent (Fine, 1982; Grob et al., 1983). Certainly some behaviors by the adolescent such as physical aggression, drug and/or alcohol abuse, and visible depression need to be responded to immediately and with parental involvement.

In instances where the adolescent shares an ideation or intention that would be harmful to him or herself, or others, the professional needs to communicate with the student as to his or her obligations and also the desirability of involving other people, mainly the parents. One way of conceptualizing the expression of such a crisis is that it is simultaneously a call for help. The crisis may reflect the unbalancing of the family homeostatic system and can represent a quest for someone or something to help put things back in order. Counselors and psychologists in the schools who deal with adolescents manifesting or expressing acute behaviors or thoughts find that the adolescent and parent will focus very quickly on some family relationship issues once they are brought together. Decisions will usually be made fairly early in the intervention process as to how to proceed, whether hospitalization is needed for the adolescent or whether the parents and adolescent can contract together to work on "their" problem.

School-Based Intervention

Families who have a history of healthy family interaction and communication are able to deal with crises as they arise, occasionally seeking some outside help. Many of the crises that come to the attention of school personnel are at a point where perhaps the history of ineffective communication patterns have rendered the involved parties relatively helpless in working toward resolution without the entree of an outsider. One can anticipate that as persons contact the school mental health professional and express their concerns about some parent–adolescent issue, that the parties experiencing the crisis are implicitly or explicitly seeking some direction and support. In the case of parents, they may be looking to the school mental health professional to do what they feel they have not been able to do, which is to correct and influence the "wayward adolescent." This temporary abdication of parental authority speaks to the frustration that the parents have experienced in their own attempts to cope with the adolescent's behavior and reactions. There is an obvious side-taking danger that requires sensitivity by the mental health professional. Because the ultimate goal is to assist the involved parties in resolving "their" crisis, the mental health professional needs to assume both a sympathetic, caring stance and simultaneously an objective and neutral stance.

A Preventive Role.   As mentioned, there is also a role for the schools in anticipating a crisis and taking the initiative. This stance is clearly different from the crisis "hot line" approach of waiting until someone calls for help. An example of a missed opportunity for such anticipation and initiative-taking involved a 16-year-old honor student who experienced an onset of headaches that led to some blackouts. She received an emergency medical study that concluded the presence of a tumor, fortunately benign. Surgery was recommended with the parents being informed of the possibility of resulting impaired functions. The surgery was successful and without any gross consequences such as paralysis or loss of motor functions, but the student did experience some slight disorientation, minor although significant learning impairments, and some slight memory problems. The teenager was placed on anti-convulsive medication as a precaution and after several weeks of recuperation she returned to school. Her parents kept school officials abreast of her medical condition and progress, however, they took no initiative in preparing her for re-entry into the classroom. She found algebra surprisingly difficult when before she had been an A student, and became extremely self-conscious regarding her wig and swollen face. Moodiness, tears, and discouragement quickly followed with the whole family sharing in her scares, anxiety, and depression. Only after several days back at school and with her emotional reactions being at a point of crisis did the school counselor initiate contact with her and establish a supportive and ultimately very helpful relationship. In the meantime, the parent–adolescent relationship had also become problematic as the parents were trying to understand their daughter's trauma and to deal with their own feelings. The parents' attempts to talk with their daughter frequently turned into yelling sessions. They were too eager to reassure her, and she in turn was continually upset by the new limitations she experienced. The counselor was able to involve the parents in some sessions separate from their daughter and assist them in better understanding their daughter's behavior, her educational problems and how they could be more supportive of her. The counselor also initiated contact with her teachers and helped them to understand what she had experienced, her current problems and educational needs, and how they could offer appropriate emotional support.

The student's medical problem was known to the school and in retrospect, it seems that the school, via the psychologist or counselor, could have initiated contact with the family. Had that happened, the student and parents could have been better prepared for her re-entry, and the teachers put in a position to play a more supportive and knowledgeable role with the student.

A Mediator Role.   Common complaints of adolescents about their parents include the perception that the parent does not listen, does not understand, is not sympathetic to what the adolescent is experiencing, is judgmental, and is not willing to give time to the adolescent. Without exactly sitting on the edge of his or her seat expressing an inordinate intensity of focus, the school mental health professional needs to convey the message of "I am here, I am interested in hearing and understanding what is happening with you, and I am available to be involved in a potentially helpful way in your situation."

When we are talking about problems that a parent or adolescent is experiencing in relation to the other the eventual bringing together of the conflicting parties is extremely important. The conflict resolution literature (Bach & Wyden, 1968; Deutsch, 1973; Gordon, 1975) speaks to how persons in conflict tend to polarize issues, draw position lines in an indelible fashion, think in terms of we/they or I/you, and engage in projection around the other persons position. A function of mediators in conflict situations is to assist the parties in obtaining a clearer understanding of each other's position, a more objective view of the respective concerns and issues, a careful examination of impasses, and consideration of new options. The perceived authority, knowledgeability, skill, and fairness of the mediator plays a very important role in the response of the "opposing" parties to conflict resolution procedures.

The mediator in the aforementioned context needs to establish his or her authority and psychological position in the conflict–mediation situation. These observations would appear to hold equally true for the mental health professional involved with parents and adolescents at a time of crisis. Their crisis is real and needs to be responded to with care and respect by the mental health professional. Both parties, parents and adolescent, typically feel vulnerable and defensive about their stance and need to receive a message from the professional that the issues and their thoughts and feelings are valid.

Specific Interventions

As indicated, the intent of crisis intervention is to restabilize a system and to reduce the crisis nature of the situation. Following that, other decisions have to be made in relation to establishing a counseling program with the individuals involved, terminating contacts, referring to another agency, or acting out some other option.

The nature and extent of the counseling that school mental health professionals should engage in is subject to some debate based on questions of competency and of the roles and function of school mental health professionals. Because the view of crisis intervention with parent–adolescent problems presented here has a family orientation, it is concerned with ways that the student and parents can be productively involved not only to cope with the immediate crisis but also to develop a better mutual understanding and more effective ways of dealing with future issues. This view can lead to some approximation of a family therapy intervention (Fine & Holt, 1983; Green, 1985). It is not the intent to present the school mental health professional as someone for whom the practice of family therapy per se is appropriate. Within the context of crisis intervention, several sessions might occur involving the respective family members, sometimes with the student and parents meeting together and other times with the student or the parents involved separately. Another option is that as student and parent meet together the mental health professional may choose to have one of the other parties leave while the professional attempts to negotiate some aspect of the situation with one of the parties following which all parties will again return.

Contact with the Adolescent

Some of the basic skills and activities in the initial crisis intervention have been discussed elsewhere in this text. It would be expected that somewhere in the early course of listening to the adolescent-in-crisis that the mental health professional would inquire as to who else is involved or who else is aware of what is happening and in particular how aware and involved are the parents. The challenge for the crisis counselor is to continue to be supportive and sympathetic to the student in what he or she is experiencing while at the same time not actively siding with the student against the parent. The other side of the coin, of course, is that the professional on hearing what sounds like distortion, overreactions, misperceptions, or inappropriate thinking by the adolescent may be pulled into speaking from the parents' point of view. However objectively the mental health professional has attempted to respond, there is a good likelihood that the adolescent will view the professional as taking the parents' side and probably not being adequately sympathetic to the student's position.

Because a key element of a person experiencing a crisis is the lack of awareness of options or the sense that one can act on those options, a function of the professional at an appropriate time is to begin helping the adolescent consider available options. An important option especially in light of conflict between parent and adolescent is to encourage the adolescent toward an involvement in a process that can generate solutions rather than necessarily coming up with concrete solutions in the crisis counseling session. It is understandable that the adolescent once having invested some trust in the mental health professional may respond in a dependent way seeking some concrete direction. Although the professional may see a role as an information giver, it may be more useful ultimately to have the student focus on ways that he or she can move into a problem solving posture with parents. To that end, the professional may need to work with the student in terms of some specific communication and conflict resolution skills and strategies that the student might venture to try with parents, continuing to use the professional as a support person.

Support and Skill-Building. A number of programs have been implemented in secondary schools to help adolescents understand themselves in their relationship with their parents and to develop more effective means of communicating and problem solving. If such a group exists in the high school as an ongoing group, then it becomes a convenient referral source for the student. It may require a few sessions with the mental health professional to prepare the student to benefit from a group process. The ongoing nature of the group means that there will be some students who have been in it for several weeks along with students who are just entering. Students who have been in the group for awhile have had the opportunity to test their new skills with their parents. The kinds of discussion and feedback opportunities that this group presents for an adolescent can be very reality orienting. This contact with reality may be especially valuable for the adolescent who feels that no one else has had this kind of problem or that his or her parents are the "worst" parents or are unapproachable. Being in a group with other adolescents who are also experiencing difficulties with their parents and who are perhaps farther down the road in coming to terms with their own inputs to the parent–adolescent problem can be extremely educative to the new group member.

Many of the programs described in the literature tend to be time-limited programs focusing on teaching the adolescent specific communication, interpersonal, or problem-solving skills. For example, Trower (1978) described a program that teaches adolescents to deal with their parents in a more adult way in terms of specific verbal skills including how to argue, console, advise, and criticize. He was also concerned with appropriate body language as a part of the message.

Brion-Meisels has published several papers describing adolescent social competency and in particular, interpersonal negotiation strategies (Brion-Meisels, Rendeiro, & Lowenheim 1984; Brion Meisels & Selman, 1984). His work derives in part from the earlier publications on problem solving by Spivak and Shure (1974) and Spivak, Platt, and Shure (1976). The proposed interpersonal negotiation model involves four social-cognitive skills: (a) labeling the problem, (b) generating alternative solutions, (c) anticipating consequences for self and other, and (d) evaluating results. These four skills interact with four levels of interpersonal negotiation strategies. The model and curriculum seem to hold a great deal of promise for training adolescents, and although not specifically focused on parent–adolescent crises, it does interface with that area.

A program entitled *Skills for Adolescence* is described by Gerler (1986) and Crisci (1986). It involves a semester-long curriculum dealing with 10 adolescent concerns. "Two of the units—one dealing with friends and the other dealing with family—focus on ways of appreciating and enchancing relationships and dealing effectively with problems and conflicts when they do occur" (Gerler, 1986, p. 438).

The curriculum has been adopted by over 500 schools and some positive outcomes have been reported from evaluation studies.

A number of other programs have been described in the literature with different populations of children, focusing on problem-solving and communication skills (Goldstein, Sprafkin, Gershaw, & Klein, 1980; Ollendick & Hersen, 1979; Sarason & Sarason, 1981). These represent program prototypes and models that can be modified and implemented with adolescents in schools around parent–adolescent conflicts.

Contact with Parents

It is important to remember that when an adolescent is experiencing a crisis involving his or her parents, that the parents also are experiencing a crisis. The decision of the mental health professional to meet once or even have several sessions with the parents is probably based on beliefs regarding the parents' needs to ventilate, develop a more positive perspective on the situation, and to think through more effective ways of communicating with the adolescent. The recommendations for the parents to be involved in sessions with the mental health professional without the adolescent present will also be predicated on the belief that the nature of the relationship at that time could not be usefully affected through having the parent and adolescent meeting together. The adolescent may be receiving some individual or group help in developing more effective communication and problem-solving skills or perhaps the adolescent has even refused any involvement. The parents can still be helped to increase their capability of negotiating differences with the adolescent and being appropriately supportive at the time of the crisis.

Programs for Parents.   In consultation with a mental health professional, one can envision the parents presenting specific incidents and utilizing the mental health professional as a back board, helping them to reflect on their thinking and behaviors and also as a source of some skill development. Those initially limited contacts with the parents can easily extend into a referral to a parent training group. In many communities there are ongoing parent education groups such as Parent Effectiveness Training (Gordon, 1975), the S.T.E.P. program (Dinkmeyer & Mckay, 1976), or Active Parenting (Popkin, 1983). These programs assist parents in understanding the complexities of parent–child relationship and support them in developing a sympathetic view toward the child and themselves in the parenting role; in addition, parents are typically offered specific communication and intervention skills. For example, Gordon's program provides a model for effective parent–child relationships in which the emphasis is on recognizing faulty communication patterns, developing effective listening skills, and managing conflict by mutually exploring and agreeing on a solution.

The time the mental health professional spends with the parents may also reveal some family problems that go beyond just communication difficulties with their adolescent. For example, some marital difficulties may be revealed along with other family happenings of a historical or contemporary nature such as abuse situations. A referral may be deemed appropriate to treatment or intervention sources that are better equipped to deal with more deep-seated, chronic family issues.

Conjoint Contacts with Parents and Adolescents

When the mental health professional schedules sessions that involve both parent and adolescent, one would hope that the professional has some appreciation for group process and the importance of his or her leadership role. These meetings of parent, adolescent, and professional should allow for ventilation, should encourage interaction between parent and adolescent, and should also present the mental health professional in a leadership-control role. The professional posture and exhibited leadership competencies of the mental health professional can go a long way toward reducing the anxiety level of the participants and in helping them to see themselves in a process that can lead to some resolution. At times, the professional may need to play a "traffic cop" role in directing people who are going off tangentially or speaking in a destructive way and in making sure that everyone's position is heard and respected. The neutrality image needs to be strongly maintained. The respective family members are likely to feel some vulnerability in the conjoint session and may tend to experience any disagreement with them or support of the other person by the professional as side-taking or not understanding their point of view. The mental health professional needs to be very sensitive to this phenomena and to do what is necessary to anticipate misperceptions and to support the image of neutrality.

There are a number of techniques and strategies that emanate from family therapy that can be useful in the short term and relatively few crisis intervention sessions. For example, as the mental health professional explores each side's point of view on events that occurred, it may be more useful to avoid "why" questions and to ask instead "what happens when" questions. Such questioning can do much to reveal some of the communication and behavior patterns in the family that precipitate conflict. Such circular questioning also avoids a blaming and a "who's right" stance and aids the family members to see and better understand dysfunctional patterns. The professional can also use the technique of reframing to present a more positive and sympathetic interpretation to someone's behavior. For example, when a parent talks about how angry he or she get when the adolescent does a certain thing, the positive reframing could be in terms of "I can see how much you care for your child and how frightened and frustrated you get when you believe he is setting himself up to get hurt."

As the session(s) continue, the sense of crisis should reduce somewhat on the part of the family members just as a function of knowing that they are in a potentially helpful process. Also, the revealing of dysfunctional patterns of communication should begin to suggest ways that the parents and adolescent can shift to a more mutually respectful, problem-solving and less combative stance. The modeling influence of the mental health professional cannot be stressed enough. As a resonable, rational, caring person who evidences logical problem-solving skills, he or she is implicitly teaching parents and the adolescent how to listen, think, and be appropriately assertive.

At some point in the conjoint session(s), it may be useful to negotiate a contract that spells out both parental and adolescent future behaviors. The preparation of the contract is a strategic device to make explicit the concerns of the respective parties. It also requires thinking and planning by the participants that at that point in the crisis intervention process can help to move them away from an excessive emotionality and into a thinking mode. Because a contract typically involves commitments by both parties, it can be "face saving" in that it is not just one party who is giving in.

An exciting approach to working with the whole family at time of parent–adolescent crisis is described by Robin and Foster (1984). The program is a behavioral-family systems approach that addresses skill deficits, cognitive distortions, structural difficulties, and functional interaction patterns. The intervention includes training in problem-solving strategies, targeting and transforming ineffectual communication habits, recognizing and restructuring cognitive sets that contribute to conflict (e.g., overgeneralization, arbitrary inference, dichotomous reasoning), and targeting and modifying family structural and functional patterns that may be maintaining maladaptive interactions. A range of "teaching" techniques are used including modeling, behavior rehearsal, and corrective feedback. Homework is utilized to encourage generalization. The program involves 7 to 15, one-hour sessions.

It would be unrealistic to believe that one or even several sessions at the time of crisis will completely resolve what may be a history of significant family dysfunction. There will be the tendency, even though important gains may have been made within the context of the crisis counseling sessions, for the family to "rubberband" back to old patterns. Therefore, in order to capitalize on the gains that may have been made, referral to another agency or resource that can work with the family on an ongoing basis may be appropriate. Examples of such services may be an ongoing family therapy program at a local mental health clinic or perhaps a family-life education program as offered through a local church or other agency.

An important consideration apropos thoughts of referring the family to another source for ongoing therapy is that the family may decide to terminate professional contacts once the crisis has abated. The views of mental health professionals are at times more idealistic than realistic. The family and its respective members may not want to work on improving relationships to a more idealized level. There may be an acceptable "discomfort level" that the family can tolerate, and only when the discomfort exceeds that level is motivation for professional involvement expressed. Szasz's (1961) view of people not experiencing mental illness as a "disease," but rather experiencing difficulties in coping with problems of daily living is a relevant consideration. Once people have improved their capacity to cope to their satisfaction with a formerly problematic situation they are often ready to terminate the help process.

SUMMARY

This chapter has examined parent-adolescent crises against the background of the child growing up within a family system. Areas such as family histories, family dynamics, intervention strategies and prevention programs were discussed with a view toward the relationship of these areas to crisis intervention. As the school-based mental health professional becomes increasingly involved in working with parent-adolescent crisis situations, she or he must be cognizant of how the family system operates, its relationship to the crisis, and how it influences the choice of intervention.

Although the "normal crises" of adolescence can be problematic for any family, they can be extremely stressful for the dysfunctional family unit. This type of family unit, with the history of ineffectual patterns of responding to normative changes, produces intensified conflictual situations that can quickly escalate to a crisis level. It is at this point of crisis that the school-based mental health professional may become actively involved through counseling, mediating, or referring to another appropriate agency, so that the system can restabilize and the crisis nature of the situation can be reduced. How well the school-based mental health professional deals with parent–adolescent crisis will depend on his or her level of flexibility, degree of decisiveness, awareness of options, knowledge of family patterns and dynamics, and how realistic his or her expectations are of the family's commitment to change.

REFERENCES

Aguilera, D. C., & Messick, J. N. (1978). *Crisis intervention: Theory and methodology*. St. Louis, MO: C. V. Mosby.

Bach, G. R. & Wyden, P. (1968). *The intimate enemy*. New York: Aron.

Brion-Meisels, S., Rendeiro, B., & Lowenheim, G. (1984). Student decison-making: Improving the school climate for all students. In S. Braaten, R. Rutherford, Jr., & C. Kardash (Eds.), *Programming for adolescents with behavioral disorders* (pp. 117–130). Reston, VA: Council for Exceptional Children.

Brion-Meisels, S., & Selman, R. L. (1984). Early adolescent development of new interpersonal strategies: Understanding and intervention. *School Psychology Review, 13*, 278–291.

Crisci, P. E. (1986). The Quest National Center: A focus on prevention of alienation. *Phi Delta Kappan, 67*, 442–446.

Deutsch, M. (1973). *The resolution of conflict: Constructive and destructive processes*. New Haven: Yale University Press.

Dinkmeyer, D. & McKay, G. (1976). *STEP-TEEN*. Circle Pines, MN: American Guidance Service.

Elkind, D. (1984). *All grown up and no place to go*. Menlo Park, CA: Addison-Wesley.

Erikson, E. H. (1968). *Identity: Youth and crisis*. New York: Norton.

Fine, M. J. (1979). *Parents versus children: Making the relationship work*. Englewood Cliffs, NJ: Prentice-Hall.

Fine, M. J. (1982). Issues in adolescent counseling. *School Psychology Review, 11*, 391–398.

Fine, M. J., & Holt, P. (1983). Intervening with school problems: A family systems perspective. *Psychology in the Schools, 20*, 59–66.

Friedenberg, E. Z. (1959). *The vanishing adolescent*. Boston: Beacon Press.

Gerler, E. R., Jr. (1986). Skills for adolescence: A new program for young teenagers. *Phi Delta Kappan, 67*, 436–439.

Ginott, H. (1969). *Between parent and teenager*. New York: MacMillan.

Goldstein, A. P., Sprafkin, R. P., Gershaw, N. J., & Klein, P. (1980). *Skill-streaming the adolescent*. Champaign, IL: Research Press.

Gordon, T. (1975). *P.E.T.: Parent effectiveness training*. New York: New American Library.

Green, B. J. (1985). Systems intervention in the schools. In M. P. Mirkin & S. L. Koman (Eds.), *Handbook of adolescent and family therapy* (pp. 193–206). New York: Gardner Press.

Grob, M. C., Klein, A. A. & Eisen, S. V. (1983). The role of the high school professional in identifying and managing adolescent suicidal behavior. *Journal of Youth and Adolescence, 12*, 163–173.

Jacobs, J. (1980). *Adolescent suicide*. New York: Irvington.

Jones, V. F. (1980). *Adolescents with behavior problems*. Boston: Allyn & Bacon.

Kidwell, J., Fischer, J. L., Dunham, R. M. & Baranowski, M. (1983). Parents and adolescents: Push and pull of change. In H. I. McCubbin & C. R. Figley (Eds.), *Stress and the family. Vol. I. Coping with normal change* (pp. 74–89). New York: Brunner/Mazel.

Ollendick, T. H., & Hersen, M. (1979). Social skills training for juvenile delinquents. *Behavior Research and Therapy, 17*, 547–554.

Popkin, M. (1983). *Active parenting: A video-based program*. Atlanta: Active Parenting.

Preto, N. G., & Travis, N. (1985). The adolescent phase of the family life cycle. In M. P. Mirkin & S. L. Koman (Eds.), *Handbook of adolescent and family therapy* (pp. 21–38). New York: Gardner Press.

Robin, A. L., & Foster, S. L. (1984). Problem-solving communication training: A behavioral-family systems approach to parent–adolescent conflict. In P. Karoly & J. J. Steffen (Eds.), *Adolescent behavior disorders: Foundations and contemporary concerns* (pp. 195–240). Lexington, KY: Lexington Books.

Sarason, I. G., & Sarason, B. R. (1981). Teaching cognitive and social skills to high school students. *Journal of Counseling and Clinical Psychology, 49*, 908–918.

Slaikeu, K. A. (1984). *Crisis intervention: A handbook for practice and research*. Boston: Allyn & Bacon.

Spivak, G., & Shure, M. (1974). *Social adjustment of young children: A cognitive approach to solving real-life problems*. San Francisco: Jossey-Bass.

Spivak, G., Platt, J. J., & Shure, M. B. (1976). *The problem-solving approach to adjustment*. San Francisco: Jossey-Bass.

Szasz, T., (1961). *The myth of mental illness: Foundations of a theory of personal conduct*. New York: Hoeber-Harper.

Trower, P. (1978). Skills training for adolescent social problems: A viable treatment alternative? *Journal of Adolescence, 1*, 319–29.

Youniss, J., & Smollar, J. (1985). *Adolescent relations with mothers, fathers, and friends*. Chicago: University of Chicago Press.

Author Index

257

Subject Index